25.1023

Brave Catherine tried in vain to keep them back (page 191)

Scotland's Story

Published by Galore Park Publishing Ltd
19/21 Sayers Lane
Tenterden
Kent TN30 6BW
www.galorepark.co.uk

The typed text used as the basis of this edition was donated by the
Baldwin Project which offers online access to hundreds of classic
children's books at www.mainlesson.com. All texts are available at
no charge for personal and educational use.

The text of this edition is copyright © Galore Park 2006

This edition first published 2006

Typeset by Typetechnique, London W1
Printed by CPI, Glasgow

ISBN-10 1 902984 77 3
ISBN-13 978 1 902984 77 3

**Also by H E Marshall published by
Galore Park Publishing**
Our Island Story
Kings and Things

Scotland's Story

A History of Scotland
for Boys and Girls

by
H E Marshall

with pictures by
J R Skelton, John Hassall
and J Shaw Crompton

Galore Park Publishing

GALORE PARK

www.galorepark.co.uk

Contents

List of Illustrations

Why this book was written

"IT IS very nice," said Caledonia, as she closed her book with a sigh, "but why did you not tell us stories of Scotland?"

"Because there was no need. That has been done already by a great and clever man."

"Oh, but children sometimes like the stories which are written by the not great and clever people best," said Caledonia wisely. "Littler children do, anyhow. They are more simpler, you know."

"Oh indeed!" said I.

"I wish you would write Scotland's Story for littler children like me," went on Caledonia, "and please put more battles in it than in Our Island Story. But you must not say that the Scots were defeated. I don't like it at all when you say 'The Scots and the Picts were driven back'."

"But you know we were defeated sometimes, Caledonia."

Caledonia looked grave. That was very serious. Presently her face brightened. "Well, if we were, you needn't write about those times," she said.

So, because Caledonia asked me, I have written Scotland's Story. I am afraid it will not please her altogether, for I have had to say more than once or twice that the Scots were defeated. But I would remind her that 'defeated' and 'conquered' are words with quite different meanings, and that perhaps it is no disgrace for a plucky little nation to have been defeated often, and yet never conquered by her great and splendid neighbour.

"Fairy tales!" I hear some wise people murmur as they turn the pages. Yes, there are fairy tales here, and I make no apology for them, for has not a grave and learned historian said that there ought to be two histories of Scotland – one woven with the golden threads of romance and gittering with the rubies and sapphires of Fairyland? Such, surely, ought to be the children's Scotland.

So I dedicate my book to the 'littler children', as

Caledonia calls them, who care for their country's story. It is sent into the world in no vain spirit of rivalry, but rather as a humble tribute to the great Master of Romance, who wrote Tales for his little grandson, and I shall be well repaid if my tales but form stepping-stones by which little feet may pass to his Enchanted Land.

H E Marshall

CHAPTER 1

The Story of Prince Gathelus

ONCE upon a time there lived in Greece a king who had a son called Gathelus. Prince Gathelus was very handsome and brave but he was wild, happy and wicked, and he caused his father much sorrow and trouble. Over and over again the King punished and imprisoned his son for his evil deeds. But in spite of all his father could do Gathelus grew no better, but rather worse. At last the King had no more patience with him and banished him from the land.

When Gathelus knew that he was banished he took a ship and, gathering as many of his friends as would come with him, he sailed away to a far country called Egypt.

When they arrived in Egypt, Pharaoh, the ruler of the land, received them very kindly for he was at that time fighting great battles and he hoped that these happy young knights would help him against his enemies.

This, Gathelus and his friends did and when Pharaoh had, with their aid, defeated his enemies he rewarded them richly and gave them a city in which they could live together. Gathelus alone was not content with the rewards, for he had seen Pharaoh's beautiful daughter, Scota, and he longed to marry her. And as Pharaoh could refuse nothing to the gallant Prince who had freed him from his enemies, he gave his consent, and Scota and Gathelus were married.

For many years Gathelus lived in Egypt, growing rich and great, and ruling over his people who became more and more numerous as the years went by. And Gathelus loved his wife so much that he commanded that in honour of her name, Scota, all his people should be called Scots.

But when Pharaoh began to be unkind to the Children of Israel, and terrible plagues fell upon the land, Gathelus wished to live there no longer. So he gathered a great fleet of ships and, with his wife and children, all his soldiers and servants, and a great company of people, he went on board and sailed far away across the sea in search of another country.

After many storms and adventures Gathelus and his company arrived, at last, on the shores of Spain. They had been tossed and buffeted about by winds and waves for many days. They had eaten all the food which they had brought with them, and they were nearly starving. So they were very glad to be safe on land once more.

But the people of Spain were not glad to see these strangers and they made ready to fight them. Gathelus too made ready to fight and a fierce battle followed in which the Spaniards were beaten.

But Gathelus and his Scots wished to live at peace with the people of the land and, although neither could speak the language of the other, the Scots found means to make the Spaniards understand that they did not wish to fight against them or to hurt them in any way. So the two nations became friends, and the Spaniards gave a part of their country to the Scots, where for many years they lived in peace.

As the years went on, the Scots grew to be still richer and greater than they had been in Egypt, and Gathelus, who had been so wild and wicked when he was young, became a wise and good king. But when the Spaniards saw that the Scots had become a powerful nation, they were once more afraid of them, and they resolved to drive them out of the country.

Then both the Scots and the Spaniards gathered their mighty men, and there was a great and terrible battle, with awful slaughter on both sides. But in the end the Scots won the victory. Then once more peace was made, and the two nations agreed again to live side by side as friends.

But when Gathelus saw how the Scots still went on growing richer and greater day by day, he feared that the Spaniards would again become angry and want to fight. So he began to think how this might be avoided. At last, hearing of the Green Island which lay in the sea not far distant, he resolved to send some of his people there.

Gathering a great number of ships, he filled them with soldiers, and making his two sons, who were called Hiberus and Himecus, captains he sent them away to seek for the Green Island.

For some days the ships sailed upon the sea seeking the Green Island in vain. But at last they came to it and landed there. The Scots soon found out that there were very few people on the Green Island, and those who were there were gentle and kindly, and had no wish to fight.

Hiberus and Himecus therefore, instead of fighting, tried to make friends with the people. This they easily did, for the inhabitants of the Green Island, seeing that the Scots meant them no harm, welcomed them gladly.

So the Scots settled in the Green Island and taught the people many useful things. They showed them how to sow and plough and reap, how to build houses, how to spin and, in many ways, how to live more comfortably. Then presently, in honour of Hiberus, who was their Prince, they changed the name of the island to Hibernia. The island is still sometimes called by that name, although we generally call it Ireland.

For many years the Scots lived in Hibernia. Gathelus died and Hiberus died and after them ruled many kings. At last, when many hundreds of years had passed, a prince called Rothsay sailed over to the islands which lay opposite Hibernia and took possession of them. The island upon which he first landed he called Rothesay, and to this day there is a town on the island of Bute called by that name.

The Scots, finding that these islands were fertile and good for breeding cattle, sailed over from Hibernia in greater and greater numbers, bringing their wives and children with them. At last they filled all the little islands, and some of them landed in the north of the big island, which was then called Albion.

After many, many years the north part of Albion came to

be called the land of Scots, or Scotland, just as the south part was called the land of Angles, or England.

Some people think that this story of Prince Gathelus is a fairy tale. But this at least is true, that in far-off days when people spoke of Scotia they meant Ireland, and when they spoke of Scots they meant the people who lived in Ireland, and Scotland took its name from the people who came from Ireland and settled in Scotland.

CHAPTER 2

A Fight with the Romans

WHEN the Scots first came to Albion they found it already peopled by the Britons and by another race called the Picts. It is not certain from where these Picts came but they were a very wild and fierce people. It is supposed that they were called Picts from the Latin word *pictus* which means painted, because they painted their bodies instead of wearing clothes.

So there were three races living in Scotland, and these were divided into many tribes who often fought with each other. There were kings of Scots, kings of Picts and kings of Britons, all ruling in Albion. Sometimes the kings and their peoples all fought against each other; sometimes the Picts and the Scots joined together against the Britons. Those were fierce and wild times and they were all fierce and wild peoples. They lived in caves or in holes dug in the ground and covered over with turf and with branches of trees. They wore few clothes except those made from the skins of animals, although the Scots knew how to weave and make cloth in bright coloured checks and stripes.

A great part of the country was covered with forests. In these forests wild beasts prowled about. Bears, wolves, wild boar, bison and a kind of tiger were the fiercest, but there were also several kinds of deer, beavers and many other animals which are no longer to be found in Scotland.

The people hunted these animals and killed them for food and also for their skins, of which they made clothes. In hunting they used bows and arrows. Bows and arrows were used too in war, as well as a long, blunt, heavy spear. And in hunting and fighting the men spent nearly all their time.

Years went on. Many kings, good and bad, lived, ruled and died, and at last a great and clever people called the Romans heard of the island of Britain, and came sailing over the sea to conquer it. They landed first in the south of the island and tried to conquer the people there, and it was not until the year 80 AD, more than a hundred years after the Romans first came to Britain, that a general called Agricola marched into Scotland against the Caledonians, as the Romans called all the tribes who lived in the north part of the island.

Agricola took some of his soldiers into Scotland by land. Others sailed there in great galleys, as the Roman ships were called. The Caledonians did not fear the Roman soldiers. They had already fought against them many times, for they had often marched into the south of the island to help the Britons against the Romans. "They were willing," says an old writer, "to help towards the delivery of the land from the bondage of the Romans, whose nestling so near their noses they were loath to see or hear of."

But if the Caledonians did not fear the soldiers, the great galleys of the Romans filled them with awe and dread. Never before had they seen so many nor such great ships. "The very ocean is given over to our enemies," they said. "How shall we save ourselves from these mighty conquerors who thus surround us on every side?"

But although the Caledonians were filled with dread, they fought bravely. As Agricola marched northward by the coast, his galleys followed him on the sea. Sometimes the galleys would come close to the shore and the sailors would land and join the soldiers in the camp. There they would tell stories to each other of the battles and dangers, of the storms and adventures through which they had passed, each trying to make the others believe that their adventures had been the most exciting, their dangers the greatest.

The Caledonians fought fiercely but Agricola's soldiers were far better trained, and gradually he drove the islanders before him into the mountains beyond the rivers Forth and Clyde. There he built a line of forts. He knew that he had neither conquered nor subdued the fierce

Caledonians. So he built this line of forts in order to cut them off from the south and shut them, as it were, into another island.

Having built this line of forts, Agricola marched still farther north. But the Caledonians fought so fiercely that some of the Roman leaders begged Agricola to turn back. Agricola would not go back but, as the winter was near and the roads were so bad as to be almost impassable, he encamped and waited for the spring before fighting any more.

The Caledonians spent the winter in making preparations for battle. All the various tribes forgot their quarrels and joined together under a leader called Galgacus. Sending their wives and children to a safe place the men, young and old, from far and near, flocked to Galgacus, eager to fight for their country.

When spring came and the roads were once more passable, the Romans left their camp and marched northward, seeking the Caledonians. They met, it is thought, somewhere upon the slopes of the Grampian Hills but no one is sure of the exact spot.

The Caledonians were little more than savages, yet they were ready to fight to the last for their country. They were almost naked. They wore no armour and carried only small shields. For weapons they had bows and arrows, blunt iron swords and heavy spears. Those in the centre of the army were mounted upon rough little horses, and there too were gathered the war chariots with swords upon the wheels ready to dash among the enemy and cut them down.

Against these savage warriors came the splendid soldiers of the Roman Empire, clad in glittering coats of mail, armed with swords and spears of sharpened steel, every man among them trained to obey, to fight and to die.

As the Caledonians stood ready for battle, Galgacus made a speech to them. "Fight today," he said, "for the liberty of Albion. We have never been slaves and if we would not now become the slaves of these proud Romans, there is nothing left to us but to fight and die. We are at the farthest limits of land and liberty. There is no land behind us to which we may flee. There is nothing but the waves and rocks and the Romans in their ships. These plunderers of the world having taken all the land, now claim the seas, so that even if we fly to the sea there is no safety from them. They kill and slay, and take what is not theirs, and call it Empire. They make a desert and call it Peace. Our children, our wives and all who are dear to us, are torn from us, our lands and goods are destroyed. Let this day decide if such things we are to suffer for ever or revenge instantly. March then to battle. Think of your children and of the freedom which was your fathers', and win it again, or die."

When Galgacus had finished speaking, the Caledonians answered with great shouts and songs. Then with their chariots and horsemen they rushed upon the Romans. Fiercely the battle began, fiercely it raged. The Caledonians fought with splendid courage, but what could half-naked savages do against the steel-clad warriors of Rome? When night fell, ten thousand Caledonians lay dead upon the field. The Romans had won the victory.

All through the night could be heard the desolate cries of sorrow and despair, as women moved over the battlefield seeking their dead, and helping the wounded. All through the night the sky was red with the light of fires. But in the morning, the country far and near was empty and silent, and the villages were smoking ruins. Not a Caledonian was to be seen. They had burned their homes and fled away to hide among the mountains.

Agricola, knowing that it would be useless to try to follow them through the dark forest and hills, turned and marched southward again beyond his line of forts. A few months later he was called back to Rome.

Agricola had been four years in Scotland, and when he left it the people were still unconquered.

CHAPTER 3

The March of the Romans

ALTHOUGH the Caledonians had been defeated they were not subdued, and they continued to fight so fiercely that the Romans gave up trying to keep the forts which Agricola had built.

Later on, a Roman emperor called Hadrian came to Britain and he built a wall from the Tyne to the Solway. This wall ran straight across the country from sea to sea, over hills and valleys, and it was so strong and so well built that, although hundreds of years have passed since then, it may still be seen to this day.

But even this great wall did not keep back the Caledonians. They broke through it or sailed round the ends of it in their little boats made of wickerwork covered with the skins of animals. Some years later another Roman emperor called Antonine came to Britain. He drove the Caledonians back again beyond Agricola's forts, and there he built a wall which is still called by his name.

But the Caledonians broke through or climbed over this wall too. The first man who leaped over the wall was called Graham, and the ruins of that part of the wall are called Graham's Dyke to this day. Dyke is a Scottish word for wall.

Many years passed. The Romans called Britain a Roman province, but the wild people of the north not only remained unconquered but they became ever more and more bold. They leaped over the wall more and more often, coming farther and farther south, fighting and plundering as they went.

At last, an emperor called Severus, hearing of the deeds of the wild Caledonians, resolved to conquer them. This emperor was old and ill. He was so ill that he could not walk and had to be carried in a kind of bed called a litter. But he was full of courage and determination and, gathering a great army of soldiers, he invaded Scotland.

Scotland at this time was covered in many parts with pathless forest, and even where there were roads they were not fit for a great army, such as Severus now brought with him, to pass over.

So Severus, as he marched his army through Scotland, cut down trees, drained marshes, made roads and built bridges. Slowly, but with fierce determination, led by a sick man who was carried about in a bed, the Romans marched through Scotland. From south to north they marched, yet they never fought a battle or came face to face with an enemy.

The Caledonians followed their march, dashing out upon them unawares, swooping down upon and killing those who lagged behind or who strayed too far ahead. In this way many were killed, many too died of cold, hunger and weariness; still on and on, over hill and valley, swept the mighty host, to the very north of Scotland. There they turned and marched back again, and at last they reached the border and crossed beyond the wall, leaving fifty thousand of their number dead in the hills and valleys of the north.

No wonder that brave old Severus gave up the task as hopeless and, instead of trying to fight any more, he strengthened and repaired the wall which Hadrian had built so many years before.

And so it went on year by year, the Caledonians always attacking, the Romans always trying to drive them back again. At last, nearly five hundred years after they first came to Britain, the Romans went away altogether.

When the Romans had gone the Caledonians found the south of Britain more easy to attack than ever. For, as the Romans took away not only their own soldiers but the best of the British whom they had trained to fight, there was now no one to guard the walls.

So the Caledonians threw down and destroyed the wall

between the Forth and the Clyde. They broke and ruined great parts of Hadrian's Wall too and overran the south of Britain as far as London.

At last the Britons were in such dread and fear of the Caledonians that they sent to their old enemies, the Romans, for help. But the Romans would not help them. The Britons then sent to the Saxons, and the Saxons came to their aid.

When the King of the Picts heard that the Saxons had come to help the Britons, he sent to the King of the Scots begging him to join in fighting them. So the Picts and the Scots joined together against the Britons and the Saxons. But when the Picts and Scots saw the great army of Britons and the strange, fierce Saxon warriors, some of them were afraid and stole away to hide themselves in the woods nearby. The two kings, when they heard of this, were very angry. They sent to seek these cowards, brought them back and hanged them, every one in sight of the whole army, so that none might be tempted to follow their example.

Then Dougall, the Scottish King, and Galanus, the Pictish King, spoke to their people and encouraged them with brave words.

When the battle began arrows flew thick and fast and it seemed as if neither side would give way. But when they came near to each other, the Picts and Scots charged so fiercely that the Britons fled before them. Then a fearful storm arose. The sky grew black with clouds and the air dark with rain and hail which dashed on friend and foe alike. In the darkness the Picts and the Scots lost their rank and order and, when the storm passed over, the Saxons and the Britons had won the battle.

It was a sorrowful day for the Picts and the Scots. They fled away, leaving the Britons to rejoice over the thousands of their enemies who lay dead upon the field.

But the Britons had no great cause for rejoicing, for the Saxons rid south Britain of the Picts and the Scots only to conquer it for themselves. And soon the Britons were glad

to ask the Picts and Scots to help them to drive the Saxons
out of their land. This they were never able to do and the
Saxons took all the south of Britain and made it their own.
But Scotland they could never conquer.

CHAPTER 4

The Story of Saint Columba

IN IRELAND there lived a priest called Columba. He was very tall and strong and beautiful. He was the son of a king and might himself have been a king, but he did not care to sit upon a throne nor to wear a crown and royal robes. He did not long to fight and kill, as kings in these fierce days did. He was gentle and loving, and he longed rather to make people happy. So he was called Columba, which means a dove.

When he was a little boy Columba had heard the story of Christ and he had become a Christian. When he grew up he spent his time teaching other people to be Christian too. For at that time nearly all the people in the world were pagans.

The Picts were pagan. Some of the Scots may have heard the story of Christ before they left Ireland, but if they had, they very soon forgot it amid the fierce wars and rough, wild life they led.

Often Columba turned his kind grey eyes across the blue waters to the islands where his fellow-countrymen had gone. He longed to sail over the sea to tell his story there and to teach the wild people of these islands to be kind and gentle.

At last he had his wish. He found twelve friends who were willing to go with him and together they sailed across the sea in a little boat.

The boat, which was called the *Dewy-Red*, was small and frail. It was made of wickerwork covered with the skins of animals and seemed hardly fit for so long a journey.

But these thirteen men were not afraid and, taking with them bread and water and a little milk, enough to serve them for a few days, they set sail. They were dressed in long white robes, their feet were bare except for sandals and, although they were going among fierce, wild people, they took no weapons. God would guard them, they said.

The sun shone brightly and a soft wind blew as the *Dewy-Red* slid out upon the waters. Columba sat at the stern, steering straight for Albion. But as the shores of Ireland faded in the distance he looked back with tear-dimmed eyes. The rowers bent to the oars, and their eyes too were dim. These men loved their country dearly, but they were leaving it for love of others.

At last they reached the islands of Albion, and they landed upon one of them. But looking back across the sea they still faintly saw the shores of Ireland. "We must go further," they said, "if, day by day, we see our dear country in the distance our hearts will for ever return to it. Let us go where we cannot see it so that we may be content to live among strangers, in a strange land."

So once more Columba and his friends entered their boat. They sailed on till they came to an island then called Hy, but which is now called Iona.

The sun was setting as the frail little boat touched the rocky shore. Once more Columba looked back. The sea shone golden in the evening light, but across the sparkling waves no glimmer of the Irish shore was to be seen.

Columba and his white-robed followers landed and, climbing to the highest point in the island, again turned their eyes westward. Still no faintest outline of the Irish shore was to be seen. They had found what they sought, and kneeling on the rocky shore, they gave God thanks who had brought them in safety over the sea. The dove and his message of peace had found a resting place.

Upon this spot a cairn or pile of stones was raised which is called *Carn cul ri Erin*. That means "the back turned upon Ireland".

For two years Columba remained in Iona. During that time, besides teaching the people, he and his men built houses to live in, and also a church. Most of the people who lived in Iona and the islands round were Scots. Many of them became Christian; then Columba made up his mind to go to the Picts to teach them too about Christ.

The King of the Picts lived then at Inverness and from Iona to Inverness the journey was long and difficult. But Columba had no fear. Through the dark forests where wild animals roared and prowled, by pathless mountain sides, among fierce pagan people, he travelled on until he reached the palace of the King.

But the King and his pagan priests had heard of the coming of Columba and the gates of the palace were barred against him and guarded by warriors.

Still Columba had no fear. Right up to the gates he marched and, raising his hand, he made the sign of the cross upon them. Immediately the bolts and bars flew back. Slowly and silently the great gates turned upon their hinges and opened wide of their own accord. At the sight, the guards fled in terror to tell the King who sat among his lords and priests.

When the King heard the wonderful story he rose up from his throne and crying out, "This is a holy man," he hurried to meet Columba.

Dressed in beautiful robes, Columba came slowly through the palace followed by his white-clad monks. As soon as the King saw him he knelt before him, praying for his blessing and protection. So the King became Columba's friend, and helped him in every way.

But not so the pagan priests. They hated Columba, they hated his teaching, and they did everything they could to keep him from speaking to the people.

One day when Columba's followers were singing hymns, the pagan priests tried to stop them, lest the people should hear. But instead of being silent, Columba himself began to sing and his voice was so wonderful that it was heard for miles and miles around. It was heard by the King in his palace and by the peasant in his hut. And yet, although it was heard so far away, it sounded sweet and low to those who were near. The sound struck terror to the hearts of the pagan priests so that they too were silent and listened to the beautiful music.

For thirty-four years Columba lived among the people of Scotland. He travelled over all the land telling to the fierce pagan the story of Christ.

Many wonderful tales are told of Columba and, although we cannot believe them all, they help us to know that in those far-off times there lived a man whose heart was large and tender, who loved the helpless and the ignorant, and who gave his life to bring them happiness.

Besides preaching and teaching, Columba spent much of his time in writing. In those days all books were written by hand and Columba copied the Psalms and other parts of the Bible. One night as he worked he grew very weary. He wrote the words: "They who seek the Lord shall want no manner of thing that is good." Then he said to those around him, "Here I must rest. Someone else must finish my work."

Then, sitting upon the hard stones which served him for bed and pillow, he spoke to his followers. "Dear children, this is what I command with my last words – let peace and charity be among you always. If you do this, following the example of the saints, God who gives strength to the just will help you. And I who shall be near Him will pray Him to give you all that is needful to you in this life, and to greatly reward you in the life that is to come."

These were his last words.

At midnight Columba rose and, going into the dark church, knelt before the altar. His servant followed him but in the darkness could not find him. So in distress he called out, "Where art thou, my father?" There was no answer.

At last, groping about the church, the man came upon Columba lying upon the steps of the altar. He raised his head and rested it against his knees, calling aloud for help.

Soon all the monks were roused and lights were brought. With cries and tears they crowded round their dying master. Columba could not speak but he smiled upon them, and raising his hand seemed to bless them. Then, with a long sigh, he closed his eyes and was at rest for ever.

CHAPTER 5

How the French and the Scots Became Friends

YEARS passed on and many kings ruled in Scotland. They were years of war and bloodshed, for the country was still divided into different kingdoms. Besides the Picts and Scots and Britons, there were Saxons who, although they could not succeed in conquering Scotland as they had conquered England, had settled in the part south of the Forth. Sometimes the Picts and Scots fought against each other; sometimes they joined and fought against the Britons; or again they would join with the Britons and fight against the Saxons. But always and always the story is of war.

At last there arose a good and wise king called Achaius. He tried to rule well and bring peace to his land.

In the time of Achaius the greatest ruler in Europe was Charlemagne, King of France and Roman Emperor. He was very powerful but even he dreaded the wild Saxons for they invaded France as they invaded Britain, and did many wicked and cruel deeds.

When Charlemagne heard how the Picts and the Scots resisted the Saxons and remained free, he resolved to make a league with them against their common enemy. He wanted too, to make his people love learning, and in all the world he could hear of no people so learned as the Scots. He resolved therefore to send to them and ask them to come to teach his people. So he called some of his greatest nobles and sent them with a message to Achaius, King of Scots.

These nobles stepped into a beautiful ship with purple sails and gilded prow and sailed away to Scotland. As soon as they landed they were led to the court of King Achaius who greeted them kindly and treated them with great honour.

"Noble King," said the messengers, bowing low before Achaius, "our master, the most Christian King Charlemagne, sends you greeting. The fame of your good name and of the love you bear to the Christian faith has come to him. He has heard too of the learning and the bravery of your people, and of how they have resisted the pagan Saxons who have invaded Britain and done many evil and cruel deeds there. Our noble King desires therefore to be in fellowship with you and with your people, so that Scotsmen shall help Frenchmen and Frenchmen shall help Scotsmen. To this end let it be sworn between us that whenever the Saxons come with an army to France the Scots shall invade England. And if the Saxons come with an army to Scotland then the French shall take their ships and invade England."

When the messengers had made this long speech they again bowed low and waited for King Achaius to answer.

"I thank your noble King for the love he shows towards me," he replied, "and when I have taken counsel with my lords and nobles you shall have my answer to carry back to him."

Then the messengers were led to splendid rooms in the King's palace. Everything was done to please and amuse them. There were great banquets and hunting parties in which some of the nobles took part, but the greatest and wisest gathered round the King to give advice.

Long they talked, for the lords and nobles could not agree. "Why should we make friends with a people from over the sea?" said one noble. "Would it not be far more sensible to make friends with the Saxons who live in the same island as we do?"

"No," said another, "we can never be sure of the Saxons, they are full of falseness and treason. What misery and trouble have fallen upon the Britons through the deceit of the Saxons. Do not mistake – they do not wish to be our friends. They have conquered Britain, they also desire to conquer our land. Therefore if we intend to avoid the hatred of our most fearful enemies, if we intend to honour the faith of Christ for whose defence the French now bear arms, if we have more respect for truth than falsehood, if we labour for the fame and honour of our nation, if we will defend our country and bring it to peace, if we will defend our liberty and our lives, which are most dear to man, let us join with France, and let this bond be a defence to our country in all times to come."

Then all the lords and nobles shouted, "It is well said. Let it be done."

King Achaius then sent to the messengers, commanding them to come to court the next day to hear his answer. That night there was great feasting and rejoicing in the palace, and next day the King in his royal robes, surrounded by his nobles, waited to receive the messengers of the French King.

"My lords," said the King, "I desire you to take to your master, the most Christian King Charlemagne, my greeting and thanks. Say to him that my people and I desire above all things to enter into a bond with him, which shall last for all time, and be for ever a joy to both nations. To make the bond more sure, I send back with you my own brother who is a true and trusty knight, and with him shall go a company of soldiers and four wise men. The soldiers shall fight for the Emperor whenever he goes against the enemy and the wise men shall teach his people."

Then the messengers rejoiced greatly and, thanking the King, they departed to their own land. The Scottish soldiers who went with them formed the beginning of a French Scots guard which afterwards became famous, and the four wise men founded schools and colleges in France, and so added honour to the name of Scotsman.

King Achaius had taken for his standard a red lion rampant (that is, standing upon his hind legs) upon a yellow ground. Now, in order that the nobles might never forget his bond with France, he surrounded the red lion with a double row of fleurs-de-lis, the emblem of France.

This was meant to show that the fierce lion of Scotland was armed with the gentleness of the lilies of France, and that the two peoples were friends for ever.

Wise people say that the story of Achaius and Charlemagne can only be a fairy tale, for that at the time when Charlemagne ruled, the people of Scotland were still a poor, half-savage, ignorant people, and that a great king like Charlemagne could have learned nothing from them, and that he would not have wished to make a bond with them.

However that may be, you will find as this story goes on that the French and the Scots were friends through many ages, and if you look at the Scottish standard you will see that the lion is surrounded by the lilies of France.

It is said that King Achaius founded the Order of the Knights of the Thistle. This is the great order of knighthood in Scotland, just as the Order of the Garter is the great order of England.

When King Achaius founded the Order of the Thistle, he made only thirteen knights – himself and twelve others. This was in imitation of Christ and his twelve apostles. So it was considered a very great honour to be made a Knight of the Thistle. There were never more than thirteen Knights of the Thistle until hundreds of years later when King George IV made a law that there should be more.

The ornament worn by the Knights of the Thistle is a picture of St Andrew with his cross surrounded by thistles and rue. The thistle was the badge of the Scots. Rue was the badge of the Picts. Thistles prick and hurt you if you do not touch them carefully; rue soothes and heals, and was supposed to cure people who had been poisoned.

Some people say, however, that this order was not founded in the time of King Achaius but in the time of King James V, a king who lived many, many years later.

*St Columba made the sign of the cross, and the
great gates opened wide (page 15)*

"Do you see that little white sail far out to sea?
Yonder is Macduff" (page 36)

CHAPTER 6

The Last of the Picts

KING ACHAIUS married the daughter of the King of the Picts, and long after his death his grandson, Kenneth Macalpine, claimed the Pictish crown as well as that of the Scots because his grandmother had been a Pictish princess. The Picts, however, did not want a Scottish king, so there was war between the two nations.

But the Scottish lords at this time did not desire to fight against the Picts so, for some years, although the war went on there was no great battle but only little fights every now and again.

Kenneth Macalpine, however, did not give up his determination to win the crown of the Picts. At last he called all his lords together to a council and tried to persuade them to gather for a great battle. He talked to them very earnestly, but, say what he might, he could not move them. They did not want to fight and they would not fight.

Seeing he could not persuade them to do as he wished, the King brought the meeting to an end, but commanded them all to come together again next day to talk once more about the matter.

Now King Kenneth Macalpine had made up his mind that as he could not persuade the lords by talking to them he must try some other plan.

That night he made a very grand supper and invited all the lords to come to it. They came and it was such a grand supper, with so many courses, that it lasted far into the night. At length it was over and all the lords went to bed. They were so tired with the long day that they fell asleep at once.

But while the lords feasted, the King's servants had been busy. No sooner were the lords asleep, than there appeared at each bedside a man dressed in fish skins, covered with shining scales. In one hand he held a torch and in the other an ox horn. The night was very dark and the light from the torches shone on the fish scales, making a soft and silvery light. When each man was in his place, they all raised their horns, and speaking through them as through a trumpet they cried, "Awake."

At the sound of that great shout each lord started wide awake and, seeing the strange being at his bedside, lay trembling and wondering what it might mean.

Then, speaking through their horns which made their voices sound terrible and unearthly, and quite unlike the voice of any human being, the dressed-up men said, "We are the messengers of Almighty God to the Scottish nobles. We are sent to command you to obey your King, for his request is just. The Pictish kingdom is due to him as his rightful heritage. Therefore, you must fight for him and win it. That is the will of the Lord of All."

Having so spoken, these pretended messengers from heaven put out their torches. The glimmer of the silver scales vanished, and in the darkness the men stole quietly away.

In fear and trembling each lord lay in his bed and could sleep no more that night. Was it a dream? each asked himself. Was it a vision? Had any other seen or heard it?

When the grey morning light streamed in through the windows, and the darkness was no longer terrible around them, the lords arose. Quickly they gathered to the great Council Chamber. With pale faces and questioning eyes they looked at each other. "You too have heard? You too have seen? Then it was no dream. A message has indeed been sent from heaven; a message which we must obey."

So they spoke to each other and, after some hurried consultation, they went quickly to the King.

"Great King," they said, "this night we have seen strange signs and visions. The Lord of Heaven himself hath sent a message to us, and we are ready to fight as you command us."

Then they told the King of the vision which each one had seen in the night.

"I too have seen a vision," said the King, "but I said naught of it, fearing lest you should think I boasted. But now I tell you as you have all seen the like."

This, of course, was not true and the King knew very well that what the lords had seen was no vision, but only his own servants dressed up.

So, in this manner, the King had his own way. His lords gathered all their soldiers together till there was such a great army as had never before been seen in the land of Scots.

When the King of Picts heard of the great preparations which the Scots were making, he too gathered all his soldiers together. But, finding that his army was not large enough to withstand so great a host, he sent to England and asked the Saxons to help him. And the Saxons, because he promised them great gain and plunder, came.

Very early one morning, when it was just beginning to grow light, the battle began. Without a shout or sound of a trumpet, the Scots rushed upon the Picts and, when the Saxons saw this silent host moving through the dim morning light like ghosts, they were dreadfully afraid. So afraid were they that they took to their heels and fled away to the mountains nearby. The noise and clattering made by these fleeing Saxons startled the Picts and threw them into great confusion. Their King tried in vain to encourage them and bring order again into the ranks. It was of no use. The Scots fought so fiercely, that in a very short time the Picts were utterly defeated and, following the example of the Saxons, they too fled away. Their King himself, seeing that all was lost, turned his horse and rode fast from the field, he and all his army pursued by the victorious Scots.

After this battle the King of Picts sent messengers to Kenneth Macalpine desiring peace. "Tell your master," replied Kenneth, "that he shall have peace when he gives the crown of Picts to me. It is mine by just right and title."

When the messengers went back to the King of Picts with this answer, he was very angry. "I will never give up the crown," he said. So the war continued.

Battle after battle was fought, sometimes one side, sometimes the other, winning. But at last, in a great and terrible battle, the King of Picts and nearly all his nobles were slain.

Then Kenneth marched through Pictland, killing men, women and children in the most cruel manner, till those who were left fled away to England to escape from his cruelty.

Thus the kingdom of Scots and the kingdom of Picts were united, and Kenneth Macalpine ruled over both. He took all the land belonging to the Pictish nobles and gave it to the Scottish nobles who had fought for him and helped him to conquer the Picts. He changed the names of all those lands and gave them Scottish names, so that the memory of the Picts might utterly perish.

Some people say that the story of the great slaughter of the Picts is a fairy tale. Perhaps it is. But this is true, that about this time the Picts did vanish away out of the story of Albion and we hear no more of them, but only of Scots.

The Picts vanished away so completely that even very wise people cannot find out what kind of language they spoke. And so these wise people cannot agree as to what race the Picts belonged to.

Kenneth Macalpine was a wise king and made good laws, and after the battles with the Picts were over he ruled his people in peace. He reigned for twenty-three years – seven years over the Scots alone, and sixteen years over the whole land. He died in 859 AD, and was buried in the island of Iona which, ever since St Columba had built his church and monastery there, had been used as a burying place for the Scottish kings. If you ever go there, you may still see the graves of some of these ancient rulers of Scotland.

CHAPTER 7

How a Ploughman Won a Battle

YEARS passed on, king following king, and still the land was filled with fighting and strife. But out of the confusion and war of these stormy times, Scotland grew.

There was war with the Saxons; there was war with the fierce sea kings who came sailing over from Norway and Denmark. Wild pagan men were these, tall and strong, with long fair hair and blue eyes. Fearless, and brave, and cruel, they landed in the islands to the north of Scotland, burning, destroying, conquering and carrying off both men and women as slaves.

Fiercely the kings of Scotland struggled and fought against these wild invaders. Again and again they were driven out. Again and again they returned. They swept round the island; they wrecked the monastery of St Columba on the island of Iona. Everywhere they carried fire and sword, leaving death and desolation behind them.

In the reign of a king named Kenneth III, these Danes were defeated in a battle called the Battle of Luncarty. The fight had been sharp and cruel, and the Danes fought with such desperate bravery that at last they drove the Scots backward. In confusion they fled from the field. Down a long lane fenced on either side with high walls they fled, hotly pursued by the victorious Danes.

But in one of the fields nearby a ploughman and his two sons were quietly at work. When the old man saw how the Scots were fleeing, he seized the yoke from the neck of his oxen and, calling to his sons to do the same, he sprang into the lane. Side by side the three men stood barring the way. They were armed only with their wooden ox yokes, and with them they beat back all those who fled.

"Would ye flee and become the slaves of pagan kings?"

cried the old man, whose name was Hay. "Nay, nay, turn back, turn back, and die rather as free men."

So stoutly did he speak, such blows did he deal, that the Scots took heart again. They turned and, led by Hay, they once more attacked the on-coming Danes. And the Danes, thinking that a fresh army had come to help the Scots, were seized with fear and fled. Then the Scots, who had been so nearly defeated, now filled with new hope and courage, chased them from the field. Many were killed in the battle, many more fell in the chase, and the victory of the Scots was great. But all the honour was given to the ploughman and his two sons who had won the day after it seemed lost.

The King then commanded that these three brave men should be dressed in splendid robes and brought before him. But they did not care for fine clothes, so they refused the robes of silk and satin which were offered to them, and they went before the King wearing their old shabby clothes, covered with dust and mud, in which they had fought.

All the people were eager to see the men who, by such bravery, had saved their King and country from the terrible Danes. So they crowded along the road to see them pass and, with cheering and shouting, a great throng of people accompanied them, doing them as much honour as if they had been kings and princes.

Thus, followed and surrounded by a rejoicing crowd, they came to the King's palace. All the courtiers wore their most splendid robes. The King sat upon his throne, his golden crown upon his head. Before him stood Hay and his sons in their old shabby clothes, carrying their wooden ox yokes upon their shoulders.

"What can I do for you? What can I give to you," asked the King, "as a reward for your great services?"

"Give me, sire," replied Hay, "as much land as a falcon will fly over without alighting."

"That is but modest asking," said the King. "Let it be done."

Then the King and all his courtiers went out into the

fields near the palace, and watched as a falcon was let loose. As soon as the bird was free it rose high in the air, then spreading its wings it flew away and away.

On and on it flew, on and on till, to those who watched, it seemed but a speck in the distance. Then it disappeared. The horsemen, who followed its flight, rode fast and they too were lost to sight. On and on the falcon flew, till at last it alighted upon a stone.

It had flown six miles without stopping, and all that six miles of land was given to Hay and his sons to be theirs for ever.

The King then made Hay and his sons knights. As you know, knights always had something painted upon their shields in memory of the great deeds which they had done. So King Kenneth commanded that Hay should have a shield of silver, and that upon it three red shields should be painted. That was to show that the ox yokes of Hay and his sons had been as shields to the King and country. On either side was painted a ploughman carrying an ox yoke, and over all was a falcon.

I must tell you that some people say that this story too is a fairy tale, but there is still a great family whose name is Hay, and who bear these same arms with the motto, *Serva jugum*, which is Latin and means "keep the yoke".

CHAPTER 8

Macbeth and the Three Weird Sisters

AFTER King Kenneth III died several other kings reigned of whom there is not much to tell. At last a king called Duncan came to the throne. He was so kind and gentle that he was called Duncan the Gracious.

He was too kind and gentle for those rough times. The beginning of Duncan's reign was quiet and peaceful, but when the people saw how kind he was and how little he punished evil-doers, they grew unruly and rebellious thinking they might do as they wished because of the weak rule of this mild king.

Some of the people rose in rebellion under a leader called Macdowald. Duncan, who did not like fighting, hardly knew what to do, but he had a cousin called Macbeth who was a great and powerful man, very fierce and stern, and a splendid soldier.

Macbeth was impatient of the King's softness. He was eager to fight, so Duncan gave the command of his army to this cousin and to another noble called Banquo.

When the rebels heard that Macbeth was coming against them they were so afraid that many of them left their leader Macdowald. Some of them stole away to hide. Others joined Macbeth. Macdowald was left with very few soldiers but he was obliged to fight, for he could not escape from Macbeth. In the battle which followed, the rebels were utterly defeated and their leader was killed.

No sooner had Macbeth put down this rebellion than the Danes once more invaded Scotland. But he defeated them too and they fled away, promising never again to return.

One day, soon after the war with the Danes, Macbeth was walking over a lonely moor with Banquo when they were met by three old women. These three old women were very ugly and dreadful to look upon. They were called the Weird

Sisters and were supposed to be witches. Nowadays no one believes in witches, but in those far-off times everyone did.

These three old women stopped in front of Macbeth, and pointing at him with their skinny fingers, spoke.

"Hail, Macbeth! hail to thee! Thane of Glamis," said the first.

"Hail, Macbeth! hail to thee! Thane of Cawdor," said the second.

"Hail, Macbeth! hail to thee! King of Scotland," said the third.

Both Macbeth and Banquo were very much astonished and wondered what this might mean, for Macbeth was certainly not King of Scotland, nor was he either Thane of Glamis or Cawdor.

Thane was an old Scottish title meaning very much the same as the Saxon title earl which came to be used later.

"You say fine things to Macbeth," said Banquo, when the old women had ceased speaking; "have you nothing to say to me?"

"Yes," said the first witch, "we promise greater things to you than to him. He indeed shall be King of Scotland, but his end shall be unhappy. His children shall not follow him on the throne. You shall never reign, but your children shall sit upon the throne of Scotland for many generations."

Then the old women vanished, leaving Macbeth and Banquo full of astonishment.

They were still wondering what it all might mean when a horseman came spurring towards them. When he came near he threw himself from his horse and kneeling at Macbeth's feet, "Hail, Macbeth," he cried, "thy father Sinell is dead, and thou art Thane of Glamis."

What the first Weird Sister had said had come true.

More full of astonishment than ever, Macbeth went on his way. But he had gone very little farther when a second messenger came hurrying towards him.

"Hail, Thane of Cawdor," cried this second messenger, kneeling at his feet.

"Why do you call me that?" asked Macbeth. "The Thane of Cawdor is alive. I have no right to the title."

"He who was the Thane of Cawdor is alive," said the messenger, "but because he has rebelled against the King his thaneship has been taken from him. The King has made you Thane in his place as a reward for all your great deeds."

What the second Weird Sister had said had come true.

Now that two things had come true, Macbeth began to think more and more of what the Weird Sisters had said, and he longed for the third thing to come true too. But unless Duncan should die there seemed no hope of that. Macbeth despised Duncan because of his gentleness, and he wished he would die. Sometimes the wicked thought came to him that he would kill Duncan. Yet he could not quite make up his mind to do the evil deed.

Macbeth had a wife who was a very proud and beautiful lady. She longed to be Queen, and when she heard of what the Weird Sisters had said, she kept urging Macbeth to murder Duncan and make himself King.

But Macbeth could not so easily forget that King Duncan was his cousin, that he had always loved and trusted him, that he had made him general of his army and Thane of Cawdor and had heaped upon him many honours and rewards. So when Lady Macbeth tried to make her husband murder the King, he reminded her of all this.

But Lady Macbeth cared for none of these things. She hated Duncan and all his family, because his grandfather had killed her brother. She longed to avenge his death and she longed to be Queen. She kept on telling Macbeth that he was weak and cowardly not to murder Duncan. So at last Macbeth listened to his wife, and giving way to his own evil wishes and to her persuasions, he killed the good King Duncan.

CHAPTER 9

Macbeth – The Murder of Banquo

KING DUNCAN had two sons, one called Malcolm Canmore, or Bighead, the other Donald Bane, or White. When these two princes heard what had happened to their father, they fled away, fearful that Macbeth would kill them too.

Malcolm Canmore fled to England to the court of Edward the Confessor. Edward received him very kindly, for he remembered that he too had been driven from his own land and had been an exile in France for many years. Donald Bane fled to Ireland. The King there also received him kindly and treated him with honour.

Macbeth then caused himself to be crowned. And because he was so strong and powerful the lords and people of Scotland accepted him as King.

And although he had come to the throne in such an evil way, Macbeth proved to be a good king. For some years he ruled well, if sternly. He made good laws; he punished the wicked, rewarded the good, and tried in every way to make people forget how he had won the crown.

But the people did not forget and they did not love Macbeth. Neither could Macbeth forget what he had done. Although he was a good king he was a most unhappy man. When he thought of the three Weird Sisters and their words he felt more unhappy still. For he remembered that they had said that Banquo's children, and not his, should rule over Scotland.

Then he began to hate Banquo and to fear him. "Will not Banquo kill me in order to get the crown just as I killed Duncan?" he asked himself. The more he thought of it the more sure he felt that Banquo would murder him, and at last he made up his mind to rid himself of this fear.

One evening Macbeth asked Banquo and his son, Fleance, to supper. Suspecting no evil, they came. Macbeth provided a splendid supper for them which lasted until very late. At last when it was quite dark and everyone else had gone to bed, Banquo and Fleance said goodnight and started homeward.

Now Macbeth intended that they should never reach home again. He dared not kill them in his own house lest people should find out that he was the murderer. So he paid a large sum of money to wicked men who promised to lie in wait for Banquo and Fleance and kill them on their way home from the supper.

In the quiet, dark night, as father and son walked home together, these wicked men suddenly set upon them and tried to kill them. They did kill Banquo but Fleance escaped through the darkness and fled away to Wales. There he lived safely for a long time and married a Welsh lady. Many years after, his son, Walter, came back to Scotland. Walter was kindly received by the King who was then on the throne, and he was made Lord High Steward of Scotland. He was called Walter the Steward. The title was given to his sons and grandsons after him and soon Steward, or Stewart, came to be used as the surname of his family. For in those days people often received their names from their work or office. At last a High Steward married a royal princess. Their son became King, and was thus the founder of a race of Stewart kings who reigned for many years in Scotland.

In this way, what the Weird Sisters had foretold to Banquo came to pass.

After the murder of Banquo Macbeth was no happier nor did he feel any safer than before. Indeed he began to dread, and to look upon every man as an enemy.

Macbeth's fears turned him into a tyrant. For very little cause he would put a noble to death and take his land and money for himself. No man knew when his life was safe and the nobles one and all began to dread the King.

At length Macbeth found pleasure only in putting his nobles to death, for in this way he not only rid himself of his enemies, but he became daily richer and richer.

With the money of the dead nobles he paid an army of soldiers, some of whom he kept always round himself as a bodyguard. But in spite of his army of soldiers Macbeth's fear of being killed grew greater and greater. At last he went to the Weird Sisters to ask them for advice.

"How shall I keep myself safe," he asked, "when everyone around me is trying to find a way to kill me?"

And the old women answered:

"Be lion-mettled, proud, and take no care
Who chafes, who frets, or where conspirers are;
Macbeth shall never vanquished be, until
Great Birnam Wood to high Dunsinane Hill
Shall come against him."

Macbeth went home feeling much comforted and quite safe, for how could Birnam Wood come to Dunsinane? They were twelve miles apart, and it was impossible for trees to uproot themselves and walk all these miles through the valley to the hill beyond. Macbeth began to believe that he would never be killed at all. Feeling safe, he treated his nobles even worse than before so that they grew to hate him more and more, and many of them turned their thoughts to the banished sons of the gracious King Duncan, and longed for one of them to come and be their King.

CHAPTER 10

Macbeth – How the Thane of Fife Went to England

IN ORDER to make himself quite safe from his enemies, Macbeth thought that he would build a strong castle on the top of Dunsinane Hill. It cost a great deal of money to build this castle because the wood and stones for it had to be dragged up such a steep slope. So Macbeth made all his thanes help. Each in turn had to build part of the castle, sending men and horses to drag the stones and wood up to the top.

At last it came to the Thane of Fife's turn to help with the building. This thane, who was called Macduff, was a very great man and he was much afraid of Macbeth. For the greater and richer a man was, the more Macbeth seemed to hate him. Besides, Macduff had loved Duncan, and secretly hoped that Prince Malcolm would one day return. Macbeth knew this and hated him the more. Macduff sent builders and workmen with everything that they might need for the work. He gave them orders to be very careful, to work diligently and well, and to do everything aright so that the King might find no fault with them. But he himself kept away, for he knew that King Macbeth had no love for him, and he feared to be seized and put to death as so many nobles before him had been.

One day Macbeth came to see how the castle was getting on. "Where is the Thane of Fife?" he asked, looking round, and seeing him nowhere among his men.

On being told that the Thane of Fife was not there, but had sent his workmen only, Macbeth fell into a violent rage. "I knew beforehand of his disobedient mind," he said. "Now I am resolved to punish it."

At this moment some oxen which were drawing a load up

the hill stumbled and fell. "He cannot even send beasts fit to work," cried Macbeth. "I will make an example of him. I will lay the yoke upon his own neck instead of upon that of his oxen."

One of Macduff's friends who stood by heard the King's angry words. This friend went quickly to Macduff to warn him to fly from the country, for it was quite certain that the King meant to do him an evil.

Macduff, as soon as he heard, mounted upon a swift horse and fled away to his strong castle in Fifeshire.

The King lost no time in following. Close behind Macduff he came with a great army of soldiers. It was a fast and furious race. Macduff was almost alone, and he had had to ride away in such haste that he had little money with him. When he came to the ferry across the River Tay, which he must pass in order to reach his castle, he had nothing with which to pay the ferryman except a loaf of bread. But the ferryman was content to take the loaf, and for many years the place was called the Ferry of the Loaf.

On again rode Macduff, faster and faster still, until at length the turrets of his castle came in sight. Now he was quite close; now he was thundering over the drawbridge; now his breathless, sweating, panting horse carried him safe within the courtyard.

"Up with the drawbridge, men, let the portcullis fall," he shouted. In olden times a castle was always surrounded by a ditch filled with water, called a moat. Over the moat there was a bridge, but the bridge was made so that it could be drawn up in time of war. In this way an enemy often found it difficult to get across the moat and enter the castle. The entrance was also guarded by a portcullis. This was a heavy, barred gate but instead of turning upon hinges as gates usually do, it was raised up and let down like a window.

As soon as Macduff had seen his orders obeyed he went to greet his wife and tell her what had happened. Together they looked out from the castle turret. In the distance they saw a dark, moving mass. Now and again, as the sun caught it, they could see the glitter of steel. It was the King's army.

"We cannot hold the castle long against such a host," said Lady Macduff, as she watched the long lines moving onward. "You must fly. Our little vessel lies in the harbour ready to put to sea. Go quickly on board. I will hold the castle until you are safe."

Macduff did not want to go and leave his wife and children whom he loved. But there was no help for it, so he said goodbye and, stepping on board his little vessel which lay in the harbour behind his castle, he sailed away. He sailed away to England to see Prince Malcolm and to ask him to come and be King.

Meanwhile, brave Lady Macduff held the castle. Macbeth and his soldiers came close below the walls, calling to Macduff to give up the keys. But no one answered.

With beating heart Lady Macduff watched the white sail grow smaller and smaller in the distance, and listened to Macbeth as he poured out dreadful threats of what he would do if Macduff did not yield himself at once.

Then, at last, when Macduff was safely beyond the reach of pursuit, Lady Macduff came to the walls. "Do you see that little white sail far out to sea?" she asked. "Yonder is Macduff. He has gone to England to the court of Edward. He has gone to bring Prince Malcolm back to Scotland. When he comes we will crown him King. You will be dragged from the throne and put to death, so you will never put the yoke on the Thane of Fife's neck."

When Macbeth heard these brave words and knew that Macduff had escaped him he was fiercely angry. He began to storm the castle at once. The few men who had been left to guard it fought bravely but in vain. In a very short time Macbeth's fierce soldiers won an entrance, and gallant Lady Macduff and all her children were put to death.

Macbeth then took all Macduff's land and money, proclaimed him a traitor and an outlaw, and forbade him ever again to return to Scotland.

But Macduff did return.

CHAPTER 11

Macbeth – How Birnam Wood Came to Dunsinane

MACDUFF sailed southward, little knowing the dreadful things that were happening at home, little dreaming that his brave wife was dead and his castle a ruin.

Through storms and dangers he sailed until at last he landed safely in England and went to seek Prince Malcolm at the court of Edward the Confessor.

Malcolm received Macduff very kindly, for he was glad to have news of his own land. Macduff told the Prince of all the sorrows and griefs of Scotland, and begged him to come to fight for the crown.

"Do not mistrust me," he said. "Your father found me ever faithful. In spite of the many hardships which I have borne, to you also I have been faithful, and am, and shall be, all my life. If you come to claim the throne nearly all the lords will support you, and the common people, I know, will joyfully shed their blood for you."

When Malcolm heard these words he was very glad in his heart. He longed to go back to Scotland to claim his crown and throne. But still he was not sure if Macduff was to be trusted. He feared that he had been sent by Macbeth to persuade him to come to Scotland so that he might be betrayed and killed. So Malcolm was silent, wondering if he should go or not, turning it over and over in his mind, while Macduff still urged and persuaded. "I am truly grieved," said Malcolm at last, "to hear of the misery which has come upon Scotland. I love my people and I would like to make them happy, but I am not fit to rule. I am a bad man. I am the most greedy creature upon earth. If I were King I should try in so many ways to get money and lands that I should put to death the greater part of the Scottish nobles, for pretended faults, in order to take their goods and possessions for myself. So it were well for you that I should not come to be your King. I am ashamed to own it, but I am a thief and a robber."

All this Malcolm said to try Macduff.

Macduff, when he heard it, was very sad but he answered, "What you tell me grieves me deeply, but when you are King you will have great wealth; when you are King you will have no lack of gold and silver, or of precious stones, or jewels, or whatever else you may desire. Be brave then. Do your best, come to be our King, and forget your greed and wickedness."

"But," said Malcolm, "that is not all. I am deceitful. I love nothing so much as to betray and deceive. No man can trust my word. I make promises but I never keep them. I am not fit to be a king." Then Macduff was silent, too sad to speak. After a minute or two he cried out, "Oh unhappy and miserable Scotsmen! Alas for us! To be subject to you, our liege lord by right – never! You confess yourself a thief, false, cunning, faithless. What other kind of badness seems to be left but that you should call yourself a traitor. A traitor you are. You shall never be lord over me. Neither shall I be subject to Macbeth. I will rather choose banishment," and bursting into tears Macduff sobbed aloud. Then looking northward he stretched out his hands. "Scotland, farewell for ever!" he cried, and turned to go.

But as Macduff, with downcast head, went slowly away, Malcolm sprang after him and, catching him by the sleeve, cried, "Be of good comfort, Macduff, I have none of these wickednesses. I only said these things to prove whether you were faithful or faithless. Wicked people have so often come to try to betray me into the hands of Macbeth that I wished to make sure that you were true to me. Now I know that you hate falseness and cunning, even as I do. Forgive me, dear friend. Let us go to Scotland together. You shall not be an exile. No! You shall be first in the kingdom after the King."

Then Macduff, who had been weeping for sorrow, wept

for joy and falling upon his knees clasped Malcolm's feet and kissed them. "If what you say is true, my lord," he cried, "you bring me back from death to life. Oh hasten, hasten, my lord, I implore you to free your people who wait and long for you!"

Malcolm and Macduff talked long, making plans. At last it was agreed that Macduff should return to Scotland at once, and there secretly gather the people together and make known to them that their true King, Malcolm Canmore, was coming.

As soon as Macduff had gone, Malcolm went to King Edward and told him that he meant to return to Scotland to fight for the crown. And Edward, who had always been kind to Malcolm, gave him leave to take with him any of the English nobles and soldiers who cared to go to help him to win the crown. So Malcolm, taking with him the Earl of Siward and ten thousand English soldiers, set out for Scotland.

It was soon seen that Macduff had spoken the truth, for nearly all the Scottish nobles joined Malcolm, and the common people flocked to his standard in hundreds. But Macbeth did not believe that he could be either defeated or killed, for he remembered what the Weird Sisters had said about Birnam Wood coming to Dunsinane. So he shut himself up in his strong castle on Dunsinane Hill and felt quite safe.

Without fighting any great battle, Malcolm marched through Scotland until he came to Birnam Wood. There he lay encamped, intending next day to attack the castle of Dunsinane where he knew Macbeth to be.

In the morning the army arose rested and refreshed. Before the march to Dunsinane began, Malcolm ordered every soldier to cut down a bough of whatever tree was near to him and to carry it in his hand. "In this way," he said, "our army will be hidden by the green branches, and Macbeth will be unable to tell what numbers are coming against him."

So each man cut down as large a branch as he could carry and held it before him as he marched.

A few hours later Macbeth stood on his castle wall looking out towards Birnam Wood. Suddenly his face grew pale and he trembled in fear. What was this coming slowly and surely onward? Trees walking? Birnam Wood had come to Dunsinane Hill. Then all was lost.

Macbeth was really brave, and now that he felt that his last fight had come he meant to fight it well. So, calling all his soldiers about him, he marched out to meet the enemy.

In the thickest of the fight Macduff and Macbeth met. "Traitor," cried Macbeth, lifting his two handed sword high.

"I am no traitor but am true to my lawful King," cried Macduff, as he sprang aside to avoid the blow. A minute later Macbeth lay dead upon the ground, slain by Macduff's sharp sword.

So died Macbeth. He had reigned for seventeen years. At first he had been a good and wise king, doing much for the happiness of his people. But in the end he had proved himself a tyrant, and was hated and despised as tyrants ever are. He was killed in 1057.

CHAPTER 12

Malcolm Canmore – How the King Overcame a Traitor

PRINCE MALCOLM was now set upon the throne. He was crowned at Scone with great ceremony, sitting upon the Stone of Destiny, or the Stone of Hope as it was sometimes called.

This stone, it was said, was the stone which Jacob had used as a pillow when he slept in the wilderness and saw the vision of angels going up and down upon a ladder set up from earth to heaven. Prince Gathelus had brought it with him from Egypt, and from that time it had always been in the possession of the kings of Scotland, for it was said that wherever this stone was, the Scots should reign.

When Kenneth Macalpine became King over the whole land, he brought the stone to Scone, and there it remained for hundreds of years, and the kings of Scotland always sat upon it when they were crowned.

Malcolm did not forget his promise to Macduff and as soon as he was King he rewarded him greatly, making him second only to himself in power.

Macduff was now called the Earl of Fife for Malcolm, having lived so long in England, had learned many English ways and words, and he brought this Saxon title into use in Scotland.

To the Earl of Fife was given the honour of placing the crown upon the King's head at his coronation. He was also chosen to be leader of the army, and over the people of his own country of Fife he was given power equal to that of the King.

Malcolm was not allowed to take possession of his kingdom without a struggle. A few nobles still refused to acknowledge him as King, and they set Lulath, Macbeth's cousin, upon the throne. But Malcolm, hearing of this, sent an army against him. In the battle that followed Lulath was killed and all his soldiers scattered.

For ten years after this the land had peace. Malcolm Canmore was a good king and ruled well. We are told that he was a king very humble in heart, bold in spirit, exceedingly strong in bodily strength, daring though not rash, and having many other good qualities.

One day a courtier came to King Malcolm to tell him that one of his greatest nobles had agreed with his enemies to kill him. But the King bade the courtier be silent, and would not listen to him. Shortly after, the traitor came to court, followed by a great company of soldiers. The King greeted him kindly and did not let him see that he knew what wicked thoughts were hid deep in his heart.

That night there was a fine supper and the King ordered a great hunting party for next day. Very early in the morning everyone was astir. Huntsmen and dogs were gathered and with a great noise and clatter they set off.

The King arranged in which direction each man was to go and he himself rode off, attended only by one knight. This knight was the wicked traitor who wished to kill the King.

Side by side they rode through the wood – the King and the murderer. On and on they went, riding farther and farther away from the others. The noise of jingling harness, the voices of men, the baying of dogs grew fainter and fainter in the distance. At last they were heard no more. Darker and denser grew the wood but still the King rode on. At last, bursting through a ring of trees, they came to a clear open space.

Then the King turned and looking sternly at the traitor, said, "Here we are, you and I, man to man. There is none to stand by me, King though I be and none to help you. Nor can any man see or hear us. So now if you can, if you dare, if your courage fails you not, do the deed which you have in your heart. Fulfil your promise to my foes. If you think to slay me, when better? When more safely? When more freely? When, in short, could you do it in a more manly way? Have you poison ready for me? Would you slay me in my sleep? Have you a dagger hidden with which to strike me unawares? All would say that were a murderer's, not a knight's, part. Act rather like a knight, not like a traitor – act like a man. Meet me as man to man. Then your treachery may at least be free from meanness, for from disloyalty it can never be free."

All the time that the King was speaking, the wretched traitor sat upon his horse with bowed head. He was ashamed to look up, and the King's words fell upon his heart like the strokes of a hammer upon an anvil. He cursed himself for his evil thoughts. The weight of shame seemed more than he could bear.

The King ceased speaking and the traitor, springing from his horse, threw away his shield and spear. With trembling hands he unbuckled his sword and flinging that too away, he knelt at the King's feet, unarmed. His face was pale and tears were in his eyes; "My Lord and King," he cried, "forgive me. Out of your kingly grace forgive me this once. Whatever evil was in my heart, whatever wicked thought was mine shall be blotted out. I swear before God that in the future I shall be more faithful to you than any man."

"Fear not, my friend," replied the King, raising him up, "you shall suffer no evil from me or through me on this account."

CHAPTER 13

Malcolm Canmore –
How Saint Margaret Came to Scotland

WHEN Malcolm Canmore had reigned over Scotland for about ten years, a great event happened in the neighbouring kingdom of England. This was the conquest of England by William Duke of Normandy.

William Duke of Normandy took possession of all England and Edgar, the rightful heir to the throne, fled with his mother and sisters. They set sail in a ship meaning to go to Hungary where they knew they would be kindly received. But great storms arose. Their ship was battered and driven about by winds and waves they knew not whither and at last, when they had lost all hope of ever seeing land again, they were driven upon the shores of Scotland. They landed there at a place on the Firth of Forth which to this day is called Margaret's Hope, from the name of Edgar's sister the Princess Margaret. The place at which they afterwards crossed the river is still called Queen's Ferry.

When Edgar, who was only a boy, and his sisters and mother found themselves in Scotland they were uncertain what to do. They did not know if they would be received in a friendly manner or not.

The country people gathered round and stared at these strange ladies. They were astonished, and a little afraid too at their grand clothes, and at the great size of the ship in which they had come.

When King Malcolm was told of the beautiful ladies and fine tall men who had come in the strange ship he sent some of his nobles to find out who they were, where they came from, and what they wanted.

When the nobles came to the ship they were almost as

much astonished as the common people had been at the splendid men and beautiful, sad ladies. So the nobles spoke gently to them and asked them how it was that they had landed upon these shores.

Then the Lady Agatha and her daughters told their sad story. "We are English," they said, "the relatives of King Edward. He is dead, and his throne and crown have been taken by the cruel Duke of Normandy. We have fled from the country. The winds and the waves have driven us upon your shores and we seek the help and protection of your most gracious King."

The ladies spoke so simply yet they looked so beautiful and so grand that the nobles felt more and more sorry for them. They talked kindly to the ladies for some time. Then they went back to King Malcolm and told him all that they had learned.

When Malcolm heard that the ladies and their brother were English, and relatives of the King who had been so kind to him, he called for his horse and set out to visit them.

Malcolm brought Edgar and his mother and sisters back with him, gave them rooms in his palace and treated them as great and honoured guests. Soon he came to love the Princess Margaret very much for she was both beautiful and good. She too loved the King and after a little time they were married.

The wedding was very splendid. Such pomp and grandeur had never before been seen in Scotland as was seen at the marriage of Malcolm Canmore and Queen Margaret.

For the sake of his wife, Margaret, King Malcolm treated all English people kindly. So at this time very many of the English, who were driven out of their own country by William of Normandy, came to settle in Scotland. Malcolm gave these English exiles both land and money and thus it came about that in after years many of the great families had lands both in Scotland and in England.

These English nobles brought English manners and

customs to Scotland. This greatly displeased many of the
Scottish nobles. The Scots had always been a very hardy
people. They were big and strong – more like giants than
like ordinary people. They ate and drank little and cared
little for fine clothes or fine houses. It seemed to them that
the English cared too much for all these things. They
thought it was a bad day for Scotland when all these grand
knights and nobles came to live there and they were angry
with Malcolm because he was kind to them.

They were angry too with Queen Margaret for she
thought it right that the King of Scotland should be
surrounded by splendour as befits a great king. So she did
away with all the old simple ways to which the Scottish
people were accustomed. Great knights, nobles, and fair
ladies waited upon the King and Queen. Their meals were
served upon dishes of gold and silver, and the clothes they
wore were beautiful and gorgeous.

Queen Margaret also encouraged merchants to come to
Scotland to trade. They brought jewels and gold and other
beautiful things, and took away woollen cloth and whatever
else the Scots had to sell. It was in the days of Queen
Margaret that the Scottish people first began to wear the
brightly coloured checked cloths which we call tartans.

But in spite of all her splendour Queen Margaret was a
very good and holy woman and after her death she was
called a saint. Every morning before she had her own
breakfast she fed nine little beggar children. Often she took
them in her arms and fed them with her own hands. At
certain times in the year the King and Queen would give
dinner to three hundred poor and wait upon them as they
sat at table in the great hall of the palace. Queen Margaret
too used to wash the feet of pilgrims and beggars which in
those days was thought to be a very holy action.

The Queen could not bear to see anyone hungry or cold
or in misery. She gave all her own money to the poor and
often, when she had nothing left to give, she would borrow
from her lords and ladies-in-waiting. They were always

willing to lend to her for they knew that they would be paid again more than they gave. Sometimes too the Queen would take the King's money to give to the poor. He knew very well that she took it but he pretended not to miss it. But sometimes he would laugh and say that he would have her tried and imprisoned for stealing. Really he loved her so much that she might do anything she wished.

Queen Margaret was learned too. In those days, when few people could read, she could read both English and Latin. The King, although he could speak Latin, English and Scotch (which were different languages in those days), had never been taught to read. But he loved to take Margaret's books in his hand and sometimes he would kiss those which she liked the best. Sometimes too he would take away one of her favourites and give it to a goldsmith who would cover it in gold and set it with precious stones. Then Malcolm would bring the book back again and give it to Queen Margaret as a sign of his love for her. Malcolm was a good king but he was rough and passionate and sometimes cruel. But however angry he was the gentle Queen Margaret could always soothe and calm him again.

When William of Normandy, who had now made himself King of England, heard that Malcolm had married the Princess Margaret he was very angry. He was afraid that now the Scottish King would help Edgar to win the crown of England again. So he sent to Malcolm demanding that Edgar should be given up to him.

This Malcolm refused to do, and there was bitter war between the King of England and the King of Scotland.

The northern parts of England, called in those days Northumbria, had always been a ground of fighting and quarrel between England and Scotland. The boundary of Scotland was always changing. Sometimes it was as far north as the Forth, sometimes as far south as the Humber.

Now Malcolm made many expeditions into Northumbria to help the Northumbrian lords who hoped to drive William the Conqueror out of England and to place Edgar upon the throne instead.

Malcolm ravaged and plundered the whole country in a fearful manner. The Scots grew rich upon the spoils of war and they carried so many captives back to Scotland that for many years English slaves were to be found in every town, every village and every cottage in Scotland.

William, seeing that he could not conquer the Northumbrians, resolved to make their land a barren waste. He marched all over it and what the Scots had not destroyed, he destroyed until the whole country north of the Humber was a blackened, ruined desert and the people who were not killed in battle died of hunger or escaped into Scotland.

Then William marched to Scotland, resolved to punish Malcolm for having helped Edgar and the Northumbrians but, as an old history says, he and his soldiers found naught there for which they were the better. So at last the two kings made a peace which lasted until the death of the Conqueror.

CHAPTER 14

The Story of Pierce-eye

WHEN William of the Red Face came to the throne of England, there was war again between England and Scotland. It is not quite easy always to know why they fought, for in those fierce days a very small cause was enough to make a war. Sometimes Malcolm fought to help Prince Edgar, sometimes he fought about the Border lands. At last it was agreed that the Scottish King should hold the northern part of England, which was called Northumbria, in fief from the English King. The Scottish King would do homage to William for it just as the English King did homage to the King of France for the lands he held there.

To hold a land in fief meant that in return for the land, the man to whom it was given promised to help his "overlord" by sending soldiers to fight for him in time of war. This way of paying for land by fighting was called the feudal system, and it first came into Scotland in the time of Malcolm Canmore.

After this agreement there was peace, but it did not last long. William of the Red Face sent for Malcolm to come into England. Malcolm went, but when he arrived the English King treated him, not as one king might treat another, but as a king might treat a subject. William tried to pretend that Malcolm was his subject and ought to do homage to him for the whole of Scotland instead of only for Northumbria. This made Malcolm very angry. Leaving William in great wrath he went straight back to Scotland and gathered his army together. Then he marched again into England, fighting and plundering as he went.

William the Red hastily gathered an army and sent it against Malcolm. At a castle called Alnwick the Scots were defeated and their brave King Malcolm slain.

The Scots were besieging the castle. The English had

almost given up hope and were thinking of yielding when an English knight, trusting to win great renown, set forth upon a bold adventure.

He begged the Governor to give him the keys of the castle. Without armour or weapon of any kind except a spear in his hand he mounted upon a swift horse. Placing the keys upon the point of the spear he rode out of the gates and made straight for the Scottish camp.

As he came near to the camp he was stopped by the guards. "Whence come you?" they asked, surprised to see an English warrior alone and almost unarmed. "Is it in war or in peace that you come?"

"In peace," replied the knight, "we can hold out no longer. I bring you here the keys of the castle which I would give to your King, in token of submission."

The guards were very glad at the news, and they led the knight through the camp to the tent of the King. With clamour and rejoicing many soldiers followed, gazing in wonder at the unarmed knight with the keys of the castle upon his spear.

Hearing the noise, and wondering what it might mean, King Malcolm came out of his tent. As soon as the English knight saw the King, he lowered his spear, as if he would present the keys to him. But instead of doing so, he suddenly made a swift thrust forward and pierced the King in the left eye. Then, before those around could realise what had happened, he set spurs to his horse, and fled away to the woods nearby.

Without a groan the King sank to the ground, and when his friends raised him, it was found that he was quite dead. Then the English, taking advantage of the sorrow and confusion into which the Scots were thrown by the death of their King, fell upon them and defeated them with great slaughter. In the battle, Malcolm's eldest son, Prince Edward, was wounded so that he died. Filled with grief, the Scots turned back to their own borders.

The English knight who killed King Malcolm was,

because of this deed, called Pierce-eye ever after. He was thus, it is said, the founder of the great family of Pierce-eye or Percy who became earls of Northumberland.

While these things were happening in England, far away in Scotland the good Queen Margaret lay very ill. She lay praying for her husband and her sons when, opening her eyes, she saw her younger son, Prince Edgar, standing beside her bed.

His face was so pale and sad that the sight of it made her afraid. "How fares it with your father and brother?" she asked anxiously.

The Prince stood silent with drooping head and eyes full of tears.

"I pray you," cried the Queen, "tell me. By the Holy Rood and by the obedience you owe to me, tell me the truth."

Then the Prince spoke. "My father and my brother are both slain," he said.

"The will of God be done," cried the Queen; and turning her face to the wall, she died.

Malcolm Canmore was killed in 1093. He had reigned for thirty-six years, which was a very long time in those wild days. He was fierce and fond of war but he was brave and generous, and a true knight. He loved his country and he loved his wife dearly. For her sake he was very kind to the English Prince Edgar, often fighting for him when otherwise he might have been at peace with the English.

It was probably for Queen Margaret's sake, too, that Malcolm built several monasteries and churches and restored others which the Danes had destroyed. One of the churches which he built was at Dunfermline, and there he was buried beside his Queen. He was the first King of Scotland who was buried in Dunfermline, instead of in Iona, but after him many Scottish kings were buried there.

CHAPTER 15

The Reigns of Donald Bane, Duncan II and Edgar

MALCOLM died in 1093. His son, Edgar, was still very young so Donald Bane, who had fled to Ireland from Macbeth, now returned and claimed the throne.

Some of the Scottish nobles had been angry with Queen Margaret because of her splendid court, and with King Malcolm because he allowed so many Englishmen, whom they looked upon as weak and idle, to live and possess lands in Scotland. These nobles now gladly welcomed Donald Bane. They placed him upon the throne and drove the English out of Scotland. All Malcolm's children also fled and took refuge in England.

Donald Bane had scarcely reigned six months, however, when another prince called Duncan claimed the throne. Duncan defeated Donald Bane and made himself King. But a year and six months later he was killed in battle and Donald Bane again became King.

This time he reigned for three years during which there was constant war and trouble. There was war between Scotsmen and Scotsmen for many hated Donald Bane and would not be ruled by him; there was war with England; there was war with the wild Northmen or Danes.

At last, tired of the unrest and trouble, some of the Scottish nobles sent messengers to Edgar begging him to come to rule over them.

Then Edgar, who had no wish to fight, sent messengers to Donald Bane asking him to give up the crown. "It is not yours but mine by right," he said. "If you will yield the crown to me, I will gladly give you great lands and possessions over which you shall be lord."

But Donald Bane, having once been King, had no mind to

There stepped from out of the crowd an old, old man
(page 70)

become merely a lord under his own nephew. So, instead of answering, he put Prince Edgar's messengers in prison and then cut off their heads.

On hearing of this cruel and insolent treatment of his messengers, Edgar made up his mind to fight. Helped by his uncle, Edgar, and by the King of England, he gathered an army and set out for Scotland.

One night as he marched northward he rested at Durham where his father, Malcolm, had built a great church. There he had a dream. It seemed to him that St Cuthbert appeared and spoke to him in the night. "Fear not, my son," said the saint, "for God has been pleased to give you the kingdom. Take my standard from the church and carry it before your army, in face of your enemies. Then I will up and fight for you. Then your foes shall be scattered and those who hate you shall flee before you."

When Edgar awoke he immediately told the dream to his friends, and they, taking the standard of St Cuthbert from the church, carried it before the army.

The sight of the holy banner put such courage into the hearts of his soldiers, that they fought and conquered Donald Bane's great army. Donald Bane himself fled away, but he was pursued and brought back. Edgar, I am sorry to say, put out his eyes and cast him into prison where he died.

Edgar was crowned at Scone with great rejoicing and for nine years he reigned quietly and peacefully. Like his mother, Queen Margaret, he was very religious and he built and restored several churches and monasteries.

CHAPTER 16

Alexander I, the Fierce

EDGAR died in 1107 and as he had no children he was succeeded by his brother, Alexander.

Alexander I was called the Fierce because he punished the robbers and other wicked men of whom there were many in the country.

Edgar had been more loved for his gentleness and goodness than feared for his justice and sternness. When Alexander came to the throne many of the nobles had become little better than robbers. They rode through all the land, burning and destroying, killing and taking prisoner men, women and children. These wild nobles imagined that Alexander would be gentle, as his brother had been. They thought that he too would be more interested in building churches and monasteries than in ruling his kingdom and that they might still continue in their wicked ways. But they were mistaken. Alexander was a good man but he was a stern and just king. He made up his mind to punish these wild nobles. So he gathered his army and went against them. And so fiercely did he hunt and pursue these robbers that very soon the worst of them were put to death. As Alexander was returning from warring against these wild nobles he was met by a poor lady. She was pale and weary, her dress was torn and dusty. Sobbing, she threw herself upon her knees beside the King.

"A boon, my lord King," she cried, "a boon."

"What troubles you, lady?" said the King, looking down at her kindly. "Tell me, and if your cause is just, you shall have my aid."

"Sire," said the lady, "the Lord of Mearns has slain my husband and my son. He has robbed me of all that I had. Now I wander about, a homeless beggar with none to help me."

As the King listened, his face grew dark with anger and

leaping from his horse he cried, "By the Holy Rood, I will never more bestride a horse till I see justice done upon this man."

Then, turning his army, he marched at the head of it against the Lord of Mearns. Nor did he rest, nor again mount upon a horse till he had taken that proud lord and hanged him for his wickedness and cruelty to the poor lady.

Thus the wicked nobles began to be in fear and dread of King Alexander and they made up their minds – as they could not kill him in battle, they must do so by treachery.

They bribed the keeper of the King's bedchamber and promised him a great sum of money if he would let some soldiers into the palace. And the keeper of the bedchamber, who ought to have guarded the King's life as his own, let these wicked men into the palace and hid them in a little room near to the King's bedroom.

In the middle of the night, when all was dark, and the King was peacefully sleeping these bad men crept softly, softly into his room. But as they came near the bed the King awoke suddenly. There was a dim light and by it he could faintly see the figures crowding round him.

In a moment Alexander sprang up and seizing his sword which hung at the head of his bed, he slew the wicked keeper with one blow. Then right and left he struck, defending himself manfully. His sword flashed and fell again and again, till six of the traitors lay dead upon the floor.

Then, seeing how brave and fierce a king they had to deal with, the others fled. By this time, however, the noise of the fight had aroused the King's servants and soldiers. Some poured into his room, others started in pursuit of the traitors. Many of them were killed and the rest were taken prisoner and brought before the King. But Alexander knew that these men had been paid to kill him and not they, but their masters, were his real enemies. So he questioned them until they told the names of the nobles who had sent them to do this wicked deed.

Then Alexander gathered his army once more and marched against these rebellious nobles. When they heard of the King's coming, they too gathered their soldiers and made ready to fight.

The two armies came in sight of each other and lay encamped on either side of a river. The rebels thought that they were safe, for it seemed to them impossible for an army to cross the river, which was both deep and wide.

But King Alexander, calling his standard-bearer, commanded him to cross the river with a company of the best soldiers.

This the standard-bearer did and the rebels were so astonished and afraid at the hardihood and bravery of the King's men that they had no heart to fight, and were utterly defeated.

After this there was peace in the land and when Alexander had rest from wars he too built monasteries and churches, as his father and brother had done. He died in 1125 having reigned seventeen years.

CHAPTER 17

David I, the Sore Saint –
The Battle of the Standard

LIKE Edgar, Alexander I had no children, so he was succeeded by another brother, David, the youngest son of Malcolm Canmore.

While Alexander was King, David had lived much in England with his sister, Matilda, who had married Henry I, the King of England. There he had married a rich and beautiful English lady who, like his sister the Queen, was called Matilda.

This Lady Matilda had a great deal of land and money both in Huntingdon and in Northumberland, so David was an English lord as well as King of Scotland, and was called the Earl of Huntingdon.

For some years after David came to the throne he continued to live in England, leaving the affairs of his kingdom to the Constable of Scotland.

Having lived so long in England David had many friends, both Norman and English. After the death of Malcolm Canmore the English had been driven out of Scotland, now both English and Norman knights came again and settled there. David gave these friends lands, so many had possessions in both countries.

About this time the King of England, Henry I, had a great grief. His son, William, of whom he was very fond, was drowned crossing from Normandy. Henry had no other son so he made all the nobles swear that when he was dead they would accept his daughter, Matilda, as Queen.

This is a third Matilda. There was Matilda, Queen of England; Matilda, her daughter, Princess of England; Matilda, Queen of Scotland; and there was yet a fourth Matilda, the wife of Stephen who was afterwards King of England.

All the great nobles of England promised what King Henry asked, and King David of Scotland was the first to take the oath. He took the oath, not as King of Scotland, but as Earl of Huntingdon. For although within his own land of Scotland he could do as he liked, as Earl of Huntingdon he was bound to obey the King of England, just as on his part the King of England, as Duke of Normandy, was bound to obey the King of France.

But no sooner was Henry dead than the English lords forgot their promise and instead of putting Matilda upon the throne they chose Stephen, Henry's nephew, to be King.

But David was true to his promise and he marched into England to fight for his niece, Matilda. His wild troops ravaged and plundered in a fearful manner, the knighthood of England rose against them and in 1138 a great battle was fought.

Stephen's army was small but it was made up of English and Norman knights and soldiers, clad in steel, fully armed and perfectly drilled.

The Scottish army was large but many of the soldiers were half savage men from the far north, some were wild men of Galloway, and only a few were well-drilled and well-armed like the Normans.

These last David wished to place in the centre, in the place of honour where the fighting would be fiercest, for he knew that they could best resist the Norman knights.

But when the men of Galloway heard what the King meant to do they were very angry and demanded that they should be placed in the centre of the army. "Why do you put such trust in iron and steel?" cried one. "I wear no armour but I dare swear I will go as far tomorrow with my bare breast as any clad in steel."

"You boast," sneered a Norman knight, "of what you dare not do."

"My arm shall prove my boast," came the fierce reply.

And so the quarrel grew until King David was forced to yield, and give the place of honour to the brave, but wild and untrained men of Galloway.

But some of the Norman knights who were now on Stephen's side, had been David's friends and vassals. They had possessions both in England and in Scotland, and they did not wish to fight. So now, as a last hope, two Norman barons rode out from the English lines and went to beg David to make peace. These two knights were Robert de Bruce and Bernard de Baliol. These are names you must remember, for the descendants of these men had much to do with Scottish history in after times. It is interesting too, to remember that they were Norman.

Robert de Bruce was an old man and he was specially anxious to avoid a battle. "You are to blame," he said to David, "for all the wicked things your soldiers do. You have said that you are sorry for them. Prove that you really mean what you say and take your wild soldiers back to your own land. It will be better for you, for although we are not many we are very resolute. Do not drive brave men to despair. My dearest master," he cried, at last bursting into tears, "you have been my friend and companion. I have been young with you and grown old in your service. It wrings my heart to think that you may be defeated, and in such an unjust war."

Tears came into King David's eyes as he listened to the words of his old friend, and he was ready to yield to his entreaties and turn back. But one of the fierce Galloway men who stood by exclaimed angrily, "Bruce, you are a false traitor. You have broken your oath to your King. Do not listen to him," he added, turning to David.

More bitter words passed and Bruce, furious at being called a traitor, left the Scottish camp swearing that he would never again be subject to the King of Scotland.

Nothing now could stop the fight.

The English were drawn up in close ranks round their standard. This standard was a ship's mast set upon a wagon. At the top of the mast was a large cross and under the cross there was a silver box containing holy relics. Round it were hung four splendid embroidered banners of four great saints.

A gallant old priest, too old to fight (for in those days priests often fought), blessed the standard and encouraged the soldiers with brave words, telling them that this was a holy war and that God would reward everlastingly those who died in it.

Then the English lords grasped each other by the hand and swore to fight for their holy standard, or die. "I swear that on this day I will overcome the Scots or perish," cried one old knight.

"So swear we all," cried the others, and the air rang with their shouts.

The knights then resolved to fight on foot and they dismounted and sent their horses away so that none might be tempted to fly, but must conquer or die where they stood.

The Scots now rushed forward and the sound of their war cry was like the roar of thunder. "Scotland! Scotland! Scotland for ever!" they shouted.

So fierce was their onslaught that for a moment the steel-clad English warriors seemed to waver. But it was only for a moment. Again and again the Scots threw themselves upon the enemy. But it was like the breaking of waves upon a rocky shore. The ranks of Normans and English stood firm.

Then Prince Henry, King David's young and daring son, galloped forward with his horsemen. Fiercely and swiftly they came dashing onward. Through the English ranks they charged, breaking them as if they had been cobwebs, scattering knights and soldiers and chasing them for several miles from the field.

It seemed as if the victory was won. But suddenly an English soldier held up a head upon the point of his spear, crying, "Behold the King of Scots."

It was not really King David's head. He was not killed nor even wounded. But seized with sudden fear, the Scots broke and fled.

It was in vain that King David, taking off his helmet, rode up and down among them bare-headed to show that he was yet alive. All was panic and confusion. The day was lost.

And so, when Prince Henry returned from chasing the English, he found the Scots flying from the field. "We have done what men may," he said to his men. "We have conquered as much as we could. Now we must save ourselves if we can."

Then his men, throwing away their banners that they might not be known, mixed with the English soldiers and so passed through their ranks. At last, after three days, having had many adventures and escapes they reached the Scottish camp. Great was King David's joy when his son returned, for he had begun to sorrow for him as lost.

Although the Scots had been defeated in the Battle of the Standard, as it was called from the famous English standard, they did not leave England. It was not until some months later that peace was made and then the terms which the Scots made were so good that they seemed to have lost little by this battle. But the cause of Matilda, Queen of England, appeared to be hopeless for the time at least, and although David helped her again, he was never able to win her kingdom for her.

King David was not always fighting. He did much besides and was a good and wise king. The chief thing for which he is remembered is that he built many churches and monasteries. Indeed he spent so much money in this way that a king who reigned long after him said that David was a "sore saint for the crown". By that, this king meant to say that David had spent so much money on churches that he made the country poor. And the kings who came after him were obliged to tax the people heavily in order to get money to pay for necessary things.

But we must remember that in those far-off days the monasteries were the only schools and hospitals, and the monks and nuns the only teachers, doctors and nurses. So in building monasteries, King David also built schools and hospitals.

King David was a just man and he protected the poor and helpless. He never lost his temper. He was always kind and gentle. The poor knew that he would always listen to their sorrows and complaints and deal justly with them. So they did not fear to go to the King whenever they were in distress.

It is told of him how one day he was going to hunt. His foot was already in the stirrup when a poor man came to him with a tale of sorrow and injustice.

The King immediately sent away his horse and returning to his palace, listened to what the poor man had to say and saw that justice was done to him.

Although David was so kind to the poor and talked to them as if he were one of themselves, he ruled his lords and knights very sternly, and made them treat him with all the reverence and respect due to a king.

At length a great sorrow fell upon this wise and good king. He too, like Henry I of England, lost his only son. Prince Henry, young, handsome and brave became ill and died and there was great mourning and wailing in all Scotland, for he had been much loved.

King David was growing old and he knew that he could not live much longer. So calling to him Duncan, Earl of Fife, he bade him take Prince Malcolm, Henry's eldest son, and travel with him through the land showing him to the people as their future King.

Prince Malcolm was little more than ten years old, but for the love they had to his father the people welcomed him and swore to be true to him as their King.

One day, soon after this, King David's servants found him kneeling as if in prayer. His head was bent and his hands clasped upon his breast. He was dead.

King David died in 1153 having reigned twenty-nine years. He was succeeded by his grandson, Malcolm, who was only eleven years old. Malcolm was allowed to take possession of the crown quietly. But in those far-off times there was nearly always rebellion when a child came to the throne. So very soon a rebellion, headed by a powerful chief called Somerled, broke out. For three years there was war but at last the rebels were subdued.

As King Malcolm was so young someone must at first have ruled for him. But strange to say, we do not know who this was. Malcolm reigned for twelve years, but very little of importance to Scotland's Story happened during that time.

King David had possessed a great deal of land in England. The king who was now on the throne of England was very fond of power. He did not like to think that so much of his land was in the hands of the Scottish King, especially as that king was only a boy. So he sent to Scotland and asked Malcolm to come to England to visit him.

Malcolm went and somehow or other Henry II, the King of England at this time, persuaded or forced him to give up his claim to all his English lands except the earldom of Huntingdon. In spite of this, Malcolm seems to have been fond of King Henry. He spent much of his time with him and even went with him to fight against the French.

This made the Scottish people very angry for the Scots and the French had been friends for many years. It was perhaps for this reason that some of the people broke out in rebellion again.

Malcolm died in 1165. He was only twenty-four years old when he died, and he was called "The Maiden", because he had a beautiful face and looked more like a girl than a man.

CHAPTER 18

William I, the Lion

MALCOLM had no children so he was succeeded by his brother, William. William was by no means meek and gentle like his brother, the Maiden, and he was called the Lion. He was very sorry that Malcolm had given up Northumberland to the King of England and he tried to get it back again. But Henry was not a man to let go anything of which he had once gained possession, so William tried in vain. But he could not forget that the kings of Scotland had once ruled Northumberland and when he had been on the throne about nine years he resolved to fight for it.

He gathered a great army and marched into England. He took several towns and castles in Northumberland. Then at Alnwick he rested, waiting for the coming of the English army.

One morning a thick mist covered all the country. Through the mist a company of English soldiers came marching from the south. They had lost their way and knew not where they were. Fearing lest they should be surprised by the Scots, some of them wished to turn back. But one bold knight named Bernard de Baliol cried out, "You may go back, but I will go on, even if I go alone, and thus preserve mine honour." So, heartened by his brave words, the soldiers pushed on as best they might.

Suddenly the mist lightened and the English saw the walls of a castle not far off. Upon a plain, near the castle, about sixty knights were holding a tournament.

A tournament was a kind of mock battle and in those days was one of the chief amusements of lords and knights. It generally took place on a large plain, round which people stood and sat looking on. In the place of honour sat fair ladies and great lords watching the knights. The weapons used in a tournament were usually blunted but in spite of this, those who took part in it were often wounded and sometimes killed.

The knights wore in their helmets the colours of their ladies and it was thought that a knight could not honour his lady more highly than by being victor in a tournament. So every true knight longed to be victor and to win the prize of bay leaves or flowers which was placed on his head by the fairest lady there.

These knights who were holding the tournament in the mist were King William and his lords. They were thus playing at war while waiting for the real enemy to appear. At first, when they saw the English, they thought that it was a party of their own soldiers. But soon they found out their mistake.

To turn and flee to the castle of Alnwick was the only safe thing to do. However, that bold King William would not do this. "Now we shall see who among us are true knights," he cried, and setting spurs to his horse he charged the enemy.

But sixty men could do little against six hundred. All that brave and desperate men could do, they did. But it was in vain. Many were slain, many more were wounded. King William fought more bravely than any. But at last his horse was killed, he fell to the ground and was taken prisoner by the English.

The English were so pleased at having taken such an important prisoner that they did not wait to fight any more. They turned southward at once carrying with them the King of Scots.

The English did not treat King William kindly. They set him upon a horse and tied his legs together under it, just as if he had been a common thief or murderer. In this manner he was brought before King Henry.

King Henry did not treat his prisoner kindly either. He put heavy chains upon his hands and feet and threw him into a dark dungeon. Then, thinking that he was not safe enough in England, Henry sailed over to France where he shut William up in a castle.

There, William the Lion was kept until he should promise to acknowledge Henry as overlord. But William, chained though he was, was still the Lion and he would not agree. So Henry sent messengers to the Scottish Parliament and they, in order to free their King, agreed that the King of Scotland should acknowledge the King of England as overlord.

William was then freed from prison and allowed to go back to his own land.

For fifteen years this wicked bargain lasted. And the King of Scotland did homage to the King of England. Then Henry II died and his son, Richard of the Lion Heart, set William the Lion free from his promise.

Richard wanted to go to join the wars of the Cross or Crusades, as they were called. They were so called because the people who took part in them were fighting for the land where Christ died upon the Cross. This land, which was called Palestine or the Holy Land, was in the hands of the Saracens. These Saracens did not believe in Christ and they were cruel to the Christians who travelled to Palestine to visit the Holy Sepulchre. So Christian people of all lands banded together to fight these Saracens and drive them out of the Holy Land.

Richard of the Lion Heart was eager to join one of these Crusades but he needed money to carry himself and his soldiers over the sea to Palestine. William gave Richard money and, in return, Richard gave Scotland her freedom once more. He wrote a letter, or charter, saying that Scotland was a free country as it had ever been, and that the King of Scotland was no longer the vassal of the King of England and need not do homage to him. This was in 1189.

This action of King Richard's did a great deal towards wiping out the bitter feeling of hate between the English and Scots, and for some years there was not only peace but even friendship between the two lands.

William the Lion lived to be a very old man. He died in 1214 having reigned fifty years all but a few days.

CHAPTER 19

The Story of Alexander II

ALEXANDER II was only seventeen years old when his father, William the Lion, died. But he was crowned at once and, young though he was, he proved to be a good and wise king.

During his reign the quarrelling over the Border lands between England and Scotland still went on. Alexander was very anxious to recover his power over Northumbria and soon after he came to the throne he marched into England to help the barons who were fighting against their own King John.

John was very angry when he heard that the King of Scotland was helping his rebellious barons and he marched northward at the head of a wild and terrible army. The names of some of the leaders of this army show what fierce men they were. They were called Buch the Murderer, Godeschal the Iron-hearted, Manleon the Bloody.

These cruel warriors marched through all the country, killing people, burning houses and laying waste the land. Every morning they set fire to the town in which they had spent the night, King John himself showing the example and setting light, with his own hand, to the house in which he had slept.

This terrible host came to within a few miles of Edinburgh, John vowing that he would "unearth the young fox," as he called King Alexander. But there he found the Scottish army ready to fight him. John dared not fight for his soldiers were almost starving. All the country round was a desert. In it John could find no food for his army so he turned and went home again.

Then, in revenge, Alexander marched once more into England and not until John died and his son ruled instead, was there peace between the two countries.

Alexander then married the sister of the new English

King, and the peace was so secure for a time that once, when the English King had to go to France, he asked Alexander to take care of the north of England while he was gone. And Alexander, like a true knight, accepted the trust and kept faith with the English King.

Having made peace with England, Alexander had time to look after his own country and people. This was no easy task. The people were wild and passionate, and so fiercely did they quarrel among themselves that, at times, they were in danger of dragging the whole country into war.

Once a tournament took place near a town called Haddington. Knights came from all sides to take part in it. Among them was a great and powerful lord called Walter Bisset. Through all Scotland he was known to be a skilful fighter. He rode proudly into the lists, his armour gleaming and his helmet plumes waving in the breeze. He was sure of winning the prize.

But there was there a young lord called the Earl of Athole. He hated Walter Bisset and he had made up his mind to conquer him. So when the heralds sounded the trumpets as a sign for the tournament to begin the Earl, singling out Walter Bisset, lowered his lance and rushed upon him with all his might. But Walter Bisset was a strong man and knew well how to use his weapons. He sat firmly upon his horse, returning blow for blow. The fight grew fierce, their lances were shivered to atoms, their swords flashed and rang. Then suddenly putting out all his strength the Earl dealt a mighty blow. In a moment Walter lay upon the ground and his horse galloped riderless away.

Walter rose unhurt but with anger in his heart and, swearing vengeance upon the Earl, he sullenly left the lists.

A few days later the young Earl was killed, his house was set on fire and burned to the ground.

As soon as the Earl's friends heard of what had happened they made sure that it was Walter Bisset who had done the deed. So he was seized and brought before the King. In vain Walter tried to clear himself. No one would believe him. He was condemned, as a punishment for his wickedness, to have all his land taken from him. He was also ordered to go upon a pilgrimage to the Holy Land there to remain for the rest of his life, praying for the soul of the murdered Earl.

But instead of going to the Holy Land, Walter went to the court of the King of England. He told the King that he was innocent and he complained that the King of Scotland had no right to punish him, even had he been guilty, without leave from his overlord the King of England.

Of course the King of England was not the King of Scotland's overlord, but the King of England was only too glad to make believe once more that he was. So he sent messengers to Alexander asking how he dared act in so great a matter without leave.

"Tell your master," replied Alexander proudly, "that I never have held, nor never will hold, the smallest part of my kingdom of Scotland as vassal of the King of England. I owe no obedience to him."

When Henry received this answer he resolved to make war on Scotland. He gathered a great army. Alexander also gathered an army and they marched to meet each other.

But there was no fighting. Even in England many people loved Alexander. The English nobles did not wish to fight against him and at the last moment peace was arranged. This peace lasted until the death of Alexander in 1249.

CHAPTER 20

Alexander III – How the Little King was Crowned and Married

ALTHOUGH Alexander II had reigned for thirty-five years, he was not an old man when he died and his son, who was also called Alexander, was only eight years old when he began to reign.

Being so young, the little Prince had not yet been made a knight. Some of the nobles said that he could not be crowned until he had been made a knight. So the old bishop of St Andrews knighted the little boy before the crown was placed upon his head.

With trembling fingers the old man fastened a big sword, with jewelled scabbard and hilt, round his waist and tried to make him understand what all the ceremony meant. Then he led the little knight to the Stone of Destiny. Sitting there, the crown was placed upon his head by the Thane of Fife, the sceptre was put into his hand and the royal robes upon his shoulders.

Then one by one the nobles knelt before the little King. Throwing their mantles at his feet and placing their hands between his, they swore to be true to him and serve him faithfully.

When the last lord had risen from his knees, there stepped from out of the crowd an old, old man. His hair and beard were long and white. His back was bent and as he walked he leaned upon a staff. His cloak, which covered him from head to heel, was brilliant scarlet. In his hand he held a harp. He was a minstrel or singer.

Kneeling before the throne the minstrel began to tell, in a kind of chant, the names of all the King's fathers and grandfathers. "Hail, King of Albion," he said, "Alexander, son of Alexander, son of William, son of Henry," and so on and on until he had told the names of all Alexander's forefathers right back to the prince called Gathelus who had come out of Greece so many hundreds of years before. Then, when he had finished, the minstrel rose from his knees and all the nobles shouted, "Hail, King of Albion."

Two years after he was crowned, the boy King was married to the little Princess Margaret, daughter of the King of England.

Alexander went to England to be married and the ceremony took place at York. The bride and bridegroom were only children but the wedding was a very splendid affair. People crowded from every part of the two kingdoms to see the sight. There were English, Norman and Scottish nobles all as grandly dressed as might be, besides merchants, farmers and common people of every description.

The feasting and rejoicing lasted many days. Hundreds of oxen were roasted whole, fountains ran with wine. A thousand knights rode behind the little Princess as she went to her wedding. Every day these knights appeared in new clothes, each suit more splendid than the last. The boy King, too, was attended by hundreds of knights, who were dressed as beautifully as those around the Queen.

But in the midst of all this splendour and feasting, the King of England tried once again to make himself master of Scotland. The little King did homage to Henry for the lands which he still held in England and Henry tried to make him do homage for Scotland too.

But young though he was, Alexander had already been taught to beware of the greed of the King of England, so he answered, "I came into England on a joyful and peaceful errand. I came to marry the English Princess, not to talk of the affairs of state. I cannot, and will not, speak of so important a matter without the advice of my lords and nobles."

And although Henry was not very pleased, he had to be content with this answer. Then, when all the feasting was over, Alexander went back to Scotland taking his Queen with him.

As the King was so young there was a great deal of quarrelling among the nobles as to who should have the power. For, of course, Alexander was too young really to rule.

The Scottish nobles had been jealous of each other, and now they were jealous of the English nobles and servants whom the Queen had brought with her. And among them all the little Queen had an unhappy time. For although she was a queen, Margaret was, after all, only a little girl. She had been taken away from her father and mother and sent to live in a strange country. There, everything seemed to her to be very dull and quiet, after the bright and lively English court. So she cried and complained and was very miserable. She cried so much that her father, the King of England, heard about it and he sent messengers to Scotland to see if they could make things brighter for his little daughter. But the Scots were so jealous of these English people that it is said they even poisoned one of them who was a doctor, and whom the King had sent to take care of the little Queen.

Then Henry came himself and he appointed a Regent to rule until Alexander should be twenty-one. But although the Queen was perhaps happier after this, no English King could settle Scottish matters. So for some years there were very sad times while the great lords plotted against one another, each struggling for power, and each trying to gain possession of the King.

But when Alexander was about twenty years old he resolved to be King indeed. He took the power into his own hands and he soon showed that he knew how to rule.

CHAPTER 21

Alexander III – The Taming of the Ravens

FOR many years the islands which lie around Scotland had been in the power of the Norsemen, these wild sea kings who came sailing over from Norway.

Now Alexander made up his mind to drive these Norsemen out of the islands and rule them himself. For he saw how dangerous it was to allow these fierce strangers to live so near his own kingdom. They were always ready to help rebels against the King of Scots, and the kings of England were always sure of their help when they wished to fight with Scotland.

So Alexander gathered an army of soldiers and sent them in ships to these islands. There was much fierce and cruel fighting but at last all the Norse nobles, who would not own the King of Scotland as overlord instead of the King of Norway, were either killed or driven away.

Those who were driven away sailed back to Norway, in hot anger, to beg help from Haco, their King.

Haco, when he heard what Alexander had done, was very wrathful, and he gathered a great army. He resolved to avenge his people. He had about one hundred and sixty ships. They were nearly all large and they were crowded with soldiers and strong men of war.

Haco's own ship was very splendid. It was built of oak and it was painted, gilded and beautifully carved with dragons. From the masthead floated his standard, embroidered with a raven with outspread wings. From this standard these fierce sea kings were known as the Ravens.

As this mighty fleet came floating onward it looked very bright and splendid. Flags fluttered in the breeze, the summer sun shone on the coats of the knights and made their weapons and armour glitter. Never before had such a fleet sailed against Scotland.

On they came, right round the north of the island, and down the west coast until they sailed up the Firth of Clyde.

When Alexander saw what a number of ships there were, he knew he could not hope to defeat them unless he had time to gather more soldiers. So when the ships sailed up the Firth of Clyde he sent some monks, with bare feet and heads, to ask Haco upon what terms he would make peace.

Haco was glad to think that Alexander wished to make peace, so he sent some of his chief men to talk to him. The King received these men kindly but he kept them waiting for a few days before he returned an answer to King Haco. And so as time went on, Alexander caused delay after delay, for he had no intention of making peace. He only wanted to gain time as he knew that every day was precious. He knew that the longer he put off fighting, the longer he had in which to gather troops, and as the summer passed there was always greater and greater chance that storms would arise and wreck Haco's ships.

Soon the Norsemen had eaten up all the food which they had brought with them. They had no means of getting more unless they landed and attacked the Scots. So the captains urged Haco to battle. By this time, too, the fine weather had gone. The sky grew grey and the wind blew cold and at last, one night, a fierce storm arose. The waves dashed high, the wind shrieked and howled, and many of Haco's ships, driven hither and thither in the darkness, were broken to pieces upon the rocky shore.

So fierce was this storm that the Norsemen thought it had been caused by the enchantments of some witch and that made them more afraid than they would otherwise have been.

The Scots were ready and watching for some such disaster to happen, and soon bonfires were lit all along the coast which carried far inland the news of the wreck of Haco's fleet. So, as the ships were dashed by the waves upon the shore, armed peasants rushed down from the heights above, eager to kill and to plunder.

In the morning, Haco resolved to land the rest of his men and to fight as best he might. When he did so, he found a great army of Scots, led by their King, waiting for him.

Among the Scots were some very splendid horsemen, both men and horses clad in steel, and so fiercely did they charge that it seemed as if they would drive the Norsemen into the sea.

But the Norsemen were strong and brave and unused to yielding, and although some fled, many stood their ground. These formed themselves into a ring and, standing back to back, their long spears made an unbroken, bristling fence upon which the Scottish horses threw themselves again and again in vain. Hour after hour the battle raged around the circle of spears. Step by step, the Norsemen were forced backward towards the sea, but still the bristling fence remained unbroken. Great deeds of valour were done on either side and many a brave knight fell. And all the time the storm raged, the roar of the waves, the shriek of the wind were mingled with the clash and clang of sword and armour and the cries of the wounded and the dying.

At last night fell and the fighting ceased. In the darkness the Norsemen fled to their boats. When morning broke, they looked with sorrow and despair towards the shore where their brave comrades lay dead. So many had been drowned during the storm, so many had been killed in battle that there were not enough left to fight any more. Haco, therefore, sent a message to King Alexander begging for peace and for leave to bury the dead.

This Alexander granted and, having gathered their dead and buried them in great trenches with piled stones upon them, the Norsemen sailed away in their battered, half-wrecked ships, never again to return. But Haco got no farther than the island of Orkney. There, overcome by grief and shame at his defeat, he died, and never more saw his native land.

This battle was called the Battle of Largs, and was fought on the 15th December 1263. By their defeat the pride of the Norsemen was broken. The Ravens were tamed.

CHAPTER 22

Alexander III – How a Beautiful Lady Took a Brave Knight Prisoner

IN THE days of Alexander III there lived a lady called Marjorie, Countess of Carrick. This lady was very young and very beautiful. Both her father and her mother were dead. Her mother had been King Alexander's cousin, her father a brave soldier who had died in a far-off land fighting the battles of the Cross. So this beautiful lady became the King's ward. That is, he looked upon her as his daughter and took care of her as a father would have done.

One day the Lady Marjorie was hunting in the woods near her castle. She was splendidly dressed and rode upon a beautiful horse. With her were other lovely ladies and fine gentlemen, all grandly dressed. As they rode through the woods, laughing and talking, they met a knight who was riding alone.

The knight was clad in shining armour and he was tall, strong and handsome. When Lady Marjorie saw him her heart gave a leap and a bound. Of all the knights and nobles she had ever seen, this was the grandest and the best.

As the knight rode past, Lady Marjorie looked after him. Then she called one of her gentlemen to her. "Ride quickly to yonder knight," she said. "Tell him that the Countess of Carrick begs him to join the chase, and to dine with her in the castle which is hard by."

The gentleman put spurs to his horse and rode quickly after the knight. "Sir Knight," he cried, "my Lady of Carrick greets you and begs the honour of your company."

The knight, whose name was Robert de Bruce, stood still and, as he listened to Lady Marjorie's message, he looked back at the lively company of lords and ladies who waited for him at a little distance. Robert de Bruce had seen the

Lady Marjorie's face as he rode past. To him she had seemed more lovely than any lady in all the world. But now he stood silent and thoughtful. He longed to go back, yet he dared not.

The Countess of Carrick was a very great lady. She was the King's ward and cousin. Robert de Bruce knew by that one look at her beautiful face that he loved her but he feared that the King would not think him great enough, nor rich enough to marry his ward. So he resolved never to see her any more. "I thank the lady humbly," he said to the gentleman who stood waiting for his answer, "but I may not stay. Pray the lady to pardon my rudeness, for I must hasten on. By nightfall I must be far from here." Then bowing low, he rode away.

The gentleman went back to the Countess and told her what Robert de Bruce had said. As Lady Marjorie listened the tears sprang to her eyes, her lips trembled, and she looked as if she were going to cry.

Then drawing herself up she said, "Who is this who dares disobey the Countess of Carrick? I say he shall come. Ride forward, gentlemen, and surround him. If he will not come in peace, then it shall be in war."

The gentlemen scattered through the wood in all directions and a few minutes later, as Robert de Bruce rode slowly forward, he found himself surrounded on all sides by a troop of brightly clad knights with drawn swords.

Seeing himself thus surrounded, Robert de Bruce drew his sword too, ready to defend himself to the last. Then Lady Marjorie rode through the ring of knights and laid her hand upon the bridle of his horse. "Put up your sword," she cried smiling, "a true knight may not fight against a lady. You are my prisoner."

Robert de Bruce sheathed his sword and taking off his helmet, bowed low before the beautiful lady. "Lady, I yield myself your prisoner," he said.

Then, laughing and merry, Lady Marjorie, holding the bridle rein of her prisoner's horse, led the way to the castle.

There Robert de Bruce remained for a fortnight as Lady Marjorie's prisoner. But he was such a willing prisoner that he never tried to run away. Indeed, as the days went on, the thought that some time he would be obliged to go away and leave her made him very unhappy. So in spite of his fear of the King's anger, he asked Lady Marjorie to marry him, that they might never be parted any more.

This was just what Lady Marjorie wanted him to do and as they were afraid that the King would say "no" they got married first, and told him about it afterwards.

When the King heard about it he was quite as angry as they had expected him to be. He was so angry that to punish Lady Marjorie, he took all her lands and money from her. But she came to him and begged to be forgiven; all her friends begged for her too, and at last Alexander forgave her. And when he saw what a splendid, strong man Robert de Bruce was, he forgave him also, and became his friend.

Robert and Marjorie lived very happily together. They had a little son, whom they called Robert, after his father. This little baby grew up to be a very wise man and became King of Scotland. You will hear a great deal about him soon.

CHAPTER 23

Alexander III – How the King Rode Homeward Through the Dark Night

ALEXANDER was a good king and after he had tamed the Ravens he spent his time making good laws. He travelled all over his kingdom to see that justice was done even to the very poor. He reigned for thirty-seven years and towards the end of his reign he had many sorrows. His wife died, his two sons died and his daughter, who had married the King of Norway, also died. She left a little daughter called Margaret and this little girl was the heir to the throne.

In those days it was very unusual for a queen to rule so, sad as he was, Alexander gathered all his nobles together and made them swear to receive the little Princess Margaret as their Queen when he died.

Alexander felt it very necessary to do this, for the King of England, Edward I, had again tried to make him own him as overlord. But Alexander had again refused. "To homage for my kingdom of Scotland no one has any right save God alone, nor do I hold it of any but God," he said. "I do homage to you only for the lands which I hold in England."

So for the time being the King of England had to be content, but Alexander felt very sure that when he was gone, and there was only a little girl to withstand him, the King of England would try once again to make himself master of Scotland. So he charged all the knights and barons to be true to their Queen and their country.

Not long after this Alexander had been to Edinburgh to a great banquet and after it was over he started to ride back to his castle at Dunfermline. The night was dark and his lords prayed him not to go, as a wise man called Thomas the Rhymer had foretold that there would be a great storm.

But Alexander was determined to go and he started off in the darkness.

He reached the River Forth in safety and there the ferryman begged him not to cross as the night was dark and the water deep. Still Alexander insisted on going. "Then will I go too," said the man; "it would ill become me if I were not willing to die with thy father's son."

The river was safely crossed. On again through the darkness went the King and his little band of followers. The road led by the riverside. The cliffs were high and steep, and the night so dark that they could not see the narrow path and they had to trust to their horses.

But on they went, the King riding first, quickly and fearlessly. Suddenly his horse stumbled. There was a cry in the darkness, the sound of a heavy fall, then silence.

"My lord King," cried a frightened attendant, "what has happened?"

There was no answer except the sound of the waves and the cry of wild birds. Far below, on the rocks of the seashore, the King lay dead.

Morning dawned clear and calm and the people laughed at Thomas the Rhymer. "Where is your storm?" they asked, pointing to the blue sky and bright sunshine. But even as they spoke a messenger came with the news, "The King is dead."

"There," said Thomas, "that is the storm of which I spoke. Never did tempest bring more ill luck to Scotland."

There was great sorrow at the death of Alexander for he had been a good king and his people loved him.

It is more than six hundred years since King Alexander died but the place is still called the King's Crag and there is a monument there to mark the spot.

CHAPTER 24

The Maid of Norway

WHEN Alexander died his little granddaughter, Margaret, who was called the Maid of Norway, was only four years old. She was living in Norway with her father but she was proclaimed Queen of Scotland and six nobles were appointed to rule the land until she grew up.

Now began a very unhappy time for Scotland, a stormy time, as Thomas the Rhymer had foretold. The six nobles, and many others besides, quarrelled among themselves. Instead of trying to keep Scotland peaceful they tried to make themselves great. This went on for about four years. Then Edward, King of England, who was still eager to make Scotland and England into one country, proposed that the little Queen, who was now eight years old, should marry his son, Edward, Prince of Wales.

The Scottish people agreed to this but knowing what was in Edward's mind they made it plain to him that Scotland should remain a free country, even though the Queen married the English Prince. The rights and customs of Scotland were to remain unchanged and Scotland was never to be made a part of England. To this, Edward had to appear to agree for he saw that on no other conditions could he have his wish. But secretly he said to one of his chief advisers, "Now the time when Scotland and its petty kings shall be under my rule has at last arrived."

The little Queen set sail from Norway in a beautiful ship filled with splendid jewels, clothes and other rich presents from her father. But she never reached her kingdom. On the voyage she became very ill and died in Orkney. How she died, or where she was buried, we do not know. In those days news travelled very slowly. There were no trains or post or telegrams and it was not for some time after her death that the people, who were waiting anxiously for their

Queen, learned that she would never come to them at all.

The death of the little Queen was a great sorrow to the people of Scotland and it also put them into a great difficulty. The Maid of Norway had been the only direct heir to the throne for King Alexander's children had all died before he did, and he had no other near relatives.

But he had a great many cousins and distant relatives, and now no fewer than twelve men claimed the throne. The chief of the twelve were John Baliol and Robert de Bruce, the father of that Robert who married the pretty Lady Marjorie. Each of the twelve thought that he had the best right to the throne. None would give way so the quarrelling became very fierce.

As the twelve could not agree among themselves as to who should be King they at last resolved to ask someone else to decide for them. So Edward, King of England, was asked to come to settle the question.

This seemed to many of the nobles the best and wisest thing to do. King Edward was king of a neighbouring country, he was King Alexander's brother-in-law and great-uncle of the Maid of Norway, and he was known to be a wise and just man. But King Edward pretended that he was asked for none of these reasons but because he was overlord of Scotland.

Edward chose John Baliol as King. Both John Baliol and Robert Bruce were descended from David of Huntingdon who was William the Lion's brother, but John Baliol was the grandson of his eldest daughter while Robert Bruce was the son of his second daughter. So Edward decided that the grandson of William the Lion's eldest child had a better right to the throne than the son of his second daughter. We might own that King Edward's choice seems the just and right one.

Unfortunately, John Baliol was a weak man and no fit king for Scotland at this time. Before Edward chose him as King he made him swear to own the King of England as overlord. To this John Baliol consented, for Edward was so strong and he so weak that he did not dare to resist. It is said that Edward had sent for Robert de Bruce and offered him the crown on the same terms, that Bruce had indignantly refused and so John Baliol was chosen instead.

Kneeling before King Edward, John Baliol placed his hands between his lord's and swore to be his man. The great seal of Scotland was broken in four and given to the King of England as a sign that Scotland was his. Then he went home, believing that at last he had made himself master of Scotland.

"Hold you, hold you, brave Wallace! The English have hanged all your best men like dogs" (page 95)

CHAPTER 25

John Baliol – The Siege of Berwick

JOHN BALIOL was made King in 1292, two years after the death of the Maid of Norway. The crown of Scotland had indeed been placed upon his head but in order to win that crown he had been obliged to own himself to be the King of England's subject. Perhaps he thought that to do homage to Edward was only a form and that once he was safe upon the throne he would be able to defy the King of England. But Edward very soon showed him that he was mistaken. Edward was a great king and to his own subjects, at least, a just one. But he loved power. He believed, perhaps, that he had really the right to be Scotland's overlord and he meant to insist on that right, not in name only, but in deed.

Whenever King Baliol tried to act as any free king would, Edward would send to scold him and ask how he dared act without leave from his overlord. If Baliol punished a rebellious noble, the noble would go to Edward and complain. Then Edward would take the side of the noble and be angry with Baliol, not perhaps because he cared whether the noble had been justly or unjustly punished, but because he wanted to make Baliol feel that he was under the King of England and must do what he was told.

No man, however unworthy of the name of king, could long suffer such tyranny and soon Baliol, weak though he was, rebelled.

Edward was at war with France and as he wanted more soldiers he sent to Baliol ordering him to come with some of his best men to fight for England against France.

But the Scottish people were tired of the insolence and tyranny of the English King. They had never agreed to Baliol's bargain so now they refused to send a single man to fight against the French. Instead, they drove all the

English from the Scottish court and agreed to help the French to fight them.

Edward was very angry about this and, gathering an army, he marched into Scotland. The Scots too gathered an army. Their Parliament declared, in the name of their King, that they no longer considered Edward as overlord. In case Baliol should be weak enough to yield again they shut him up in a strong castle and went to war without him.

But, unfortunately, all the Scottish people were not united. As many of the great lords owned lands in both countries, they owed obedience both to the King of Scotland and to the King of England. In times of peace that did not matter much, but in times of war it caused great difficulties. As you know, they only held their lands on condition of fighting for their overlord in battle so, as their two overlords were fighting against each other, many of them, as was natural, sided with the stronger, which was Edward.

Besides this, many of the Scottish lords were angry because Baliol was kept a prisoner, so they would not join in fighting Edward.

Among those who fought for Edward was Robert Bruce, the husband of Lady Marjorie. Bruce joined Edward because he was an English as well as a Scottish lord, because he hated Baliol and because he hoped Baliol would be driven from the throne. Then, he hoped, Edward would help him to become King.

Edward marched north as far as Newcastle-upon-Tyne. From there he sent a message to the King of Scotland, ordering him to come to him. But, after waiting a few days and finding that Baliol did not come, he marched on again and, crossing the Tweed, laid siege to the town of Berwick. Berwick was at this time the most important seaport in Scotland.

To lay siege to a town means to surround it on all sides so that the people in the town cannot come out and no one can go in carrying help and food. Sometimes, if a siege lasts a long time, the people within a town suffer terribly from hunger.

The siege of Berwick did not last long for although the town was protected by the sea on one side, on land there was only a low mud wall to keep the enemy back. Edward attacked it both by land and sea. The Scots set the English ships on fire and drove them back. But on land the English army broke down the walls and entered the town.

The King himself, mounted upon his great horse, Bayard, was the first to leap over the wall. After him swarmed his soldiers, eager to kill.

There was terrible bloodshed and slaughter. Such was the fury of the English that none were saved and the streets ran red with blood.

In the town was a place called the Red House. It belonged to Flemish merchants who had come to live in Berwick and who had helped to make the town rich and prosperous. It was a very strong place and when the rest of the town had been taken the merchants of the Red House still held out and fought bravely. These gallant men, although they were not Scotsmen, had made up their minds to die for the land in which they had found a home.

When the English saw that they could not take the Red House, they set it on fire. Still these brave Flemish merchants would not yield to the English King and they died, every man of them, amid the roaring flames. They were buried beneath the ruins of their Red House.

Then King Edward, lest the Scots should take their town again, dug a ditch and built a wall round it to make it strong. King though he was, he wheeled a barrow and used a spade himself, so eager was he to encourage the men and help on the work. The remains of these fortifications can be seen to this day. Fortification comes from a Latin word which means "strong" so, to fortify means to make strong.

CHAPTER 26

John Baliol – The Last of Toom Tabard

BERWICK was taken. Instead of yielding the people made Baliol send a letter to Edward saying he would not come to do homage as he was ordered to do.

"Ah, the foolish traitor," cried Edward when he read the letter. "What folly is this? Since he will not come to us, we will go to him."

And so he went, fighting battles and taking towns all the way. Town after town, castle after castle fell before Edward and his victorious army. The great lords and barons knelt to him as their master. There seemed no help for it. They must yield or die.

At last, at Montrose, Edward and Baliol met again. And there Baliol, forgetting his proud words, came to Edward begging for pardon. With no crown upon his head, with no royal robes about his shoulders, with neither sword nor sceptre, clad only in a plain dark dress like a penitent and carrying a white wand in his hand, he came. Standing before his master he confessed that he had been led away by evil counsels. He gave up his right to the throne of Scotland and put himself into the hands of Edward.

Edward, strong and stern and filled with contempt for so weak a man, sent both Baliol and his son prisoner to England. A few years later Baliol was allowed to go to France. There, on his own lands, he lived quietly till he died. In Scotland's Story we have no more to do with this weak-spirited king. His own people called him Toom Tabard, which means empty coat, because he looked rather fine in his splendid robes, but there was neither courage nor manhood in him. And for many years to come Scotland suffered for his weakness and folly.

Now that Baliol was no longer King, Robert Bruce thought that the time for which he had hoped had come. He thought that he should now be King. But Edward had no mind to give up what he had won. "Have we nothing, think you, to do but to conquer kingdoms and give them to you?" he asked scornfully, and Robert Bruce went back to his own lands sad and angry.

Edward placed English governors over Scotland, filled the Scottish castles with English soldiers then, thinking that he had subdued the people, he went home.

He took with him many things that were dear and sacred to the hearts of Scotsmen. Among these was the Stone of Destiny, which remained in England for many hundreds of years. It is said too that Edward caused to be taken away and destroyed, many old books and records of Scotland. He did this so that the people might be made the more easily to forget their ancient freedom and become his willing subjects.

But all these things he did in vain.

CHAPTER 27

The Adventures of Sir William Wallace

THOSE were sad days for Scotland. The people seemed crushed and almost in despair but they were still unconquered. They had no king, no leader. But in this dark hour a man arose who became their leader and although he never wore the crown he was the king of every true Scotsman's heart. This man was Sir William Wallace.

Wallace was not one of the great nobles. He was only the younger son of a country gentleman. But he loved Scotland with all his heart and soul and he hated the English who had brought so much sorrow and trouble on his dear land.

At the time when John Baliol was driven from the throne, Wallace was very young. He was indeed little more than a boy but he was far taller than most men and was very strong and handsome. He had a great deal of brown, wavy hair and his eyes were bright and clear. Far and wide he was known as a gallant fighter and there were few who could stand against the blows of his sword. Yet although he was so big and strong and fierce in battle, he was very kind and generous. He gave nearly all his money to poor people and those who were in need never came to him in vain.

When everyone else was in despair, when everyone else had yielded to Edward, Wallace alone would not yield and would not quite despair. But his heart was full of hot anger against the English and he longed to free his country from them.

Wallace had hated the English all his life, and he had his first fight with them when he was quite a boy. One day he had been out fishing and had caught a good many fish. On his way home he met some Englishmen.

"What have you in that basket?" asked one of them.

"Fish," replied Wallace.

"Fish? Where did you get them?"

"I caught them."

"Give them to me," said one of the Englishmen. "What need have beggarly Scotsmen of fish?"

"No," said Wallace, "I will give you some if you ask nicely, but I won't give them all to you."

"What insolence," cried the Englishman, drawing his sword. "Give them to me at once!"

Wallace had only his fishing rod with which to defend himself but he was very strong and with it he gave the Englishman such a blow on the head that he fell dead. Wallace then seized the dead man's sword and he used it so well that the others soon ran away. Then Wallace went home quietly with his fish.

The English Governor was very angry when he heard of what Wallace had done. He sent soldiers to take him prisoner. But kind friends warned Wallace and he escaped into the mountains. There he lived until the matter was forgotten and it was safe to return home again.

Wallace had many adventures with the English and as he always got the best of the fighting they soon began to fear him. But he did not spend all his time in fighting.

One Sunday, as he was going to church, he met a beautiful lady. She too was going to church and was dressed in her best clothes. She looked so lovely that Wallace could not help looking at her and when he could no longer see her he kept thinking about her. He soon found out that she was the daughter of a gentleman called Hugh Braidfute. Not long afterwards they were married.

William Wallace and his beautiful young wife were very happy together. They were so happy that perhaps he began to think a little less about Scotland and the sad state of the country. But one bright spring day Wallace and his friends were walking through the town. It was the Scottish custom to dress in bright green in springtime. Wallace and his friends were all finely dressed in green and he wore a jewelled dagger at his belt. As they walked, some Englishmen began to jeer and laugh at them.

"What business have Scotsmen with such fine clothes?" they said.

"You are so grand we thought you must be from the court of France."

"What right have you to wear such a fine dagger?"

So they went on, jeering and tormenting until a quarrel broke out. Swords were drawn and blows fell thick and fast. In the fight Wallace killed a man and when at last the Englishmen had been driven back he and his friends fled to his house.

Wallace knocked at the door which was quickly opened by his wife. As fast as possible he told her all that had happened. Then Wallace, knowing that it would not be safe long to stay there for the Governor would certainly send to look for him, said a sad farewell. He and his friends stole out by a back way and fled to the woods beyond, while Lady Wallace barred the doors and the windows and made ready to fight the Governor, should he come.

She had not long to wait. Soon a body of horsemen came clattering down the street led by the Governor, whose name was Hazelrigg. They battered and banged at the door and at last broke it open. Then they poured into the house. But Wallace was not there. High and low they hunted. He was nowhere to be found.

Then Lady Wallace was dragged before the Governor.

"Where is your traitor husband?" he asked.

But brave and beautiful Lady Wallace stood silent. She would not tell.

Mad with anger, Hazelrigg drew his sword and pierced her to the heart. She fell to the ground dead. Never again would Wallace see her lovely, merry face. Then Hazelrigg killed all the servants and friends of Wallace he could find and set fire to his house. He proclaimed him a traitor and an outlaw. An outlaw means a man whom the laws no longer protect. Anyone might kill him without fear of being punished. The Governor, indeed, promised a large sum of money to anyone who would bring Wallace to him, alive or dead.

In the darkness of the night a brave woman, who had loved Wallace and his beautiful wife, crept out from the silent and deserted ruins of their house. Down the still streets and lanes she crept till she reached the wood. Through the woodland paths she hurried until she came to the secret cave where she knew that Wallace and his friends would be hiding. There she threw herself on her knees before him, sobbing out the dreadful story.

As he listened, Wallace, who feared no danger, covered his face with his hands and wept. His great friend, Sir John the Graham, was with him and, seeing his master in such sorrow, both he and his men wept too.

But Wallace soon rose. Dashing the tears from his eyes, "Let us be men," he cried. "Tears are but useless pain. They cannot bring her back who was so blithe and bonny. But hear me, Graham," he added fiercely, drawing his sword, "this blade I will never sheathe until I have avenged her death. For her dear sake ten thousand shall die."

Back to the town marched Wallace and his men. Straight to the Governor's house they went. Fierce wrath gave Wallace double strength and setting his shoulder to the door he burst it open. Up the stairs he sprang and entered the Governor's bedroom. There he lay, quietly sleeping, having finished his cruel day's work. As Wallace rushed in he started up, "Who makes so much noise there?" he cried.

"'Tis I, Wallace, the man whom you have sought for all day," and as he spoke Wallace clove the Governor's head, cutting through flesh and bone to the shoulder.

Very soon the whole town was in a stir. The news of the Governor's death spread fast. The English fought fiercely to avenge their master but the people of the town rose to a man to help Wallace. When morning dawned hundreds of Englishmen lay dead in the streets and Wallace was master of the town.

CHAPTER 28

William Wallace – The Black Parliament of Ayr

AFTER this many people gathered round Wallace so that he was soon at the head of an army of men all eager to drive the English out of Scotland. These men were nearly all of the common people for most of the great lords were too proud to follow a leader who was only a poor gentleman. Besides, many of the great lords had lands both in England and in Scotland and it did not seem to them to matter much whether Edward of England ruled over Scotland or not. Indeed, as in any case they had to do homage to him for their lands in England, some of them would have been glad that he should have been King of Scotland also, so that they might have only one master instead of two.

Wallace was clever as well as brave and in a short time he had driven almost all the English out of the south of Scotland. The people loved him. Men, and women too, were ready to fight and die for him.

At last the English, seeing that they could not conquer Wallace, tried to take him by treachery. They pretended that they wished to make peace and they invited Wallace, and all the Scottish nobles who had joined him, to meet in a council in the town of Ayr.

The meeting was to be held in a large house, built of wood, just outside the town. This place was called the Barns of Ayr.

Glad at the thought of peace and suspecting no evil, the Scottish knights and nobles agreed to come to the council. So, lightly armed and brightly clad, they rode along by twos and threes to the place of meeting.

All seemed peaceful and quiet. But as each man leapt from his horse and entered the barn he was seized, a rope was flung round his neck and before he could utter a word he was hanged from the beams of the roof.

Knight after knight entered that awful house. Many went in, but none came out again. The English soldiers stood ready, waiting silently and quickly did their cruel work.

Knight after knight came but Wallace, Wallace the chief of all, the man whom they most wished to seize and kill, did not come.

He never came. For a woman, unseen by the soldiers, had crept close up to the barn. Something had warned her that within all was not fair and true. So she watched and waited and at last she found out what deadly work was being done.

Not a moment did she waste. Fast as feet could carry her she sped away to warn Wallace. As she ran she met him galloping towards the Barns. He knew he was late, but he hoped yet to be in time to help to make peace for his country so he urged his horse to greater speed.

"Oh hold you, hold you, brave Wallace!" cried the woman, as soon as she saw him. "Go not near the Barns of Ayr for there the English have hanged all your best men like dogs."

Wallace stopped his horse and as he listened to the woman's tale he reeled in his saddle, as if he had been struck. Then he turned and went back to his men, his heart brimming over with rage and pain.

That night the English soldiers feasted and rejoiced over their cruel deeds. Then they lay down to sleep. Some of them slept in the very house in which they had killed so many brave and unsuspecting Scotsmen; others lay in houses nearby.

When all was dark and quiet, the woman who had warned Wallace went through the town. On every house in which the English slept she set a white mark.

Behind the woman came Wallace and his men. Wherever they saw the white mark, they piled up branches of trees and firewood against the house. When all was ready they set light to each pile. The houses were all built of wood, and soon the whole town was filled with the roar and crackle of flames and the shrieks of the dying.

The English tried in vain to escape for Wallace and his men stood round ready to kill them or to drive them back again into the flames. They cried for mercy but the Scots had none. It was a cruel death but those were cruel times and the Scots had terrible wrongs to avenge.

In the morning nothing remained but smoking ruins strewn with dead. This was called the Black Parliament of Ayr. Some of the English had been quartered in the monastery nearby. When the Prior heard of what Wallace was doing he bade all the monks to rise and arm themselves. Then they fell upon the soldiers and put them all to death. The monks were as merciless as Wallace and his men had been and the people called the slaughter the Friar of Ayr's Blessing.

CHAPTER 29

William Wallace – The Battle of Stirling Bridge

Day by day the army of Wallace grew. From castle after castle he drove the English. And because he had not soldiers enough to guard these castles he pulled many of them down.

At last King Edward, hearing of all that Wallace was doing, sent a great army to conquer him. Wallace was then laying siege to the castle of Dunbar. Dunbar was now the only fortress in the north which still remained in the hands of the English, although it was but a year since Edward had gone home thinking that he had conquered Scotland.

As soon as Wallace heard that the English were coming, he left Dunbar and marched to meet them. The two armies came in sight of each other near the Forth. That night they camped one on each side of the river, not far from the town of Stirling.

Wallace had many men but the English had three times more and he knew that it would take both skill and bravery to win the day. So he had chosen his position well and carefully. He had encamped on high ground above the Forth and in such a position that most of his men could not be seen by the English or tell how many men he had.

The river was swift and deep and crossed only by one narrow bridge. So narrow indeed was the bridge that only two men could walk abreast. To take a whole army across this narrow bridge was very dangerous. Yet it was the only way of reaching the Scots who lay securely awaiting the enemy on the opposite side.

The English leader felt it to be so dangerous that in the morning he sent two friars to Wallace, asking him to make peace and promising him pardon if he would lay down his arms.

"Go back," replied Wallace proudly, "and tell your master that we care not for the pardon of the King of England. We did not come here in peace. We came ready for battle. We are determined to avenge our wrongs and to set our country free. Let the English come and attack us: we are ready to meet them beard for beard."

The friars went back and the English general was so angry at this bold answer that he resolved to attack at once, cost what it might. So, two by two, his men marched across the narrow bridge. On and on they came, yet the Scots moved not hand or foot. But when a good part of the English army had passed over, a company of Scots stole quickly round the hill and, taking possession of the end of the bridge, they cut off those of the English who had already crossed from those who were still on the other side.

Then, as soon as Wallace saw that the English army was thus cut in two, he thundered down the hill upon them. The English had had no time to form in proper order after crossing the bridge and now, when the Scots dashed down upon them, they were thrown into utter confusion.

Fearful bloodshed followed. Hundreds fell beneath the long spears and broadswords of the Scots. Hundreds more were drowned in the river. Men and horses struggled together in wild disordered masses. Of all who crossed that narrow bridge, only three returned alive.

When the soldiers on the other side saw what was happening they turned and fled, their leader with them. He who had been sent to subdue Scotland galloped madly southward, never stopping until he had reached Berwick. Then, after a few hours' rest, he fled still further, far into England.

Half the English army lay dead upon the field. Scotland rang with shouts of joy. The power of the English King was broken once more.

But the land was wasted, barren and desolate. The fields lay untilled. The people starved and there was not even bread for the army. So Wallace led his men into England.

There they found bread enough and to spare. There for three months they lived, fighting, ravaging and carrying off great spoil from the English.

Wallace was now made Governor of Scotland. But although the people chose Wallace to be Governor, the lords and barons were not pleased. They were jealous of the great love and fame which Wallace had won by his bravery. They were so proud that they could not bear to think of being ruled by a man who was only a simple gentleman and not a great lord. But this simple gentleman had shown that he was the one man who could break the power of England and he was the best ruler for Scotland at the time. Much sorrow might have been spared the land, if those proud nobles had put away their foolish jealousies and had thought, not of themselves, but only of their country.

CHAPTER 30

William Wallace – The Battle of Falkirk

DURING this time King Edward had been in a far-off land called Flanders. Now he returned and, full of anger against Wallace, gathered an army and once more marched to Scotland. "Had I been in England," he said, "Wallace durst not have done such cruelties to my people."

"I chose but my time in England," replied Wallace, "I chose but the time when King Edward was out of it, as King Edward chose his time in Scotland when he found the same without a leader. For when the nobles took him as a friend to decide upon the rights of those who were struggling for the throne, he tried to conquer the kingdom for himself."

It was a great and mighty army that now marched into Scotland with King Edward at its head. Horsemen and footmen, great lords and barons, and all the proudest and best warriors of England were there. Wallace, too, had a large army but his were mostly foot soldiers. Only the great in Scotland rode in those days and, as you know, few of the great nobles had joined Wallace.

Wallace knew that it was best not to try to fight a battle against the whole strength of Edward's army. He hoped rather to weaken the English by hunger and weariness. So he laid waste the country through which they would have to pass. And when Edward came, he found only a desolate, deserted land with no food for his men to eat, and no enemy for them to fight.

But Wallace and his army were never far off. Whenever they saw a chance of attacking a small company of the English, they came out of their hiding place and fell upon them. Having killed as many as they could, they would dash away again and wait for another chance.

Thus with many little fights, or skirmishes as they are called, by the way, Edward marched far into Scotland without fighting any great battle or even finding out where Wallace and his men really were.

At last Edward grew tired of marching through a barren land in search of an enemy who would not fight an open battle. He had given orders to his men to turn and march home again when a sad thing for Scotland happened. Two of the jealous Scottish nobles came to Edward and told him where the Scottish army lay. They were not far off, in a forest, near a town called Falkirk. These wicked nobles not only told Edward where the Scottish army lay but they also told what plans Wallace had made. "Hearing that you are turning homeward," they said, "he is going to take you by surprise at night and attack you from behind."

"Thanks be to God who hitherto hath brought us safe through every danger," cried Edward, when he heard the news. "They shall not need to follow me since I shall forthwith go to meet them."

Not a moment was lost. The order to advance was given. The King himself was the first to put on his armour, the first to mount his horse. Without rest, the soldiers marched onward while daylight lasted. When night fell they lay down where they were, clad in their armour, their weapons beside them and their shields for pillows. Horse and horseman lay together, so that each man was ready at the least alarm to vault into his saddle. Among them, like any other soldier, lay the King beside his horse.

In the middle of the night a sudden cry arose. The enemy was upon them! Their King was wounded! In a moment all was bustle and preparation. Every man seized his weapon and stood ready in his place. But there was no enemy. The King indeed was wounded but by his own horse which had kicked him in the side and broken two of his ribs.

As the camp was now thoroughly aroused and as morning was not far off the King gave the order to advance.

He himself, in spite of his hurt, mounted upon his horse and led the way.

Through the grey morning light the army marched and as the first beams of the sun shone out they were flashed back from the glittering spears of the Scots army. At last the long-looked-for enemy was in sight.

It was but a little army compared with the English. But Wallace was not afraid. He divided his men into four companies and placed them to the best advantage. "I have brought you to the ring," he said, "now let me see how you can dance," meaning, "I have brought you to the battlefield, let me see how you will fight."

And bravely and well did these Scotsmen fight. But it was the people only, the foot soldiers, who fought. For hardly had the battle begun than the horsemen turned and rode from the field without giving or taking a blow. Oh bitter was the heart of Wallace as he watched them go! The nobles had forsaken him.

The famous English archers showered arrows on the Scottish spearmen. So true was their aim that it was said that every archer carried twenty-four Scottish lives beneath his belt. Which meant that he carried twenty-four arrows in his quiver and with every arrow he killed a man.

The English horsemen, splendid in glittering steel armour, charged the sturdy Scottish archers. They, armed only with their bows and arrows and short daggers, still would not yield. To a man they fell where they stood. So gallant and brave were they that even their enemies praised them.

But no bravery could stand against such numbers and such skill. Wallace, seeing that the battle was hopelessly lost, commanded his men to retire. With his best knights round him he fought bravely to the last, keeping the enemy off until his soldiers had found shelter in the forest behind.

Nearly fifteen thousand Scots were slain upon the field, among them Sir John the Graham, the dear friend of Wallace.

So he mourned his loss.

When the rough soldiers saw how sad their master was they mourned with him. Then, taking up the dead body of the Graham, they carried him to the church at Falkirk. Over his grave they laid a stone and carved these words upon it,

"Here lies Sir John the Graham, both wight and wise,
One of the chiefs who rescued Scotland thrice,
A better knight not to the world was lent,
Than was good Graham of truth and hardiment."

Thus Wallace had lost his wife and his friend and, in spite of his brave struggles, it seemed as if he would lose his country. He gave up his post of Governor of Scotland. The happiness of his country was all he longed for. He saw that it was useless to struggle against the jealousy of the barons. They would never consent to be ruled by him. He could not even hope to lead his army to victory when the nobles were ever ready to desert him, as they did at Falkirk.

So Wallace once more became a simple country gentleman.

It is said that in this Battle of Falkirk Robert the Bruce, who afterwards became such a good king in Scotland, fought on the side of the English. After the battle Bruce and Wallace met. They were both brave men and Bruce was filled with admiration for the courage and skill of Wallace. "But," he said, "what is the use of it? You cannot overcome so great a king as Edward. And if you could, the Scots would never make you King. Why do you not yield to him as all the other nobles have done?"

"I do not fight for the crown," replied Wallace, "I neither desire it nor deserve it. It is yours by right. But because of your sloth and idleness the people have no leader. So they follow me. I fight only for the liberty of my country and should surely have won it if you and the other nobles had but done your part. But you choose base slavery with safety rather than honest liberty with danger. Follow, hug the fortune, then, of which you think so highly. As for me, I will die free in my own country. My love for it shall remain as long as my life lasts."

At these words Bruce burst into tears and never again did he fight for Edward.

Edward now marched through Scotland but he found only a deserted country. Burned towns and ruined castles met him everywhere for the people had destroyed their homes rather than that they should fall into the hands of the English King. His soldiers began to starve and, at last, angry and sullen he was forced to march back to England, leaving the north still unconquered.

Hardly had he left the country when messengers came to him, telling him that the southern Scots had again risen and were driving out every English soldier whom he had left to guard his conquests. So again he gathered an army and marched back to Scotland. For seven long years the struggle lasted. Five times during those years did Edward's army ravage Scotland. Broken, crushed but still unconquered the people fought on. Had they only been united under some strong leader, the struggle would not have lasted so long. But since Wallace had given up in despair no great leader had arisen.

CHAPTER 31

William Wallace – The Turning of a Loaf

NEARLY every lord in all broad Scotland bowed to Edward and owned him as his master. From every castle the flag of England floated. Every battlement was manned by English soldiers. Yet Edward was not content, for the common people would not yield and Wallace was still free. Among the mountains and the woods he lived with his faithful band of followers. Outlawed and hunted, with a price upon his head, he still was free. For he was so brave and skilful that he could not be taken by fair means, and the people loved him and would not betray him for all King Edward's gold.

But at length, alas! a man called Sir John de Menteith was found who was wicked enough to consent to betray Wallace for a large sum of money. Shame it is to say this man was a Scotsman and greater shame still, he had been one of Wallace's trusted friends.

Sir John laid his plans and waited. He had not long to wait. One night Wallace lay down to sleep, attended only by two of his men. One of them was Sir John Menteith's nephew. Wallace and his other friend slept, while Sir John's nephew kept watch. But he was in league with his wicked uncle. As soon as Wallace was fast asleep he stole his sword and dagger and then crept quietly away. Menteith and his soldiers were sitting at supper, waiting for news of Wallace, when his nephew arrived. He went to the table and turned a loaf upside down. It was the signal agreed upon. By that the soldiers and Sir John knew that all was ready and that it was time to march out and take Wallace.

Ever after it was considered very rude to turn a loaf upside down if anyone called Menteith happened to be at table because it seemed to mean, "One of your family betrayed Wallace, our hero, to his death." This of course was taken as an insult as it was something which every honest man would wish to forget.

Wallace was sleeping soundly when he was suddenly awakened by the sound of armed men. He started up and felt for his sword. It was gone. Gone, too, his dagger and even his bow and arrows.

Seizing a stool, he defended himself as well as he could and succeeded in killing two men with it before the soldiers closed in upon him. He was so big and strong that it took many of them to seize and bind him. But at last they succeeded.

The false Menteith then swore to Wallace that his life was safe and that he would only be kept as an honourable prisoner of war. And Wallace, knowing that Menteith had been his friend, believed him. But Menteith lied.

By lonely ways they led Wallace southward, for they dared not take him through towns and villages lest the people should rise and rescue him. On they went till they crossed the Border. There, Wallace turned to take a last long look at the hills of his dear land which he was never more to see.

On and on they went, right through England and at last they reached London. The fame of Wallace was so great and such crowds came to look upon him that it was difficult to pass through the streets. Men and women pressed and crushed, and almost trod on each other in order to catch a glimpse of him.

For a short time Wallace was kept prisoner. Then, crowned in mockery with a wreath of laurel, he was led to Westminster. There he was tried for treason, for having invaded England and for many other crimes.

He was no traitor for he had never sworn to obey Edward. He was a patriot and a hero. That he loved his country was his only crime.

But Edward meant that his great enemy should die. For

as long as Wallace lived and was free, he could never hope really to conquer Scotland. So Wallace, the brave, was condemned to die. Those were fierce, wild times and Edward's anger was cruel. His death was made as horrible as possible and his dead body was treated with all dishonour. But the cruel triumph of the Englishmen over his dead body could matter little to Wallace. He had fought his fight, he had done his work and after his life of struggle and hardship he rested well.

The hatred between England and Scotland has long ago died out. The two countries are now united into one kingdom, under one queen.

Wallace, in his life, did his very best to prevent that union. Yet both Englishmen and Scotsmen will ever remember him as a hero for they know that in preventing Edward from conquering Scotland, he did a good work for the great empire to which we belong. If Scotland had been joined to England in the days of Edward, it would have been as a conquered country and the union could never have been true and friendly. When hundreds of years later the two countries did join, it was not because one conquered the other but because each of the two free nations, living side by side, wished it. Thus the union became firm and unbreakable and all Britons may honour the name of Wallace for the part he had in making it so.

CHAPTER 32

Robert the Bruce – How the Bruce Received a Letter and Struck a Blow

WALLACE was dead. After a struggle of fifteen years Edward had triumphed, Scotland had reached her darkest hour and English tyranny made the life of Scotsmen a daily burden and misery. But not for long. Scarcely six months after the death of Wallace, the Scottish people had chosen and crowned a king who was utterly to break down the power of England.

John Baliol had a nephew called the Red Comyn. He now claimed the throne. Robert the Bruce also claimed the throne, for the Bruces had always thought that they had the better right, even when Edward of England had chosen in favour of Baliol. So Bruce and Comyn hated each other and quarrelled bitterly. In those days great nobles quarrelled and fought among themselves very often and it was these quarrels that had helped Edward many times to defeat the Scots. Bruce, as you know, was an English as well as a Scottish noble and at one time he had fought for Edward. But now he made up his mind to fight for Scotland only and he determined to make friends with the Red Comyn. This Robert was the grandson, you must understand, of that Bruce who had been among the twelve who claimed the throne after the death of the Maid of Norway.

One day as they were riding from Stirling together Bruce began to talk to Comyn. "We must no longer quarrel," he said. "We must work together. Help me to get the crown, and I will give you all my land in return. Or, if you wish to be King, give me your land and I will help you to win the crown."

"I do not want to be King," replied Comyn. "If you will really give me your lands and possessions I will help you."

So it was agreed between them. Then they wrote down what they had agreed to do. Each signed and sealed the paper, each keeping a copy of it.

Bruce then went back to the English court for his plans were not yet ready and he did not wish Edward to find out what he was doing. But the Red Comyn did not mean to help Bruce. He still hoped to win the crown for himself. So, no sooner had Bruce gone back to England than Comyn sent the paper which they had written, with a letter to Edward.

When Edward had read the letter and the paper he was very angry but he wished to make quite sure of catching Bruce and all the people who were helping him. So, although he was planning how he might seize Bruce and his friends and put them all to death, he was kind and pleasant to them as usual, pretending that he knew nothing of what they meant to do.

But one of Bruce's friends discovered the King's plan by accident. He dared not write a letter to warn Bruce lest it should fall into King Edward's hands. So, instead of writing, he sent a pair of sharp spurs and twelve silver pennies to Bruce.

Bruce was clever enough to understand what this message meant. It meant: "You are in danger. Mount upon your horse and ride away as fast as you can. Here are spurs; here is money for the journey." That was how Bruce read this strange letter.

The snow lay thick upon the ground. Few people travelled in the wintry weather and Bruce knew it would be very easy to trace which way he had gone by his horse's hoof marks in the snow. So he sent his horse and those of two faithful servants to a blacksmith, telling him to take off all the shoes and put them on the wrong way round. In this way the horses' hoof marks looked as if someone had been galloping towards, and not away from London.

By midnight all was ready and in the darkness three men rode quietly out of the town. As soon as they were beyond the houses they set spurs to their horses and galloped swiftly northward. The night was cold and clear but as they rode the snow again began to fall, so that the hoof marks of the horses became more and more indistinct.

In the morning a breathless messenger came to King Edward. "My liege," he cried, "Robert the Bruce has fled in the night."

Edward was furious at the escape of his enemy, and sent horsemen in all directions in search of him. But it was in vain; no trace of him was to be seen.

Meanwhile Bruce spared neither spurs nor money. So fast did he ride that in five days he had reached the Border. Still on he went and presently he met one of Red Comyn's servants riding southward.

Robert the Bruce stopped him. "Whither go you?" he asked.

"To the King of England with letters from my master," replied the servant.

"Show them to me," said Robert sternly. And the servant, knowing Bruce to be a great lord, gave them to him.

Without more ado Robert the Bruce broke the seals and read the letters. As he did so his face grew dark with anger. "The foul traitor," he cried, crushing the letters in his hand. "Where is your master?" he then demanded, turning to the servant.

"He is at the convent of Dumfries, my lord," replied the man, trembling, for he saw how angry Bruce was.

Turning his horse, Bruce rode towards Dumfries. His heart was hot with anger as Red Comyn had written to King Edward that if Robert the Bruce were not speedily slain there would be great trouble in Scotland.

Robert the Bruce had a fierce, passionate temper but as he rode his anger cooled and he made up his mind to reason with Red Comyn and be calm.

In a quiet church, in the little town of Dumfries, the two men met. As was the fashion in those days they kissed each other and together they walked up the aisle, talking earnestly. But Bruce could not long control his temper and with bitter words he accused Red Comyn of having betrayed him to the King of England.

"You lie," cried Comyn.

The two men were now close to the altar steps; the face of Christ looked down upon them, seeming to say, "A new commandment I give unto you, that ye love one another." But Bruce, blind and speechless with passion, drew his dagger and struck at Red Comyn. He fell and the steps of the altar were stained with his blood.

Bruce had had no thought of murder. In the blind passion of a moment, he had slain a man. He had slain him too in the church, and before the holy altar. White and sick with horror, hardly seeing what he did, he turned and groped his way to the door.

Outside, his friends were waiting for him. "How fares it with you?" they asked, seeing him look so white and wild.

"Ill, ill," replied Bruce, "I doubt I have slain the Red Comyn."

"You doubt?" cried Kirkpatrick, one of his friends. "You leave such a weighty matter in doubt? I will mak' siccar," meaning "I will make sure." And going into the church, Kirkpatrick stabbed the wounded man again and again till he died.

CHAPTER 33

Robert the Bruce – How the King was Crowned

THE murder of Red Comyn was wrong and cruel, and Robert the Bruce suffered for his passionate deed. It made his struggle for the freedom of Scotland more difficult for now, besides fighting King Edward, he had to fight the friends of Red Comyn too, who were many.

But the deed was done. There was now no turning back. So Robert the Bruce gathered his few friends and followers around him and boldly marched to Scone to be crowned.

The precious Stone of Destiny, upon which the kings of Scotland were used to sit, was no longer there. There were no royal robes, no crown, no sceptre. But an old bishop, who in his heart had ever been true to Scotland although he had seemed to yield to Edward, brought out the ancient royal standard which for ten years he had carefully kept hidden. He gave his bishop's throne to be used instead of the Stone of Destiny, and his beautiful bishop's dress for a coronation robe. A plain gold band was quickly made to take the place of the crown, glittering with gems. All was ready but the man who should have placed the crown upon the head of the King was not there.

Long ago, you remember, Malcolm Canmore had given to the Thane of Fife, and his sons and heirs after him, the right of placing the crown upon the head of the King. There was now indeed an Earl of Fife but he was in the power of the King of England. This was a very real misfortune for the people would not think that their King was truly their King if he were not crowned with all the ancient rites and ceremonies.

The Earl of Fife, however, had a sister called the Countess of Buchan. Her husband, the Earl of Buchan, was a follower of King Edward; he was also the near relative of the Red Comyn. In spite of all that, the Countess loved her country and when she heard of the difficulty in which Bruce and his friends were, she made up her mind to take her brother's place and to set the crown upon the King's head.

Calling her knights and gentlemen around her she mounted upon her horse and rode southward as quickly as she could. And one day in March, the people of Scone heard the thunder of horses' hoofs and the clatter and jangle of swords and armour as the Countess rode up to the abbey door.

So the King was crowned, and as he knelt at the altar under the ancient royal banner it was no gallant knight in shining armour who placed the crown upon his head and led him to the throne – it was a brave and beautiful lady, whose bright eyes shone with love for her country.

But not yet could Robert the Bruce be truly called King of Scots. "Alas!" said his wife sadly, "we are but Queen and King of May, such as boys and girls crown with flowers in their summer games." It was true, for the King's friends and followers were but a very small band. He had to win Scotland to himself before he could win it from the English.

But Bruce was wise as well as brave, and he used every means in his power to force and persuade the people to join him, and his little band soon grew.

Meanwhile, King Edward, who was now an old man, was filled with furious wrath against Bruce. He gathered an army, made many new knights, and at a great feast he swore that, living or dead, he would go to Scotland, there to avenge himself upon Bruce and his friends. He also swore that when they were conquered he would never again draw sword to fight Christian men, but would make a journey to the Holy Land, and there die fighting for the Cross.

Then the Prince of Wales, also called Edward, set out for Scotland, the King himself following more slowly.

Through the land the English marched, fighting, burning and destroying. They had reached the town of Perth and were safely within the walls when King Robert marched upon them with his army.

The King rode to the walls. "Come out and fight," he called to the English leader. "Come out and fight like men and do not hide behind stone walls."

"The day is too far spent," replied he. "Abide till tomorrow. Then will we fight."

To this King Robert agreed. He believed that the English leader meant what he said and that he would not fight until the next day. So he marched his men a little way off to the shelter of a wood. There they laid down their weapons, took off their armour and began to cook their supper. Then they rested so that next day they might be strong to fight, for they had walked far that day.

But suddenly there was a loud cry. The English had stolen out of the town and were upon the weary soldiers. Snatching up their arms and buckling on their armour as quickly as might be, the Scots prepared to defend themselves.

The fight was fierce, and never did king fight as Robert the Bruce fought. Three times his horse was killed under him. Once he was taken prisoner. "I have taken the King of Scots," cried an English knight. But hardly had he uttered the words than a Scottish knight struck him to the ground, and Bruce was once more free. Again he was taken. But this time it was by a Scottish knight who, although he was fighting for Edward, set his prisoner free as soon as he saw that he was the King.

But no bravery could save the day. Slowly the Scots were beaten back, fighting to the last with their faces to the foe. This was called the Battle of Methven. In it many of King Robert's best friends were taken prisoner and afterwards cruelly put to death by the English. And the King, so lately crowned, became a hunted man obliged to hide and to wander among the hills and valleys of his own land.

CHAPTER 34

Robert the Bruce – If at First You Don't Succeed, Try Again

ALL seemed lost. The King was a hunted beggar. A great sum of money was offered to any who should betray him. Death threatened any who should help him. Yet a few friends were still faithful to him and shared his wanderings and hardships.

Their clothes were torn and shabby, their shoes worn out. For food they hunted wild animals and gathered roots and berries from the woods. They found shelter from the cold, wind and rain, under dark pine trees or in wild, rocky caves.

It was a hard life for men, yet women shared it too. For the Queen and her ladies refused to live in comfort while the King was hunted among the hills. So, one day, accompanied by Nigel Bruce, the King's young brother, they rode out from Aberdeen to seek him.

The King was very glad to see his dear wife again and he and his brave followers did their best to make the Queen and her ladies comfortable. None worked harder than Sir James the Douglas. He shot the deer and fished for salmon and trout; he gathered heather for beds; he was always busy and always happy, and kept everyone from despairing, even when things looked darkest. The King too did his best to keep up the spirits of the little company. At night, when they gathered round the watch fires, he would read stories out of old books or tell tales of bygone days and of far-off countries, and listening to these stories the little company would forget for a time their own sufferings and dangers.

They were driven about from place to place. Sometimes they were attacked and had to defend themselves. Often the ladies were in great danger, and at last King Robert was so beset by his enemies that he persuaded the Queen to leave him and to go with her ladies to the castle of Kildrummie which was the only castle still left to him. So the Queen took a sad farewell and went away under the care of Nigel, King Robert's brother. She little guessed that long years were to pass before they should see each other again.

Bruce was now left with only two hundred men. He had no horses as he had given them all to the knights who had gone to take care of the Queen and the other ladies. The enemy were close upon him and with all haste he sought a still safer hiding place.

He and his men went quickly through the land until they came to Loch Lomond. To cross the loch seemed impossible. To go round it would have been very difficult and would have taken a long time, yet what was to be done? They were almost in despair when they found a little boat. It was old and leaky, and so small that only three could cross in it at a time. But it was enough for those brave men, used to every kind of danger. Those who could swim tied their clothes into bundles, placed the bundles upon their heads, and so swam over. The others, by two and by two, crossed in the little leaky boat until all were safely over. It took a long time, but while the men were waiting for the boat to return, King Robert told stories to them, so that the hours seemed to pass quickly.

At last, after many difficulties and dangers, the little band arrived safely at the coast. There they found a ship in which they sailed over the sea to an island off the coast of Ireland. Here Bruce spent the cold winter months, safe, for a time, from his bitter enemies, and happy, no doubt, in the thought that his Queen too was safe in his strong castle of Kildrummie.

But Edward was very angry when he knew that Bruce had again escaped him. So he sent soldiers to storm the castle in which the Queen was. The castle was taken, the brave knights who defended the ladies were killed, and the ladies themselves were all made prisoners.

At night, when they gathered round the watch fires, the King would read stories out of old books (page 115)

Full of new hope, Bruce sprang to land (page 119)

The Queen, her daughter, the little Princess Marjorie and the King's sisters were sent to prisons in England and Scotland, where they remained for many years. The brave Countess of Buchan was also with the Queen, and Edward now determined to punish her for having set the crown upon the head of Robert the Bruce.

He ordered a great cage of wood and iron to be made, and in this the Countess was shut up like an imprisoned wild animal. The cage, some people say, was hung upon the walls of Berwick Castle, so that all passers-by might see the poor Countess and be warned by her fate not to displease the King of England. Other people think that King Edward was not quite so cruel as that and they say that the cage was placed inside a room. However that may be, the poor lady was kept caged up like an animal for four years. During all that long time no one was allowed to come near or to speak to her, except the servants who brought her food and drink, and care was taken that they should not be Scottish.

One by one the friends of Bruce were taken prisoner by the English and, by Edward's orders, put to death in the most cruel fashion. Among them was Nigel, the King's brave and handsome young brother. It seemed truly as if the cause of Robert the Bruce was lost.

When news of all these misfortunes was brought to Bruce, he did indeed almost despair.

Sad, disappointed and weary of the struggle he lay, one day, upon his bed of straw in the poor little cottage where he had found a refuge. What should he do, he asked himself. Everything seemed against him. Was it worthwhile fighting and struggling any more? "I will give up my right to the throne," he thought. "I will send away all my brave men and tell them to make peace with Edward, for if they stay with me nothing but death and imprisonment awaits them. Then, alone, I will go to the Holy Land and die fighting for the Cross. Perhaps, then, heaven will forgive me for having killed Red Comyn, for surely these evils come upon me in punishment for my sin. It is no use fighting for the crown any longer."

Full of such sad thoughts King Robert looked up at the bare rafters of the cottage roof. They were brown with smoke and covered with dust and cobwebs. From one of the cobwebs hung a spider. The spider seemed to be working very hard and, idly at first, the King began to watch it. He soon saw what it was about. It was trying to swing itself from one rafter to another. It tried and failed. Again it tried and again it failed. The King began to be interested in the little creature. "It is just like me," he thought, "I have tried and failed." Six times the spider failed. The King became more and more interested. More and more anxiously he watched. "If the spider can succeed, why should not I?" he said. Again the spider tried and this time, hurrah! it succeeded and landed safely on the opposite rafter. "Bravo," cried Bruce, and he rose from his bed, cheered and comforted, and quite decided to try again.

CHAPTER 35

Robert the Bruce – The King Tries Again

AT LAST the winter passed. In the spring Bruce sailed over to the island of Arran, bringing with him thirty-three boats and three hundred men. He was within sight of Scotland, yet he did not dare to land on the mainland for he knew not how great an army of English soldiers might be there ready to fight with him. So first he sent a messenger over. It was agreed that if this messenger found that the English were not in great force or if he found many friends willing to help Bruce, he was, upon a certain day, to light a beacon fire on a hill near Turnberry, Bruce's own castle. King Robert would then embark at once and sail over to Scotland.

The day arrived and, as the hours went by, Bruce waited upon the Arran shore, hoping and longing. Minute after minute passed but no light appeared. At last, about noon, a little column of smoke shot up growing denser each minute, till at length the fire blazed forth so that Bruce had no doubt but that it was the signal for which he waited.

All was in readiness in the hope that the signal would come. Now with a cheer the men sprang into the boats and pushed off. Eagerly they bent to the oars, and when night fell they were well on their way across the channel, steering still by the beacon light, for they had no other compass or guide.

But on the shore of Scotland, Bruce's messenger anxiously awaited his master's coming. He hoped against hope that the King would not come, for the fire had not been lit by him, and the whole country was full of English soldiers. There was no chance of success.

The boats drew near. They touched the shore. Full of new hope, Bruce sprang to land only to be met by his trembling servant who begged him to fly. "The English leader, Lord Percy, is in possession of your castle. He has a strong garrison there. Besides that, the whole country is full of English soldiers," he said.

"Traitor, why then did you light the fire?" cried Bruce.

"Oh, sire," replied the man, "as God sees me, the fire was never lit by me. Indeed, until the night came I knew nothing of it. As soon as I saw it, I hastened here to warn you, for I knew that you would start, thinking the signal to be mine."

Angry and disappointed, Bruce turned to his brother, Edward. "What shall we do?" he asked. "Must we go back?"

"Nay, here I am, and here do I stay," replied bold Edward Bruce.

"Brother," said the King, "let it be as you say. It is good to take what God sends to us, disease or ease, pain or play."

Then, in the darkness of the night, the Scots attacked the English and defeated them. Lord Percy, hearing a great noise and not knowing how strong the Scottish army might be, did not dare to fight. He shut himself up in the castle until he found an opportunity to leave it and flee to England.

The tide had begun to turn.

But the King had yet many adventures to pass through, many misfortunes to endure. To tell all the stories of these adventures would take too long, so I can only tell a few. Perhaps, when you are older, you will read a book called *The Bruce* which was written by a man named John Barbour who lived soon after the time of Bruce. There you will find all the stories.

Bruce was now much in need of more soldiers, so he sent two of his brothers to bring men from Ireland. There they gathered seven hundred and set sail once more for Scotland. But, as they landed, they were attacked and utterly defeated by a Scottish chieftain who was fighting for the English. Many were slain, many were drowned in the sea, and the rest were taken prisoner. Among these were

Bruce's two brothers whom Edward at once put to death. Thus, within the space of a few months, the King had lost three brothers and many dear friends.

He had lost, too, the help of the Irish soldiers. Again his little army was scattered, again he was hunted from place to place, his enemies trying to take him in many ways, by force or by treachery.

Among Bruce's own men there was an ugly one-eyed villain. Bruce had been warned against this man but still he trusted him and believed him to be faithful. But the man was greedy, and when the English offered him money if he would kill Bruce, he consented to do it. So this wicked man waited until he could find Bruce alone, that he might the more easily kill him.

One morning, as Bruce walked in the woods, accompanied only by a little page, he met the one-eyed villain with his two sons. One was armed with a sword and spear, the other with a sword and battle-axe, and the man himself held a drawn sword in his hand.

King Robert had not expected to meet with any enemies so he wore no armour and carried no weapon except his sword, without which he never went anywhere. His little page had a bow and one arrow. Now, when the King saw these three men coming towards him with fierce looks and in their hands drawn swords, he knew that what he had been told was true: that the one-eyed villain was a traitor.

"What weapon have you there?" he asked, turning quickly to the page.

"A bow and one arrow, sire," said the boy.

"Then give them to me," said the King, "and stand back a little and watch. If I get the better of these traitors I will give you weapons enough in return. If I am killed, then run as fast as you can to save yourself and tell my men what has happened to me."

The boy did as he was told, although he would have liked to fight for his master and shoot the arrow himself.

While Bruce had been speaking, the three men had been

coming nearer and nearer. Now they were quite close. "Stop," cried the King, "move not another step if you value your lives."

"Sire," replied the old man, "why do you greet me with such words? Surely you know that I love you. Who should be nearer to you than I?"

"Traitor," replied the King, "you have sold my life for English gold. Come one step nearer and you shall die."

As he spoke the King fitted his arrow to the bow and took aim at the one-eyed man. Seeing the King stand there so fierce and bold, the man hesitated. Then he thought of the English gold which had been promised to him. "After all," he said to himself, "it is but one man to three. Surely we can conquer him." So he made a step forward. That moment the bow string twanged and the man fell dead, pierced through his single eye, for Bruce was a splendid archer and never missed his aim.

With yells of anger, the two sons sprang upon the King. But quick as lightning, he threw away his bow and drew his sword.

One son raised his battle-axe but as he did so his foot slipped. He missed his aim and before he could recover himself he fell dead, pierced through the heart by the King's mighty sword. The spear of the second son was levelled at Bruce but with one great blow he cut the wooden shaft of it in two, and with a second blow struck the villain's head from his shoulders.

The fight had lasted but a few minutes. When it was over, the King put up his sword, looking sadly at the three dead men. "They might have been gallant and faithful soldiers," he said with a sigh, "had they not been so greedy of gold."

CHAPTER 36

Robert the Bruce – The Fight at the Ford

KING ROBERT'S little army grew smaller and smaller until at last he had only sixty men. The English, knowing this, resolved to attack the band, kill them all and take the King prisoner. They made quite sure of success, but in case Bruce should get away they took bloodhounds with them with which to trace him.

A bloodhound is a kind of dog which is trained to follow a man by the smell of his footsteps. Their sense of smell is so strong that even if they have never seen the man upon whose track they are put, they can follow every turn he has gone, simply by smelling the path along which he has passed. The only way to escape from a bloodhound is to walk through running water. Then the scent is carried away and the hound loses the trace.

Bruce heard that his enemies were coming, so he encamped with his little army in a safe place, above the steep banks of a river. The river was swift and deep. There was no bridge across it and only one ford in many miles.

A ford is a place in a river shallow enough to let men and horses walk through it. This ford was very narrow so that only one man could cross at a time. The banks of the river were very high, and the path which led from the ford to the top of them, steep and dangerous.

When night came, Bruce made all his men lie down to sleep, and he, taking only two soldiers with him, went to guard the ford. For some time they sat in silence, hearing nothing but the rushing of the water and the whispering of the night wind in the trees. Then suddenly, from far away came the baying of hounds.

The King listened eagerly. What was it? Was it the

enemy or not? Should he awaken his men? "No," he said to himself at last, "I shall not awaken my men for the barking of some stray sheepdog. They are very tired. Let them sleep on until I make sure, at least, that something is really the matter."

So he waited and listened. Soon the baying of the hounds came nearer and nearer. Other noises too came to him from far across the river. Nearer and nearer they sounded, until at last he could make out the trampling of horses, the clatter of weapons and armour and even the voices of men. The enemy, two hundred strong, were close to the ford.

"If we go back now to awaken my men," thought the King, "the English will be able to cross the river before we can return. That must not be. At all costs we must guard the ford." Then he bade the two soldiers to run to the camp, awaken the men and bring them to the ford as quickly as possible.

The two soldiers ran off as fast as they could, and the King was left alone by the ford – alone and on foot, in the face of two hundred men on horseback.

He looked to his armour and his weapons, saw that all was right, then calmly waited.

The enemy was now very near. The moon shone out and Bruce could see the glint of steel armour and the glitter of many spears as they crowded upon the opposite bank. Then, as they looked across, they saw that the ford was guarded by one man only whose still, dark figure showed clearly against the sky.

The ford was theirs! One man alone stood between them and certain victory. Without a moment's hesitation the foremost rider urged his horse into the river, dashing the water in a white spray all around him. He reached the further bank. Up the steep path he sprang. But as he gained the top a battle-axe flashed in the moonlight, and horse and rider fell crashing down the bank again.

Another and another rider followed. Again and again the King's mighty axe was raised. Again and again it fell, until the dead formed a ghastly barricade before him, over which no warrior could pass.

Below, in the river, all was confusion. The riders in front, unable to climb the bank, were thrown back upon those behind. Crowded upon the narrow ford and unable to turn, the horses lost their footing and, with their riders, were carried away by the swift current. Wild panic seized those who yet remained on the further bank and, at last, filled with a nameless terror, they turned to flee.

When at last Bruce's soldiers came up, they found their master sitting in the moonlight, alone, as they had left him. He was hot and tired, and had taken off his helmet in order to get cool. Around him lay heaps of dead but he himself was not even wounded.

CHAPTER 37

Robert the Bruce – How the King Escaped from Traitors, and How He Met a True Woman

SOON after this, the King's enemies got possession of a bloodhound which, at one time, had belonged to Bruce himself. The hound had been very fond of his master and now, not knowing that he was being used by enemies to betray his master, eagerly followed his trail. But Bruce was warned in time and fled away with one faithful follower. Hungry and tired, for they had walked many weary miles, they at last reached a wood through which ran a brook. "Here is safety," said Bruce. "Let us wade down this stream a great way so that my poor hound may lose the scent."

This they did and thus, once more, Bruce escaped from his enemies.

But the danger was not over. Having rested in the wood for a short time, Bruce and his follower set off in search of something to eat, for they were very hungry. On and on they walked, hoping to find some cottage but no cottage could they see, nor indeed any sign of a living creature.

At last, in the very thickest part of the wood, they saw three men coming towards them, one of whom carried a sheep upon his shoulder. These men seemed rough and they looked more like robbers than like honest folk.

"Where are you going, my good men?" asked King Robert.

"We are looking for Robert the Bruce," replied they. "Do you know where he is, for we wish to join him?"

Now King Robert was not sure if these were friends or foes, so he answered, "If you come with me I will take you to the King."

But something in his way of speaking made one of the

men guess that it was the King himself to whom he was talking. Robert, who was watching him sharply, knew by the look which came into his eyes that he had guessed the truth. But neither the man nor the King wished to show that they knew.

"My good friends," said Bruce quietly, "I will take you to the King. But as we are not well acquainted with each other, do you go on first and we will follow."

"You have no reason to think evil of us," said one of the men sulkily.

"Neither do I," said Bruce, "but I choose to travel in this way."

And seeing that there was nothing for it, the men did as they were told and went on first, the King and his man following.

For some time they walked in silence and at length they came to a ruined and deserted cottage. Here the three men stopped and proposed to kill the sheep and roast some of it for supper.

The King was near fainting with hunger and fatigue so he gladly agreed. "But," he said, "we will not eat together. You must sit at one end of the cottage while my friend and I sit at the other." With evil looks and much grumbling, the men did as they were ordered. The sheep was killed and cut up and some of it was roasted, and at last they all sat down to supper. They had neither bread nor salt, nothing indeed except the newly killed and hastily cooked mutton. Yet to the hungry King and his man it seemed delicious.

Having eaten a large supper, the King began to feel very sleepy. He tried for some time to keep awake for he did not trust the three men. But, at last, do what he would, he could no longer keep his eyes open. So, begging his man to watch while he took a short rest, he lay down on the hard floor and immediately fell asleep.

The King's man was very tired too. He had promised to watch and he tried his best to keep his promise. But very soon his head fell forward on his breast, and in a few minutes the ruffians at the other end of the room knew by his breathing that he, too, was fast asleep.

Now was their time.

Rising quietly, they drew their swords and softly crept towards the sleeping King. They were quite near when suddenly he awoke. It was growing dark within the cottage but by the light of the fire which they had made, he saw the three men creeping towards him with their swords in their hands. Springing up, he drew his sword, at the same time giving his man a great push with his foot to awake him. But, before the man could rise to his feet, one of the villains pierced him to the heart. So the King was left alone to battle against the three. It was one weary man to three who were rested and fresh, but Robert the Bruce was such a brave and skilful fighter that very soon all three lay dead at his feet. Then, grieving for the loss of his faithful follower, he left the cottage and went on his way alone.

The next day, weary and hungry, the King knocked at the door of a farmhouse to beg for food and rest. "Come in," said the old woman who opened the door, "come in, all travellers are welcome here for the sake of one."

"And who is he for whose sake you make all travellers welcome?" asked the King, as he entered the house.

"It is our lawful King, Robert the Bruce," replied the woman. "He is now chased about from place to place, and hunted with hounds like a wild animal, but I hope to live to see him yet King over all Scotland, for he alone is our rightful lord."

"Since you love him so well, good wife," said the King, "let me tell you that he is now standing before you. I am Robert the Bruce."

"You," cried the woman. Surprised and delighted, she fell upon her knees to kiss his hand. "But where are all your men? Why are you thus alone?"

"My men are scattered far and wide," said Bruce sadly. "At this moment there is no man that I can call mine, so I must go alone."

"'That shall not be," cried the old woman, "for I have three tall sons and they shall be your men." And hastening away she called her sons, and there and then they knelt to the King, and swore to be his men, and to fight for him to the death.

The King then asked his new men to shoot, that he might see what they could do. So they fetched their bows and arrows, and shot before the King. The first son saw two ravens sitting upon a rock some way off and, taking aim, he shot them both with one arrow.

The second saw another raven flying high above his head. He shot and the bird fell dead with the arrow through his heart.

The third son, seeing his brothers shoot so cleverly, aimed at a raven still further off but although he was a good archer, the shot was too difficult for him, and he missed.

The King was well pleased with his new men and they proved to be good and faithful soldiers, and afterwards served him in many ways. And when at last the wars were over, and King Robert sat safely upon the throne, he did not forget the old woman who had helped him when he was alone and in trouble. One day she was told that the King wished to speak to her. When she came before him, he said, "Good wife, you helped me when I was in sore need and trouble. What can I do for you now in return?"

"Oh," said she, "just gie me that wee bit hassock o' land atween Palnure and Penkiln."

The "wee bit hassock o' land" as she called it, stretched over many miles, but the King gave it to her willingly. The old woman divided the land between her three sons, and so founded three noble families. The eldest son, when he became a knight, took for his device or picture, which he had painted upon his shield, two ravens shot through with one arrow, in memory of the day when he first became one of the King's men.

But meantime, while the sons were shooting and their mother preparing a meal for the King, they heard the

tramp of horses. At first they feared that it might be the
enemy, and the King went into the house to hide. But soon,
to his great joy, he heard the voices of his brother, Edward,
and of his dear friend, Lord James the Douglas.

Right glad were they to meet again after so many
dangers past and when the King saw that they were
followed by a hundred and fifty men, he forgot all about
being tired and hungry, and felt ready to fight at once.

"We have just passed a village where two hundred
English are quartered," said Douglas. "They are keeping no
watch, for they think that your army is utterly scattered. If
we hurry we can take them by surprise and beat them."

That was good news indeed. So without more ado the
King mounted and rode away at the head of his little army.

It was as Douglas had said. The English were keeping no
watch and when the Scots swooped down upon them they
were taken by surprise and utterly defeated.

From that time, more and more men gathered to the
standard of Bruce. He gained victory after victory, until the
English would no longer come out to fight him but shut
themselves up in the castles and towns of which they had
taken possession, hoping that King Edward would soon
send them help.

CHAPTER 38

Robert the Bruce – The Taking of Perth

ALL THIS time King Edward had not himself come to Scotland. He had only sent his generals and soldiers, but now that things seemed to be going badly with them he resolved, old and feeble though he was, to come himself.

He was so ill that he could not walk nor ride but had to be carried in a litter. His spirit, however, was keen and fierce as ever and he longed to conquer Scotland before he died. But that was not to be and, at a place called Burgh-on-Sands, within sight of the Scottish border, he died. When he felt that he was dying, when he knew that his dearest wish could never be fulfilled, that he would never conquer Scotland, never be received as Scotland's King he called his son, Edward, to him.

The Prince came and knelt beside his dying father to receive his last commands. "My son," said the great King, "I die, but to you I leave my unfinished task. Swear to me before my lords and barons that you will never give up this war until Scotland is conquered. Let my bones be carried with the army and never lay them to rest until you have subdued the Scots."

The Prince of Wales swore by the saints and by all that he held holy to do as his father wished. But he did not keep his promise.

When his father was dead, the Prince sent his body back to Westminster where it was buried. He himself marched a little way into Scotland then, growing tired of the hardships and discomforts of camp life, he turned and went back to England without having fought a single battle.

But although Edward II and his army marched away from Scotland, there were many English left there and all the castles and strong towns were theirs. These, King Hobbe, as Edward used scornfully to call Bruce, had to conquer one by one before he could call his kingdom his own.

For a time, however, little could be done for Bruce became very ill and, without their great leader, the soldiers had no heart to fight.

Edward Bruce, the King's brave brother, did his best to comfort the soldiers but it was a sorrowful band that he led into the mountains, carrying their King in a litter.

Bruce had gone through such terrible hardships, had suffered so much from cold, hunger and weariness, that it was little wonder that even he, strong though he was, had broken down. No medicine seemed to do him any good. But one day, hearing that his soldiers had been put to flight by the English, he rose from his bed and, in spite of all that his friends could say to him, he mounted upon his horse, determined to lead his men to avenge their defeat. He was so weak and ill that a soldier rode on either side of him to support him. But his men were so filled with gladness to see him amongst them once more that they fought with such new courage that they again won a victory. From that day King Robert became quite well again.

Fighting still went on but many of the Scottish nobles, who had before fought for Edward, now joined Bruce. Among these was his own nephew, Thomas Randolph. During a battle, Randolph was taken prisoner by Lord James Douglas and brought before the King. "Nephew," said Bruce, "you have for a time forgotten your obedience to your King. Now you must return to it."

"I have done nothing of which I need be ashamed," replied Randolph proudly. "You blame me but it is you who are to blame. You have chosen to defy the King of England, yet you will not meet him like a true knight in the open field."

"That may come," replied Bruce calmly, "and before long perhaps. Meanwhile," he added sternly, "since you are so rude of speech, it is fitting that your proud words should meet their just punishment. You shall therefore go to prison until you learn to know better my right and your duty."

Randolph went quietly to prison, but he was not kept long there, for he soon made up his mind to join his brave uncle and to fight for Scotland. Robert then made his nephew Earl of Moray, and he became one of his greatest friends and generals, second only to James Douglas.

Perth, at this time one of the strongest places in Scotland, was in the hands of the English. It was surrounded by a moat. The walls of Perth were high and thick and there were stone turrets upon them at short intervals. For six weeks King Robert besieged this town but it was so strong that, do what he would, he could not take it.

One night, however, the King crept unseen close up to the walls. He carefully examined the moat and discovered that there was one place at which it would be possible to cross it. Then he went back to his camp and next morning the English within Perth rejoiced to see the Scottish King and his army march away.

A week passed. There was no sign of the enemy and the English, feeling quite safe, kept no watch.

But one dark night the King and his army came quietly marching back again. Robert led his men to the shallow part of the moat. He was the first to jump into the water and show the way across it. He wore all his heavy armour and in one hand he carried a ladder, in the other a spear. With this he carefully felt his way but at one part the water was so deep that it reached his throat. At last, however, he landed safely on the other side. Quickly, one after the other, his soldiers followed him over the moat. They reached the wall and setting their ladders against it, clambered up. Then with a wild war cry they leaped over into the town.

A French knight happened to be in the Scottish army. When this knight saw the King so full of bravery and courage, when he saw that he was among the first to place the ladder against the wall, among the first to leap into the town, he was filled with admiration. "What shall we say to our French knights," he cried, "who sit at home feasting and idle when so gallant a prince puts his life in danger for a wretched village?" and dashing through the moat, he too joined the fight.

The English were so completely taken by surprise that the battle was soon over. Every Scotsman who was found within the walls fighting for the English was put to death but the English soldiers were spared. Then Bruce broke down the wall and ruined the towers for, as he had not enough soldiers to defend the towns and castles which he won from the English, he thought it was better to destroy them, lest they should again fall into the hands of the enemy.

CHAPTER 39

Robert the Bruce – How Two Castles Were Won

THE CASTLE of Linlithgow was in the hands of the English but it was won from them by the help of a poor farmer called Binning.

The castle was very strong. It was surrounded by a loch and a moat crossed by a drawbridge. Under the archway of the entrance there was a portcullis.

It seemed hopeless to attempt to take the castle, it was so strong.

One day the English Governor ordered Binning to bring a cartload of hay to the castle as he was in need of some for his horses. Binning promised to bring it but he made up his mind to take the castle at the same time. Quickly and quietly his plans were made. During the night some Scottish soldiers crept as near to the castle walls as they dared and hid where they could not be seen by the English. Then, very early in the morning, Binning loaded his cart. But he did not load it with hay only. In the cart lay eight strong men, clad in steel and armed with swords and battle-axes. Over these men, so as to cover them, Binning placed a light load of hay.

He then harnessed his oxen with ropes to the heavy cart and set out for the castle. A servant sat in front, driving, and Binning himself walked by the side of the cart, with a stick in his hand and his woodman's axe at his belt.

Slowly the cart creaked along the silent street until it reached the castle gate. The drawbridge was lowered at once, for the sentinels knew that hay was expected and asked no questions. The heavy load passed over the wooden bridge, the hoofs of the oxen sounding loud in the still morning air. With beating heart, but seemingly calm,

Binning walked along. The portcullis was slowly raised and the cart passed under it. But, just as it was directly under it, Binning sprang forward and, quick as lightning with a blow from his hatchet, cut the ropes which bound the oxen to the cart. The oxen moved on. The cart was left beneath the portcullis.

"Call all, call all," shouted Binning. It was the signal agreed upon. "Call all, call all," cried the soldiers in the cart as they threw off the hay which covered them, and sprang to the ground with drawn swords. "Call all, call all," replied the men from without, rushing in to help them.

The portcullis was lowered, but it was of no use. The heavy cart stood underneath it and prevented it from falling to the ground. The gates could not be shut for the same reason, so the castle was taken and all the English soldiers were put to death.

Bruce rewarded Binning by giving him a great estate and even to this day the name of Binning is remembered in Linlithgowshire.

Roxburgh was another strong castle and it was so near the Borders that the English were very anxious to keep it. But Douglas had quite made up his mind to take it, however difficult it might be.

Douglas was a great soldier and a gallant knight. By his friends he was called the Good Lord James but by his enemies, because of the fear they had of him and because he was very dark, he was called the Black Douglas. Indeed the terror of his name was so great that mothers would frighten their naughty children by saying to them, "Be good now, or I shall fetch the Black Douglas to you."

On Shrove Tuesday there was great feasting and drinking, and on that day Douglas and his friends made up their minds to take Roxburgh Castle.

The only hope of doing this was to take it by surprise. But to get to the castle some fields had to be crossed. If the Scots had marched across these fields they would have been seen by the garrison who would then have had time to prepare for them. So, waiting until it was dark, they threw black cloaks over their bright armour and, crawling on their hands and knees, passed through the fields to the bottom of the wall. They went a few at a time so that in the dusk they looked like straying cattle.

Some were safely over and were hiding close against the walls when the watch went their rounds. The watchmen paused on the wall, just above the spot where were Douglas and his men, and looked across the fields. "There be cattle late afield," said one soldier, pointing to the slowly moving objects in the distance.

"Yes," said the other, "the farmer is making merry this Shrovetide and has forgotten to shut up his cattle. If the Black Douglas comes across them before morning he will be sorry for it."

Then the men moved on, little dreaming that the Black Douglas was listening to what they were saying and that the "cattle" were no other than the Black Douglas's own men.

At last all had safely reached the walls. The ladders were placed, the men mounted. Everything was quiet within the castle. Only a woman, the wife of one of the soldiers, sat upon the walls with her child in her arms, singing it to sleep.

"Hush ye, hush ye, little pet ye,
Hush ye, hush ye, dinna fret ye,
The Black Douglas will no get ye."

"Don't be so sure of that," said a voice close beside her and a steel-gloved hand was laid upon her shoulder. With a scream the woman looked round. Beside her, tall, dark and strong stood the very Black Douglas of whom she sang.

In a moment the alarm was given. The fierce cry of "Douglas! Douglas!" with which his men always rushed into battle, sounded through the night and the fight began. Nearly all the English were killed. But Douglas took care of the woman and her child, so she lived to know that he was not so dreadful as his name.

CHAPTER 40

Robert the Bruce – How the Castle of Edinburgh was Taken

EDINBURGH Castle stands upon a high, steep rock up which it is almost impossible to clamber. Randolph, Earl of Moray, who was now fighting valiantly for the King, was very anxious to get possession of this castle. But how to do it he did not know. At length a gentleman named William Francis came to tell him that he knew of a way. Many years before, Francis had been a soldier in Edinburgh Castle. He had loved a lady who lived in the town and because he was not allowed to visit her openly, he had found a way by which he could clamber up and down the steep rock in secret. He still remembered the path and he offered to lead Randolph and his men by it. It was a very dangerous plan, for only one could go at a time and, should the sentry see them, every man would certainly be killed. Still, it was worth trying and Randolph resolved to try.

So one dark, moonless night a little band of thirty brave men gathered at the foot of the castle hill. Francis led the way and one by one they followed him up the rocky path. It was a fearful climb and besides being fully armed they had to carry ladders with them, with which to scale the walls. On and on they went in silence, gripping the rock with hands and knees, clambering round boulders or up the face of cliffs where there was scarcely the smallest foothold. Not a word was spoken. If a stone slipped or a twig crackled, their hearts seemed to stand still. On and on they went till, hot and breathless but unseen and unheard, they neared the top.

When they were almost at the top they heard the watchmen going their rounds on the wall above. As they clanked along so close above, each man pressed himself against the face of the rock, keeping as still as possible, scarcely daring even to breathe.

Suddenly the guards stopped and looked over the wall. One of them, thinking to have a jest with his comrades, picked up a loose stone and throwing it over the cliff, cried out, "Aha, I see you well!"

For one horrible moment Randolph believed himself to be discovered, but not a man moved. The stone crashed down and down, bounding from rock to rock till it reached the bottom far below. Then all was still again and with a laugh the sentry moved on. He had had his jest, he had frightened his companions for a moment. But he little knew how fast he had made thirty hearts beat. He little knew that just below him thirty men clung motionless to the rock, every moment expecting discovery and death.

As soon as the sentries moved away, the men began their climb again and a few minutes later the top was reached. The ladders were quickly fixed, and the men sprang over the wall. Except for the watchmen, the whole garrison were asleep, and before they had time to rise and arm themselves, the castle was taken.

Thus in one way or another, castle after castle fell into the hands of Bruce. From town after town the English were driven out, until hardly one remained to them, except Stirling. And that was sore beset by Edward Bruce.

At last the Governor of Stirling, seeing that he could not hold out much longer, made a bargain with him. He promised to yield the castle if by midsummer the King of England did not come to his aid.

To this, Edward Bruce agreed. But King Robert was angry when he heard what bargain his brother had made. To fight a great battle against the whole force of the English army was just what he did not want to do, and to give Edward of England nearly a year in which to make ready seemed to Bruce, true knight though he was, to allow the enemy too great an advantage.

"Let Edward bring every man he has," said Edward

Bruce, "and we will fight them, ay even if they were more."

"So be it, brother," said King Robert. "Since so we must, we will manfully abide battle, and let us gather all who love us and greatly care for the freedom of Scotland to come and fight against Edward."

Edward II was a weak and changeable king, not wise and brave as his father had been. How changeable he was, you may know from the fact that he appointed six different governors for Scotland in one year – not that it was much use appointing governors at all over a country which refused to acknowledge them.

Edward II was weak and he was easily led by favourites. He often quarrelled with his barons and nobles, but now they and their men gladly joined him against Scotland. Never, even in the gallant days of Edward I, had such a knightly army poured over the Border. From all his dominions Edward called his followers – from France, from Wales, from Ireland.

On they marched through a deserted country, watched only by sad-eyed women who, as they saw the mighty host roll on, prayed and trembled for their husbands and brothers and fathers who were gathered at Stirling to oppose the foe.

CHAPTER 41

Robert the Bruce – How Sir Henry de Bohun Met his Death

ON SUNDAY 23rd June 1314, the day before the Governor of Stirling had promised to give up the castle, the two armies came in sight of each other. King Robert's army was much smaller than that of the English. But in Bruce, the Scots had a brave and gallant leader. He knew how much depended upon this battle and he took every care to make the best of his men, and the best of his position. Courage alone he knew could not beat the mighty host that was coming against him, so he thought and planned carefully.

He chose a very strong position. It was a plain guarded in front by bogs and marshes. At one side flowed a little river called the Bannock with steep rocky banks; on the other rose the castle rock. In front, wherever the land was firm, Bruce made his men dig holes a few feet deep. These holes were then filled with branches and twigs of gorse, over which the turf was again lightly placed. From a distance the plain seemed firm and solid when really it was filled with pits. Besides digging these holes, Bruce made his men scatter iron spikes, called calthrops, over the field.

Having finished his preparations, the King sent all the servants, camp followers and untrained men out of the army and made them go behind a hill. This hill was afterwards called the Gillies' Hill, that is, the servants' hill.

When Bruce heard that the English were near he drew his soldiers up in line and made a speech to them. He reminded them of all they had suffered, of what they had so hardly won, of what they might so easily again lose if they were not brave and determined; he prayed every man who was not ready to fight to the death, to leave the army.

Edward Bruce led the right wing of the army, Douglas,

the centre, and to Randolph was given the left, with a command that he should let no Englishman get into Stirling. The King, mounted upon a little pony, rode up and down in front of the lines making sure that all was ready, although he did not expect to have to fight that day. He wore a golden crown on his helmet so that all might see that he was the King. He was clad in complete armour but carried no weapon except a battle-axe.

The English host swept on, their armour and weapons glittering in the June sunshine, their colourful banners fluttering in the breeze. On they came with sound of music and trumpets, till the hills echoed and re-echoed.

As Bruce rode up and down he watched everything with his keen eye, and presently he saw the glint of steel away to the left. A party of English horsemen were quietly making their way towards Stirling.

"Ah! Randolph," said the King, pointing to the horsemen, "a rose has fallen from your crown." By this he meant that Randolph had been careless of the trust given to him and had lost a chance of renown.

Ashamed of himself, Randolph made no reply, but calling to his men dashed off at full speed towards the English. He was upon them before they reached the town, and a fierce fight followed. But the English were twice as many as Randolph's little band and it seemed for a time as if the Scots were getting the worst of it. Douglas watched the fight uneasily. He and Randolph were King Robert's best generals and greatest friends, yet there was no jealousy between them.

"I pray you, sire," said Douglas at last, "let me go to Randolph's aid."

"You shall not stir a foot," replied the King; "let Randolph free himself as best he can. I will not endanger the whole battle for a careless boy."

"My liege," said Douglas again, "I cannot stand thus idly and see him perish when I may bring him help. So by your leave I must away to him."

Unwillingly then the King gave his consent and Douglas, with his men, hurried off to help Randolph. But when he drew near he saw that Randolph was beating the English without his aid. "Halt," he cried, "yonder brave men have no need of us. We will not take any of the honour of the day from them." Then he turned back to the King without having struck a blow. A little later Randolph followed, flushed and triumphant.

He had recovered his rose.

But meanwhile, the King too had been fighting. An English knight, called Sir Henry de Bohun, had seen the King of Scotland as he rode in front of the line, and saying to himself that he would win great fame and settle the battle at one stroke, he set spurs to his horse and dashed furiously upon Bruce.

Fully armed, riding upon his great warhorse, the English knight came thundering on. Bruce, on his little pony, could have no chance against him. There was a dreadful moment of suspense. The two armies watched breathlessly. Bruce waited calmly and when Bohun was almost upon him, he suddenly turned his pony aside. Bohun dashed on. As he passed, the King, rising high in his stirrups, brought his battle-axe crashing down upon the knight's head. The steel helmet was shattered by the mighty blow, Bohun fell to the ground dead and his frightened horse dashed riderless away.

Cheer after cheer rose from the Scottish ranks and the generals gathered around their King. They were glad that he was safe, yet vexed that he should so have endangered his life. "Bethink you, sire, the fate of all Scotland rests upon you," they said.

But the King answered them never a word. "I have broken my good axe," was all he said, "I have broken my good axe."

CHAPTER 42

Robert the Bruce – The Story of the Battle of Bannockburn

AFTER the death of Bohun there was no more fighting that day. All night long the two armies lay opposite each other and very early next morning both were astir. The Scottish soldiers were formed in battle array and then they knelt to receive the blessing of a holy friar who passed along their lines, his head and feet bare, and carrying a great crucifix in his hand.

"Think you, will these Scots fight?" Edward had asked one of his knights a short time before.

"Ay, that will they," was the reply, "to the last."

But now, seeing them kneel, Edward cried out, "They kneel, they kneel; they ask for mercy."

"They do, my liege," was the answer, "but it is from God and not from us. Believe me, yonder men will win the day or die upon the field."

"So be it, then," said Edward, "let us to the fight." Then the trumpets were sounded and the battle began in right good earnest.

The English arrows fell fast and thick till one would have said it snowed. But Bruce knew these deadly arrows of old and was prepared for them. He sent a body of horse to attack the archers and they, having no weapons except their bows and arrows, were soon scattered in flight.

As the English cavalry advanced, the horses fell into the pits prepared for them, stuck fast in the bogs or were lamed by the sharp iron spikes with which the field was sown.

Soon all was terrible confusion. The English began to waver. "On them, on them, they fail!" shouted the Scots, and charged more fiercely than before.

At this moment, when the English were beginning to feel

themselves beaten, they saw what they thought was a fresh army come over the Gillies' Hill. Then they lost all heart. The confusion became complete. They fled.

This new army was, however, no army, but only the servants and camp followers who had grown tired of idly watching the battle. So, with sticks for weapons and with sheets tied upon tent poles for banners, they marched down the hill to join the fight.

The slaughter now became terrible and the noise terrific. Banners were trailed in the dust, maddened, riderless horses rushed wildly through the flying ranks, broken armour and weapons strewed the ground. The groans of the wounded and the dying mingled with the clang of arms and the shouts of victory.

Many were slain upon the field, many fell over the rocky banks of the Bannock burn, others were drowned trying to cross the River Forth. Thirty thousand English perished that day.

The King fled with the others. First he fled to Stirling but the Governor reminded him that there was no safety there, for he had promised to deliver the castle to the King of Scotland next day. So again Edward turned and fled away. He was followed closely by Douglas but he reached Dunbar without being overtaken. From there he escaped to Berwick in a fishing boat and so, at last, after many dangers, landed safely in England.

The English left so much spoil behind them that it was said if the chariots, wagons and wheeled carriages, which were laden with stores and spoil, could have been drawn up in a line they would have reached for twenty leagues.

The Scots too made many prisoners. Bruce was far more kind to these prisoners than was usually the case in those wild days. Few, if any, were put to death and those of them who had friends were soon bought back. For it was the custom then to ransom prisoners, that is, to buy their freedom. As numbers of the prisoners were knights and nobles, their friends paid such great sums of money for them, that it was said Scotland grew rich in one day.

To the noble dead, Bruce gave honourable burial instead of chopping their limbs in pieces and placing them on the gateways and walls of castles throughout the kingdom, as was too often the fashion.

Now, too, Bruce was able to buy back, or rather exchange for English prisoners, his wife, daughter and sisters, and the other noble ladies who had been kept in English prisons for eight years. So at last the Queen was Queen indeed, and not a mere Queen of the May as she had said so long ago.

By the Battle of Bannockburn, English power over Scotland was completely broken. Scotland was free at last. Robert the Bruce was seated firmly upon the throne. Although dark days came again, although the kings of England again and again revived the old foolish claim of being Scotland's "overlord", the freedom of the country was never more in real danger. So it is right that we should remember and honour the name of Bruce, as also the name of Wallace. They stand together as the preservers of Scottish freedom.

CHAPTER 43

Robert the Bruce – How the Scots Carried the War into England

FOR some years after Bannockburn King Robert ruled Scotland wisely and well. The war with England still went on but it was the Scots who won the battles.

At last King Robert became very ill. He could no longer sit upon a horse or lead his soldiers to battle but he still thought, and planned, and ruled his kingdom, living quietly in his castle near the River Clyde.

About this time Edward II of England was dethroned and his son, Edward III, was crowned instead. Robert the Bruce, having sent a message to the new King telling him that he would invade England, gathered an army and sent it across the Border. Randolph and Douglas commanded this army which was about twenty thousand strong. The men wore little armour and were mounted upon rough ponies so that they moved about from place to place far more quickly than the heavy English horse. The ponies were so swift and sure-footed that they could go through valleys and among hills where the English found it impossible to follow with their heavy cavalry.

Besides his weapons each man carried a bag of oatmeal and an iron girdle. A girdle is a flat, round piece of iron, something like a frying pan without sides, upon which scones and oatcakes are baked. Except their bags of oatmeal, the Scots carried no other provisions, for they were always sure of finding cattle in the country through which they passed. They used to kill these and cook the flesh. But they carried neither pots nor pans. They boiled the flesh in the skins which they made into pots by slinging them on crossed sticks above a fire.

After a day's march the ponies were turned loose to

graze. Bullocks were killed and skinned. Water and beef were put into the bag-pots, fires were lit under them; every man brought out his girdle and oatmeal. After a supper of boiled beef and oatcakes the men lay down to sleep round the warm camp fires.

In this way the Scots moved from place to place, burning and destroying at will, pursued by the English who tried in vain to come up with them. The English could often see the smoke of the Scots' fires as they followed them over hill and dale till, weary and hungry, they encamped for the night, hoping next morning to catch the Scots. Day by day this went on till the English army was well-nigh exhausted.

Sometimes during the march there would be a cry. Those behind, thinking that at last the enemy was in sight, would hurry forward with drawn swords in their hands, ready to fight. But, after having run for a mile or so over hill and valley, they would find that what had aroused their hope was only a herd of deer or wild cattle which fled swiftly away before the army.

Wandering about in this manner, the English leaders lost their way and one day, just as the sun was setting, they arrived at the River Tyne. This they crossed with great difficulty and lay down for the night on the bank.

The men had only a loaf of bread each to eat and there was nothing but water from the river to drink. They had no hatchets to cut down wood so they could make neither fire nor light. Wet and hungry they lay down to sleep, wearing their armour and holding their horses by the bridle, lest they should stray during the night.

In the morning, some peasants passing told them that they were eleven leagues from the nearest town. Hearing this, the King immediately sent messengers to the town with a proclamation saying that anyone who wished to earn some money had only to bring provisions to the army.

The next day the messengers returned with what they could get, which was not much. They were followed, however, by many of the townspeople, who brought badly

*Bruce brought his axe crashing down upon the head
of Bohun (page 143)*

When a stone hit the walls, Black Agnes would bid her
maids wipe the spot with a clean white cloth (page 157)

baked bread and poor, thin wine for which they made the soldiers pay very dearly. Even then, there was not enough for everyone and the men would often quarrel fiercely over a piece of meat or loaf of bread, snatching it out of each others' hands. To add to the discomfort it began to rain, and kept on raining for a whole week. Hungry, cold and wet the soldiers began to grumble bitterly. Still there was no sign of the Scots.

At last the King made a proclamation, that anyone who could find the Scots should have a hundred pounds a year and be made a knight. Upon that, about fifteen or sixteen gentlemen leaped upon their horses and rode off in different directions, eager to win the reward.

Four days later, a gentleman came galloping back to the King. "Sire," he cried, "I bring you news of the Scots. They are three leagues from this place, lodged in a mountain where they have been this week, waiting for you. You may trust me – this is true. For I went so near to them that I was made prisoner and taken before their leaders. I told them where you were, and that you were seeking them to give battle. The lords gave me my liberty on condition that I rested not until I found you, and told you that they were waiting, and as eager to meet you in battle as you can be to meet them."

As soon as the King heard this news he ordered his army to march forward. About noon next day they came in sight of the Scots. But when they saw in what a strong position the long-looked-for enemy lay, they were very much disheartened.

The Scots were encamped upon a mountain at the foot of which flowed a strong, rapid river. The river would be difficult and dangerous to cross. If the English did cross, there was no room between the mountain and the river for them to form into line. Seeing this, King Edward sent his heralds to ask the Scots to come down into the plain and fight in the open.

Douglas and Randolph replied that they would do no

such thing. "King Edward and his barons see," they said, "that we are in his kingdom. We burn and pillage wherever we pass. If that is displeasing to the King he may come and amend it, for we will tarry here as long as it pleases us."

Seeing that the Scots would not come out of their stronghold, King Edward resolved to starve them out. For three days and nights, his army lay in front of the Scots. But the Scots had plenty to eat, they had comfortable huts and great fires, whereas the English lay opposite in cold and hunger, without shelter or proper food.

But on the fourth morning, when the English King looked towards the Scottish camp, behold it was empty. Not a man was left. They had decamped secretly at midnight.

Immediately, Edward sent scouts on horseback to search for them. About four o'clock in the afternoon they came back with news. The Scots were encamped upon another mountain, in a far stronger position than the last.

So again the English marched forward and took up a position opposite the Scots.

That night the English camp was suddenly aroused by the fierce war cry, "Douglas! Douglas! Ye shall die, ye thieves of England."

It was Lord James Douglas with two hundred men, who had silently left the Scottish camp and, finding the English keeping but careless watch, dashed suddenly upon them.

Three hundred Englishmen were killed and the King narrowly escaped. Douglas reached his tent and, cutting the ropes, tried to carry off the King in the confusion. But his servants stood bravely round their master and, the camp being now thoroughly aroused, Douglas was obliged to call his men together and escape. After this, the English kept a strong and careful watch but the Scots did not again attempt to surprise them.

For three weeks the English lay watching the Scots, hoping to starve them out. During this time the Scots were not idle. Behind them was a marsh and while the English watched in front, they were busy making a road through the marsh behind. One morning, behold, again the Scottish camp was empty!

Two Scottish trumpeters alone remained. "My lords," they said, coming to the English camp, "why do you watch here? You do but lose your time, for we swear by our heads that the Scots are on their homeward march and are now four or five leagues off. They left us here to tell you this."

The English were very angry with this message and on going to the Scottish camp they found that what the trumpeters told them was only too true. Not a Scot was to be seen. They had vanished in the night but they had left behind them many signs that they had been by no means starving. In the deserted camp there lay the dead bodies of many cattle which the Scots had killed because they could not take them away, as they moved too slowly. There were hundreds of fires laid, ready to light, under skin pots filled with meat and water. There were thousands of pairs of worn-out shoes. These shoes the Scots used to make out of the raw, rough hide of the bullocks which they killed for food. They wore them with the hairy side out and from that were often called "the rough footed Scots", or "red shanks",

Besides these things, the English found a few prisoners whom the Scots had taken and whom they had now left behind tied to trees. They also left a message saying that if the King of England were displeased with what they had done, he might follow them to Scotland and fight them there.

But Edward had no wish to follow so wily a foe, and he turned southward and disbanded his army.

Shortly afterwards a peace was made between the two countries, and a treaty was signed at Northampton. By this treaty the English King gave up all claim to Scotland, and acknowledged Robert the Bruce to be the rightful King. It was also arranged that Edward's young sister should marry Bruce's son. And so at last the land had rest.

CHAPTER 44

Robert the Bruce – The Heart of the King

KING ROBERT did not live long to enjoy the peace which at last had come to the land. He was not an old man but he had lived such a hard life that he seemed older than he was. Now he became so ill that he knew he could not live long.

When he felt that he was dying, he called all his nobles and wise men to him. As they stood round him, Bruce told them that he must soon die, and bade them honour his little son, David, as their King.

With tears of sorrow the nobles promised to do as the King asked.

Bruce then turned to the good Lord James. "My dearest and best friend," he said, "you know how hard I have had to fight for my kingdom. At the time when I was sorest pressed, I made a vow that when God should grant me peace, I should go to the Holy Land to fight for the Sepulchre of Christ. But now that I have peace, my body is feeble and I cannot fulfil my heart's desire. Yet I would fain send my heart whither my body cannot go. There is no knight so gallant as you, my dear and special friend. Therefore I pray you, when I am dead take my heart from my body, carry it to the Holy Land, and there bury it."

At first Douglas could not speak for tears. After a few minutes he said, "Gallant and noble King, I thank you a thousand times for the honour you do me. Your command shall be obeyed."

"Dear friend, I thank you. You give me your promise?" said the Bruce.

"Most willingly. Upon my knighthood I swear it."

"Thanks be to God. Now I die in peace, since I know that the bravest knight in all my kingdom will do for me what I cannot do for myself," said the King as he lay back content.

Not many days after this the great King died. From all the land there arose a cry of mourning and sorrow. With tears and sobs, with the sound of sad music and wailing, the people followed their King to his last resting place in Dunfermline Abbey.

Wrapped in a robe of cloth of gold the great King was laid to rest, and a beautiful tomb of white marble was raised over his grave. Long ago the tomb disappeared but the place where Robert the Bruce lies is still pointed out in the abbey of Dunfermline.

True to his promise, the Douglas ordered the heart of Bruce to be taken from his body after he was dead. The heart was then embalmed. That is, it was prepared with sweet-smelling spices and other things to keep it from decay. Douglas enclosed the heart in a beautiful box of silver and enamel which he hung round his neck by a chain of silk and gold. Then, with a noble company of knights and squires, he set sail for Palestine.

On his way he passed through Spain. There he heard that the King of Spain was fighting against the Saracens. The Saracens were the people who had possession of Palestine. They were unkind to the Christians and insulted their religion. Douglas therefore thought that he would be doing right to help the King of Spain, before passing on to the Holy Land.

The armies met and there was a great battle. The Scots charged so furiously that the Saracens fled before them. But thinking that the Spaniards were following to help them, the Scots chased the fleeing foe too far. Too late, Douglas found that he and his little band were cut off from their friends and entirely surrounded by the fierce, dark faces of the enemy.

There was no escape. All that was left to do was to die fighting. Taking the silver box containing King Robert's heart from his neck, Douglas threw it into the thickest of the fight, crying, "On, gallant heart, as thou wert ever wont, the Douglas will follow thee or die." Then springing after it, he fiercely fought until he fell, pierced with many wounds. Round him fell most of the brave company of nobles who had set sail with him.

When the battle was over, the few who remained sought for their leader. They found him lying dead above the heart of Bruce. They had now no wish to go on to the Holy Land so they turned home, taking the body of Douglas and the heart of Bruce with them. Douglas was buried in his own church at Castle Douglas, the heart of Bruce in the abbey of Melrose.

CHAPTER 45

David II – The Story of Black Agnes

WHEN Robert Bruce died in 1329 his son was at once crowned under the title of David II. David was only a little boy so, of course, could not himself rule and Randolph, Earl of Moray, was made Regent. For three years Randolph ruled. He was very just but very strict and even cruel, so he made many enemies. One day he died suddenly. Some people thought that he had been poisoned but that has never been proved.

Another Regent was chosen but he turned out to be neither a good soldier nor a good ruler, and so once more troubles began. There were, as you know, many great lords who had lands both in England and in Scotland. During the wars, many of these lords who had fought for Edward lost their Scottish lands. This made them very angry. Now that there was only a child upon the throne they rebelled, hoping to win their lands again. They found a leader in Edward Baliol, the son of John Baliol, who had been King before Robert the Bruce.

Edward Baliol said that he had a better right to the throne than David and, in spite of the treaty of Northampton, he was helped and supported by Edward of England who hoped once more to become Scotland's overlord.

Once again Scotland was torn in two by civil wars, some taking the part of Baliol, some that of David. A battle called the Battle of Dupplin Moor was fought, a few miles from Perth. In this battle the loyalist Scots, that is those who were fighting for the King, were utterly defeated.

A base Scottish baron showed Edward Baliol where to cross the river, on the other side of which the King's army lay. Silently, at midnight, Baliol led his soldiers over and broke into the Scottish camp while the soldiers were all

asleep. The Scots were soon awake and sprang to arms.
Randolph, Earl of Moray, the son of the famous Earl,
gathered his men together quickly. They fought so bravely
that in spite of the surprise the battle might have ended in
victory instead of defeat, if only the Regent had known how
to command his men. But he drew up his soldiers in such
close lines that they fell over each other and crushed each
other to death without ever getting near the enemy. Thus,
far more of the Scots were killed by their friends than by
their foes. So dense was the crowd, so awful the slaughter,
that in one part of the field the dead lay in heaps of a spear
length in depth. The Regent and most of the bravest and
the best of the Scottish nobles were among the slain. After
this battle Edward Baliol hurried to Scone, and there he
was crowned. So there were two kings in Scotland – David
Bruce and Edward Baliol. But King David and his young
wife, who you remember was Edward of England's sister,
fled away to France.

One of the first things Edward Baliol did after he was
crowned was to own himself, as his father had done, vassal
of the King of England. But Baliol's triumph was not for
long. There were many Scotsmen who were still true to
their King. They chose another Regent to rule in David's
name, and one dark night they suddenly attacked Edward
Baliol. They slew many of his barons and Edward himself
barely escaped with his life. He had to flee so fast that he
had not even time to dress but throwing himself on a
barebacked horse he galloped away through the darkness.
So in less than three months after the crown had been
placed upon his head, he was chased from his kingdom,
penniless and almost naked.

He fled back to England, to his master, Edward. Edward,
gathering a great army, marched against the Scots and in a
battle called Halidon Hill, the Scots were once more
defeated.

Edward then overran the country, plundering and
conquering, till no one dared call David King any more,

except the little children in their games when they played at being kings and queens.

But Scotland would by no means yield to England and fighting still went on. Among those who fought most bravely for their country was the Countess of March. She was called Black Agnes because she was so dark. Her husband, the Earl of March, was away fighting for the King when the English besieged his castle of Dunbar. Dunbar was a very important castle and Black Agnes made up her mind that nothing would make her yield it.

In those days cannon had not yet come into use. Instead of cannon, armies carried about with them great engines, with which they threw enormous stones at the walls of the castles which they wished to take.

The English brought their strongest engines against Dunbar but Black Agnes laughed at their big stones. She used to stand on the walls with her ladies and her maids and when a stone hit the walls she would bid them wipe the spot with a clean white cloth, as if to say that she liked to keep her castle clean and tidy, and all the harm the English could do was to make a little dust.

She was always on the walls or at the gate and in the most dangerous places, taunting the English and encouraging her own men by her brave words.

> "She kept a stir in tower and trench,
> That brawling, boisterous Scottish wench;
> Came I early, came I late,
> I found Black Agnes at the gate."

Angry as they were, the English could not but admire Black Agnes for her courage and they accepted her gibes and jeers with a rugged chivalry. "There goes one of my lady's tiring-pins," said the English leader one day as a knight fell dead beside him, pierced by a Scottish arrow. "Black Agnes's love-shafts go straight to the heart."

For five months Black Agnes kept the castle. By the end

of that time the men and women within the walls were near starving. Dunbar is by the sea, but the English watched so carefully that no help could be brought to the brave little garrison either by land or by sea. One night, however, a bold Scotsman managed to slip between the English ships which lay close about the castle. In his little vessel were forty men and plenty of food for the brave defenders.

After this the English lost all hope of taking the castle, so they went away, angry and ashamed at having been beaten by a woman. But the Scottish people were proud of Black Agnes, and the minstrels made poems about her and sang of her valiant deeds.

CHAPTER 16

David II – The Battle of Neville's Cross

SLOWLY but surely, and with much fighting, the Scots began to win their country again. Robert the High Steward, or Robert Stewart as he came to be called from the name of his office, was now Regent. He at length decided that the King, who had been living in France for nine years, might safely return.

David was by this time eighteen years old and as soon as he came back Robert Stewart gave up his office of Regent. But the King was too young and too ignorant to be able to rule well, and he was jealous of Robert Stewart. So there was no love between the King and the man who had fought for and ruled his kingdom while he had been away.

The war with England still went on. In those days there was no regular army as there is now. In time of war each man left his work, put on his armour, took his weapons and went to fight for his master. The war now had lasted so long that the fields had neither been ploughed nor sown; the country was wasted and barren; there was no corn with which to make bread, and the people starved. After famine came a horrible disease called the Black Death from which hundreds and hundreds died, and the whole land was filled with misery and mourning.

The Scots, having driven the English out of Scotland, now often marched into England to fight there. They plundered the rich fields and brought back food for the starving people. Sometimes these fights were little more than skirmishes or border raids as they were called; sometimes they were great battles. One of these battles was called Neville's Cross.

King Edward of England was fighting with France as

well as with Scotland. The French and the Scots were friends, so while Edward was in France the French King persuaded the Scots to invade England. He hoped that this would help the French for Edward would be obliged, he thought, to send home some of his soldiers to protect England. The Scots too thought that it would be a good time to invade England for the King and all his best fighting men and greatest generals were far away. "None but cowardly clerks and mean mechanics stand between us and a march to London," they said. But they were mistaken for there were still many brave fighters left in England, and an army of thirty thousand marched to meet the Scots.

David was brave but he was not a great soldier as his father had been, nor would he listen to the advice of his generals. So when the two armies met at Neville's Cross the Scots were defeated.

For three hours the battle raged with terrible slaughter. The nobles at last formed a ring round their young King and fell, one by one, fighting to protect him. Twice he was wounded but still he fought bravely, till at last an English knight succeeded in disarming him and he was taken prisoner.

Many Scottish nobles lay dead upon the field; many more, like their King, were taken prisoner. In triumph they were led through London. The King, clad in beautiful robes and mounted upon a splendid black horse, was followed by the Mayor and his counsellors and by a great procession of people all dressed in their holiday clothes. Everywhere they passed the streets were brightly decorated and filled with gaping crowds come to see the sight. Then David and his nobles were led back to the Tower of London and there kept prisoner.

After the battle of Neville's Cross, Edward Baliol once more came back to Scotland and pretended to be King. But the Scots would neither submit to the rule of Edward Baliol nor of Edward of England, and they again chose Robert the High Steward as Regent.

Then Baliol, seeing himself powerless, knelt to King Edward placing his crown at his feet and giving him a handful of Scottish soil as a token that he yielded to the English King all over Scotland. This ceremony was a mere empty show for Baliol could not give away what he did not possess. Edward, however, in return for this homage, granted Baliol a large sum of money and Baliol, who was already an old man, went away quietly and was heard of no more.

Edward now set David free on condition that he should own the King of England as his overlord. But the Scottish people would not agree to be subject to Edward, so David had to return again to prison.

Edward then gathered a great army and marched once more into Scotland carrying before him, among his other banners and pennons, the Scottish royal standard. He pretended no longer that he was fighting for Baliol. Henceforward he fought for himself. But wherever he went he found a deserted country. He reached Edinburgh without fighting any great battle but having wrecked every town and village on his way. So fearful was the havoc he made that this raid was known for long after as the Burned Candlemas.

By the time Edward reached Edinburgh his army was starving – even bread was scarce. At last, seeing nothing but famine before him, he gave the order to march back to England. This was the fifth time that Edward III had invaded Scotland. Every time he had said that he would conquer the country. Every time he had failed.

At last a truce was made. The Scots agreed to pay a large sum of money to Edward and their King was set free. It was such a large sum that it could not all be paid at once and Scotland, already made poor by so many wars, was made poorer still. But the people were so anxious to have their King again that they paid the money willingly.

When at last the King returned, there was great rejoicing. Wherever he went the people crowded around him cheering. But the King, instead of being pleased with this show of love, was angry. One day on his way to Parliament, when the people were pressing round him as usual, David seized a mace from one of his servants. With this he gave the man nearest to him a blow on the head and threatened to knock down any other who came nigh him. After that the national joy at the return of their King was not so great.

It was soon seen that David did not care for his people at all. He was selfish and fond of pleasure and greedy of money. When he died no one was sorry. He had reigned forty-two years, nine of which he had spent as an exile in France, eleven as a prisoner in England.

CHAPTER 47

Robert II – How the French and the Scots Made War on England

DAVID II died in 1370 and as he had no children he was succeeded by Robert the High Steward. Robert was the son of Lady Marjorie, the daughter of Robert the Bruce. Thus Robert was, through his mother, the grandson of Robert the Bruce and he was the first of a long line of kings called the Stewarts. You remember that Walter, the first High Steward, was descended from Fleance, the son of Banquo, who fled to Wales when Macbeth tried to kill him. Now, as the Weird Sisters had foretold, his children sat upon the throne for many years.

Robert II had already proved himself to be a good soldier and a wise Regent. But now he was fifty-five years old. He was worn with wars and weary with ruling. He was no longer able to fight as he had done, no longer strong enough to curb the power of the great barons who, through the long years of war, had grown ever prouder and fiercer.

Nor was Robert allowed to take the throne without opposition. Douglas, the head of one of the proudest and greatest of the noble families claimed it too. But Robert did not wish to quarrel with this great lord so he proposed that his daughter should marry the eldest son of the Douglas. This satisfied the Douglas, and Robert was then crowned at Scone with great pomp and ceremony.

Although there was peace between England and Scotland, Edward would not call Robert King but spoke of him as "our enemy of Scotland" and Robert returned the insult by calling Edward "that reiver Edward, calling himself King of England". In spite of the peace, there was very often war on the Borders between the great Scottish lords and the northern English chiefs. The Scots and the French were fast friends and leagued themselves together against the common enemy. And presently some French knights came to Scotland and offered to fight against England.

The countries were at peace but in spite of that the Scottish lords told the French knights that they should see some fighting. Without telling King Robert anything about it they marched across the Border and laid waste Northumberland, returning with much spoil.

Soon after, the French knights went home and told their King of all that they had seen and done in Scotland. Then the French King determined, that when the truce between the two countries was over, he would send a great army to Scotland to fight against the English. For the French were always anxious that there should be war between Scotland and England, as then the English King had fewer soldiers to send to fight against the French.

So the following summer an army of Frenchmen sailed from France and landed in Scotland. The Scottish nobles, especially Earl Douglas and Earl Moray, received them very kindly. But when it became known in Scotland that so large a body of Frenchmen had arrived, the people were not pleased.

"What has brought them?" they asked.

"Who sent for them?"

"Can we not carry on our own wars with England without aid from France?"

"We do not understand their language and they cannot speak ours."

"Let them be told to go back again. We can fight our own quarrels and do not require their help."

The Scottish people spoke like this because they were afraid that the French, instead of helping them, might in the end try to conquer them as the English had done.

But if the Scots were not glad to see the French, the French were just as sorry that they had come. They were accustomed to handsome houses, splendid castles, soft beds and every luxury. Scotland had been made so poor by constant wars with England, their houses had so often been burned and destroyed that they had none of these things to offer their guests. So the French nobles began to laugh and to say to their leader, Sir John de Vienne, "What could have brought us here? We have never known before what poverty and hard living were. Now we will find out the truth of what our fathers and mothers used to tell us when they said, 'If you live long enough you shall have in your time hard beds and poor lodgings.' Let us be quick and get on to England, for there is nothing to be gained here."

But Sir John replied, "My fair sirs, it becomes us to wait patiently since we have got into such difficulties. Take in good humour whatever you can get. You cannot always live in Paris or in some great city. In this world, those who wish to live with honour must endure good and evil."

King Robert had been in the Highlands when the Frenchmen arrived. Now he came to Edinburgh and the Frenchmen were again disappointed when they saw him. Instead of the gallant leader they had expected here was an old and worn man with red bleared eyes.

But Robert did not go with the army to England; he sent his sons in his place.

The French and the Scots had marched some way into England, taking castles and doing much damage by the way, before they met the English army. At last they heard that the enemy was near.

At this the French were greatly delighted and hoped for a battle at once. But the Scots had learned to be very careful how they attacked the English in open country so instead of advancing they went back.

This made the French leader very angry. "Why will you not fight?" he said. "You told us before we came that if you had a thousand good men of France you would be strong enough to conquer the English. I will warrant you have now a thousand if not more, and five hundred crossbows to boot. And I must tell you, the knights who are with me are valiant men who will not fly."

And Douglas answered, "By my faith, my lord, we are sure that you and your men are brave. But all England is on the march to Scotland. We will take you to a place where you may see all their host. If after that you still advise a battle, we will not refuse it."

"By heaven, then," said Sir John, "I will have a battle."

Douglas and the Scottish leaders then took Sir John to a high hill from which he could see the whole of the English host.

Thousands of foot soldiers, thousands of archers, horsemen, knights and nobles were there. In silence the Frenchman looked upon the mighty company as it lay before him.

Then turning to Douglas, "You were right," he said, "in not wishing to fight. But what is to be done? The English are in such numbers that they will overrun and destroy your whole country."

"Let them," said the Scots. "They will find only a deserted land. Meanwhile we will march into England. It is a rich country and we will gather great spoil."

And so it happened. The Scots allowed the English army to pass them and to march into Scotland. There they did all the damage that they could which was not much for, as Douglas had said, they found only a deserted land, all the people having fled away to safe places in the hills and forests taking their cattle and goods with them. It was in this way that the Scots had learned to fight the English. As soon as they had gone the Scots came out of their hiding places, rebuilt their wooden houses which the English had burned and were not much worse off than they had been before.

In the meantime the Scots army overran all the north of England, ravaging and plundering to their hearts' content and finding none to oppose them for all the English soldiers had marched into Scotland, leaving no one to protect their homes.

Then when the two armies had each wasted the other's

country as much as possible, they turned home again, the Scots laden with spoil, the English poorer than when they came.

Soon after this the French knights went back to France, many of them little pleased with their visit to Scotland.

CHAPTER 48

Robert II – The Battle of Otterburn

THE SCOTTISH nobles now resolved again to invade England. They made all their preparations secretly, keeping them from the King as they would from an enemy, for they knew that he desired peace. But the Scottish nobles knew too that the English King was in trouble, that he was quarrelling with his own family and with his people and that it was therefore a good time to avenge themselves upon England.

So, secretly, and in spite of the King they gathered to arms and crossed the Border.

The Scottish army was divided into two bodies one of which, led by Earl Douglas, marched into Northumberland. There, after having done much damage, they met the English under the Earl of Northumberland's two sons, Henry and Percy. Henry, the elder, was so gallant and eager a knight that he was called Hotspur. He and his brother were among the bravest of the English knights, just as Douglas was among the Scottish.

Near Newcastle, Douglas and Hotspur met and in the fight which took place Douglas captured and carried off Hotspur's pennon.

"I will carry this with me to Scotland," cried Douglas, waving it aloft. "I will place it upon the topmost tower of my castle that it may be seen from far."

"By heaven, Earl Douglas," cried Hotspur, full of anger, "you shall not even bear it out of Northumberland. You shall never have that pennon to brag about."

"You must come then this night and take it," replied Douglas scornfully. "I shall fix it before my tent. Come and take it if you dare."

It was now late in the evening so each army went back to camp to rest and have supper. The Scots had plenty of food and having had a good meal, they lay down to sleep. But a strict watch was kept, for they expected Hotspur to make good his proud boast and to come to take his pennon.

But the night passed. Hotspur did not come and next morning the Scots began to march homeward.

They might have gone safely home, without more fighting, but Douglas decided to remain for two or three days near the castle of Otterburn. "For," said he, "I conquered Hotspur's pennon in fair fight and I will give him a chance of winning it back again. He will find it well defended if he comes."

In those days knights looked upon war almost as a game, and Douglas was anxious to play fair and to keep the rules.

In the meantime, Hotspur was greatly ashamed that he had not kept his word and won his pennon again from Douglas. The knights who were with him tried in vain to comfort him. "Many such losses happen in war," they said.

"If Douglas did take your pennon, he had to fight hard for it."

"We are not strong enough now to attack so great a host. Let us wait until more men come to help us. It is better to lose a pennon than two or three hundred knights."

Very unwillingly Hotspur yielded to this advice. But when some English knights came galloping into the camp with the news that the Scots were near Otterburn, and that they were not more than three thousand strong, Hotspur sprang up. "To horse, to horse," he shouted. "By the faith that I owe to my God and to my lord and father, I will yet recover my pennon this very night."

It was a warm, calm August evening and the moon shone brightly as Hotspur and his men galloped impatiently along.

The Scots had had supper, many of them had already fallen asleep, when the whole camp was aroused with the cry of "Percy! Percy!"

Hotspur had come for his pennon.

Quickly the Scottish knights armed themselves, the soldiers fell into fighting order and soon the cry of "Douglas!" answered that of "Percy!"

Although it was night, it was not very dark for the harvest moon shone brightly and calmly on the raging battle. Lance met lance, sword rang on sword, great deeds of valour were done and many a brave man fell on either side.

"Douglas! Douglas!" shouted the Earl, pressing with his banner where the fighting was most fierce.

"Percy! Percy!" came the answering cry.

The two banners met. Round them the battle raged most furiously. Cowardice was unknown. With splendid courage, Scottish and English knights fought courteously, as if in play. Never had there been such a chivalrous, knightly battle fought. Yet it was no play, but deadly earnest.

At last, pierced by three lances, Douglas, fighting desperately, was borne to the ground. His standard-bearer was killed and his banner, trampled and bloodstained, lay beside him. Only his chaplain still fought fiercely, guarding his master's body, as the English swept past little knowing how great a general lay dying upon the field.

"How fares it, cousin?" asked a knight as he knelt beside him.

"But so and so," answered Douglas. "But thanks be to God, there are few of my ancestors who have died in their beds. Now I bid you avenge my death, for I have but little hope of living. Raise my banner. Shout 'Douglas' and do not tell friend or foe that I am not with you. For, should my enemies know that I am dead, they would greatly rejoice, and should my followers know, they would lose heart. There is an old saying in our house that one day a dead man shall win a battle. Please God, this night it will come true."

So speaking, upon the battlefield the Douglas died.

Then the knight drew his dead body out of the press of battle, raised the fallen banner and shouted, "Douglas! Douglas!"

The Earl's men, who had been scattered, hearing again the sound of their master's battle cry, gathered once more round his banner and so well did they fight that at last the English were scattered and beaten.

Many prisoners were taken, among them both Hotspur and his brother. So Hotspur, as well as his pennon, was carried to Scotland. But Douglas could never place the captured pennon on his castle walls, for he lay quiet and still in the fair abbey of Melrose and over his grave was hung the torn and bloodstained banner which had won the battle.

After this a nine years' truce was made, and in 1390 King Robert died. He had grown so ill and feeble that for some time the power had really been in the hands of his second son who was called Robert, Earl of Fife.

As Regent, Robert Stewart had been a good ruler and had fought valiantly against the kings of England. But as King, he had been idle and weak. He had allowed the great lords to carry on war with England, although he himself wished for peace, and knew that peace would have been best for the country. For when the King of England gave up trying to make himself overlord of Scotland the great reason for fighting had gone. But, during the wild years of war, the great barons had grown to love war and they were glad of the smallest excuse for fighting. Only a stern, strong king could have repressed them and forced them to keep peace. Robert II was neither strong nor stern and so the barons carried on war in spite of his wishes.

CHAPTER 49

Robert III – The Story of a Fearful Highland Tournament

THE ELDEST son of King Robert II was called John. But that name was thought to be unlucky. The people remembered John Baliol and his unhappy reign. They had also heard that King John of England and King John of France had been unfortunate, so they changed John Stewart's name to Robert and he was crowned as Robert III. But changing his name made no difference either to his fortunes or to his nature.

Robert III was not a strong man and he was lame, having been kicked by a horse when he was a boy. He was kind and gentle and quite unfit to rule the fierce lords and barons. So, even after he came to the throne he allowed his brother, who was also called Robert, to continue to rule as he had done at the end of their father's life.

King Robert had a son called David, to whom he gave the title of Duke of Rothesay. To Robert his brother he gave the title of Duke of Albany. These were the first dukes ever made in Scotland.

Rothesay was young and handsome. He was wild and wicked too, and often caused much sorrow to his father, who loved him dearly.

Albany was silent, dark and cunning. He hated Rothesay because he knew that one day he would be King, and he himself wanted to be King.

When Robert III came to the throne there was peace with England. But not having England to fight against, the great lords fought all the more fiercely among themselves. They fought, too, with the Highland chieftains who lived in the wild and mountainous parts of Scotland. These Highlanders were so fierce that the English called them the

Wild Scots. They were formed into various clans and families and fought often among themselves, as well as with the Lowland lords.

Had the King been a strong man, he might have tamed the wild nobles. But he left everything to his brother, Robert, the Duke of Albany. Albany tried to make friends with the nobles by leaving their wicked deeds unpunished, for he hoped that some day they would help to put him upon the throne. So the whole land was full of fighting, quarrelling and oppression. Those who were strong took from those who were weak. There was neither justice nor mercy to be found anywhere and Albany, although he was a strong and clever man, allowed these things to be.

Among the wildest of the Highland clans were two called Clan Kay and Clan Chattan. There was a deadly hatred between them. They were always fighting, and they filled the whole country round with war and bloodshed. At last they decided to settle their quarrels by a great tournament, thirty of the best men from one clan fighting against thirty from the other.

The place chosen for this battle was a beautiful plain close to the walls of Perth. Wooden galleries were built all round for the people who came to watch, and the King and all his court consented to be present. This was no ordinary tournament such as knights often took part in, for the knights fought in full armour and often with blunted weapons. These Highlanders, when they entered the lists, wore no armour and carried not only bows and arrows, but swords, battle-axes and short, keen daggers. They were all fierce, strong men and they meant to fight to the death.

But at the last moment, when the trumpets sounded for this fearful tournament to begin, one of the Clan Chattan men lost heart. Throwing down his weapons he fled from the lists. Full of fear he leaped the barriers, plunged into the river and, swimming across it, disappeared into the wood beyond.

The King, who did not love bloodshed, was not ill pleased

at the thought that the fight could not take place. For the numbers were now uneven and no man of the Clan Kay would retire lest he should be thought cowardly. But from the bystanders a little crooked-legged man, who was a blacksmith in Perth, stepped forward.

"I will take the coward's place," he cried, "if you pay me half a French crown." The offer was at once accepted, for there was no time to send to the Clan Chattan country for another man and rather than not fight at all, they were glad to have the little crooked-legged blacksmith.

So the trumpets sounded and the bagpipes screamed, and with mighty yells the two clans closed upon each other. A terrible fight it was. The great battle-axes swung and fell, sword and dagger flashed, and the fair meadow was red with blood.

In the middle of the fight the crooked-legged blacksmith, having killed a man, stood still. "How now," said the Clan Chattan chief, "are you afraid?"

"Not I," replied the smith, "but I have done enough for half-a-crown."

"On and fight," cried the chief, "I will not grudge wages to him who does not grudge his work."

So the smith fell to again and fought as fiercely as any. Both sides fought, filled with bitter hatred of each other, till at last only one man of Clan Kay was left alive. Of Clan Chattan there were ten, and the little crooked-legged blacksmith, all sorely wounded.

Then the King flung down his baton and cried out that Clan Chattan had won the day.

This was a very terrible way of settling a quarrel but probably some of the great Lowland nobles encouraged the clans to fight in the hope that if some of the fiercest of the Highlanders were killed, the others would be more easily kept in order. And indeed, for a long time after this slaughter, the Highlands remained more peaceful.

CHAPTER 50

Robert III – The Story of the Duke of Rothesay

THE DUKE of Rothesay, although he was wild and wicked, was handsome and had pleasant manners and the people loved him. He had many friends and Albany had few. Parliament decided that as the King was ill and could not himself rule his son, the Duke, should be Governor.

Albany had always hated Rothesay; now that he was obliged to yield the power to him, he hated him more than ever.

Soon after this the truce with England came to an end and the Scottish Borderers, who had been waiting eagerly for that time to come, once more broke into England and laid the country waste. The English Borderers too were not slow to fight and soon the terrible wars were raging as fiercely as before.

The King of England, who was now Henry, remembering the old claim of the English kings to be overlords of Scotland, determined to conquer the country. He sent a letter to King Robert telling him that he meant to march to Edinburgh, there to receive his homage.

King Robert took no notice of this letter but treated it with silent scorn. Then Henry, gathering a great army, marched into Scotland. He marched right on to Edinburgh. There Rothesay, who commanded the castle, sent a fiery letter to King Henry. In it he told Henry that he had only come into Scotland for love of plunder and dared him to settle the quarrel by a tournament between an equal number of knights from either side. To this Henry would not listen and he began to besiege Edinburgh.

Albany had meanwhile gathered an army and he now came marching toward Edinburgh. But instead of helping his nephew he encamped a little way off and did nothing. This made the people very angry, for they believed that Albany wanted King Henry to defeat the Duke of Rothesay, and either to kill or take him prisoner.

Winter was coming on. The English had eaten up all the food they had and they began to starve. Many of them, too, had died of sickness and cold. And last of all Henry heard that the Welsh were rebelling, so he gave up the siege and marched back again to England.

This is the last time that an English King ever brought an army into Scotland. When armies came again they were not led by the King but by one of his generals. Unlike all the other armies which had come before, this one did little damage. For Henry did not allow his troops to burn and ravage as they went, but made them march peacefully and quietly through the land.

While his country was in danger, the Duke of Rothesay had fought well and kept the castle of Edinburgh from falling into the hands of the King of England, but now that the danger was over, he again took to his former wild ways. Albany, who hated his nephew, was not slow to tell the King all the evil things that he had heard about him. At last, the poor old King, hurt to the heart that his son should do such things, ordered Albany to imprison him until he should promise to behave better.

Then Albany was very glad. For many years he had longed for the death of Rothesay. Now he felt that he could safely kill him. In those days it was easy for prisoners to be killed, for the dungeons were dark and hideous and it was not wonderful that few should come out alive. And Albany had the King's orders, signed and sealed by the King's ring, telling him to put the Prince in prison.

So one day as the Duke rode towards St Andrews, attended only by a few followers, he was suddenly seized by Albany and his friends. Rothesay was first taken to the castle of St Andrews but that was not secret or safe enough to please his wicked uncle. So in a storm of wind and rain, mounted upon a carthorse, and with only a rough peasant's cloak thrown over his beautiful clothes, he was rudely hurried away to the castle of Falkland which belonged to Albany. There he was thrown into a dark and gloomy dungeon under the castle walls.

He had no light except what came through the tiny barred window, just above the ground. He was given no food, no drink. His cruel uncle meant him to die by one of the most terrible of deaths. He meant him to starve.

In this dungeon he remained day and night without food, or drink, or light, until he cried aloud in pain. The daughter of the Governor of the castle heard his cries and she came to the window. She knew that dreadful things often happened in these dark dungeons and when the poor Prince, dragging himself to the window, told her that he was being starved to death, she was full of pity. She hurried away and returned as quickly as she could with some thin oatcakes hidden in the white muslin veil which it was then the fashion for ladies to wear on their heads. It was all that she dared to bring, for fear of the soldiers who watched. Day after day she went, pretending to walk in the garden, and always she stopped at the little window and let the oatcakes drop through the bars. Another woman gave the Duke milk, but all that those two kind women could bring him was not enough to satisfy his terrible hunger. Soon even that was stopped, for the cruel jailors began to wonder why the Duke did not die. They watched more carefully than before and when they found out what the Governor's daughter and her servant were doing, they put them to death. The poor Duke was now left without a single friend, and one morning his groans ceased and there was silence in the little cell. He was dead.

Then the Duke of Albany caused it to be made known that the Prince had become ill and had died in prison. Everyone believed that he had been murdered by his uncle but no one dared to tell this to the poor old King, who wept and mourned greatly for the loss of his son, whom he had loved very dearly, in spite of his wildness and wickedness.

Albany now once more became Regent, for although King Robert had another son called James, he was only a little boy, too young to rule. But King Robert began to be afraid of his brother. He began to feel sure that he had murdered Rothesay. So to keep his son, James, safe he made up his mind to send him to France, pretending that he thought he would receive a better education there than in Scotland.

A ship was fitted out and, accompanied by several nobles, the young Prince James, who was about nine years old, set out for France.

The weather was fine and they sailed along without fear, for there was a truce between England and Scotland at that time. But in spite of the truce, they had not gone far when an armed English ship came sailing towards them and attacked them. The Prince was taken prisoner and carried away to the King of England.

When they were led before him, the nobles fell upon their knees and begged him to set the Prince free, reminding him that the two kingdoms were at peace and that to take the Prince prisoner was an act of war. But King Henry only laughed at all they said. "If King Robert had been truly friendly," he said, "he would have sent his son to England to be taught. For I know French indifferently well, and nowhere could he find a better master."

So instead of going to France, the poor little Prince was put into an English prison.

When this news was brought to King Robert he was sitting at supper. As he listened to the messenger, his face grew pale and he fell forward senseless. His servants thought that he had died. They carried him to his room and laid him upon his bed. There he lay like one dead, and indeed he was so full of grief that he did not care to live, and soon after, on the 1st April 1406, he died. He had reigned for sixteen years. He was a good and gentle man, but no fit king for those troubled times.

CHAPTER 51

Regent Albany – The Story of the Battle of Harlaw

THE OLD King was dead and his young son was a prisoner in England, so the Duke of Albany had his wish. If he was not King he was at least Regent. He did not try to make the English King release his nephew the Prince. He was glad that he should be prisoner, for now there was no one to interfere with him or to question his power. So he made and kept peace with England. This was a good thing for Scotland although Albany did it for his own selfish ends. But he also wanted to make friends with the barons so that they might continue to let him rule. He allowed them therefore to oppress the people and to fight with each other, and he also divided among them many lands which belonged to the King. All this was bad for Scotland. In order to rule, the Regent dared not enforce the laws, so the whole land was filled with bloodshed and sorrow.

Among the wild barons was a fierce chieftain called Donald, Lord of the Isles. He was ruler over the islands of the west and had much land on the mainland itself, and he thought himself as great as any king. But not content with his many possessions he claimed, as a right, the earldom of Ross. This earldom Albany gave to his son, Murdoch.

Full of dreadful wrath, the island Prince gathered an army and swearing that he would burn the city of Aberdeen and make all Scotland a desert to the shores of Tay, he marched with his wild soldiers through the land. Where they found quiet farms and peaceful homes they left only blackened ruins. Making themselves rich with plunder, they swept on, a trail of fire and smoke telling the story of their passage.

But the men of Aberdeen rose and, headed by their brave

provost, they marched to meet the Highland host. They joined the Earl of Mar who with an army of knights and gentlemen, was coming to fight Donald. At Harlaw, about five miles from Aberdeen, a great battle took place.

The Highlanders wore little armour and were wild and undisciplined, but they far outnumbered the Lowlanders and they fought with a fierce and savage courage. Round the steel-clad knights of the south they swarmed, yelling madly, fighting with long, two-handed swords, short, sharp dirks and mighty battle-axes. They sprang upon the horses behind their riders and clung there like wild cats, driving their dirks again and again into the backs of the knights through the joints of their armour. Or with the hooks upon their battle-axes they pulled the knights out of their saddles, dealing them deadly blows as they lay upon the ground.

But the Lowland men fought calmly through the yelling horror that surrounded them and although many were slain, the Highlanders were at last driven back.

On the red field of Harlaw hundreds of the noblest men of Lowland Scotland lay dead, along with hundreds of Highlanders and islanders.

The Highlanders had the worst of the battle. They did not take Aberdeen as they had threatened, but went back to their islands subdued if not conquered.

For thirteen years Albany continued to rule. He was a very old man, over eighty when he died. Including the time he had ruled during his brother's life, he had governed Scotland for thirty-four years. Little good can be said of him, he was not even brave, as nearly all the Stewarts have been.

It was during the years in which Albany ruled that the first Protestant martyr was killed in Scotland. A martyr is a person who dies for his religion. Up to this time much of the world had belonged to the Roman Catholic Church, of which the Pope was the head. But now a few men began to doubt if all that the Pope commanded them to believe was

"But thanks be to God, there are few of my ancestors who have died in their beds" (page 170)

For there in the garden walked the fairest lady
he had ever seen (page 186)

right. These men came to be called Protestants because they openly protested or bore witness to what they believed. But the Pope, and all those who thought as he did, were very angry with the Protestants. They ill-treated them and often put them to death.

The first martyr was called John Resby. He suffered a very cruel death, being burned alive at Perth in 1407. His books and all that he had written were burned with him so that people might forget what he had taught. But this was not a good way to make people forget and in the years to come many died as he did, rather than pretend to believe what they did not believe.

CHAPTER 52

Regent Murdoch – The Scots in France

As soon as Regent Albany was dead his son, Murdoch, began to rule instead of sending to the King of England and asking him to allow Prince James to come back to his kingdom. Murdoch was not so crafty and treacherous as his father but he was weak and simple, and the barons became more powerful than ever and more unwilling to submit to rule and order.

Regent Albany had always tried to be friends with the English King because he wanted him to keep Prince James a prisoner. But many of the Scottish nobles did not care for the friendship of England and some of them would have been glad to see their Prince free. So these now sailed across the sea to help the French against the English. For Henry of England had claimed the crown of France and as the French King would not give it up there was war between them. The first battle of the Scots in France was at a village called Baugé.

The English were led by the Duke of Clarence, brother of the King of England. He was just sitting down to dinner when news was brought to him that the Scots army was near. "On them, gentlemen," cried the Duke, springing up. "Let the men mount and follow me at once." And leaping upon his horse, he rode to meet the enemy.

The Scots were not thinking of battle because there was a three days' truce at the time. They were amusing themselves playing football when they heard that the English were advancing. Quickly they left their play and prepared to fight.

Between the Scots and the English there flowed a river which was crossed only by a narrow bridge. Clarence pressed eagerly on and some of his soldiers passed over the bridge. But the Scottish knights charged down upon them

before they could form again and won the battle much as
Wallace had won Stirling Bridge.

The Duke, riding first and cheering on his men, was easily
known by his splendid armour and by the glittering band of
gold and jewels which he wore over his helmet. As he rode,
one of the Scottish knights dashed upon him with his lance.
So great was the shock that the Duke was thrown to the
ground. There another noble killed him with his battle-axe.

Many a brave English knight fell upon the field; many
more were taken prisoner. Of the Scots and French very few
were killed or even wounded.

The King of France was so pleased when he heard of this
victory that he made the Scottish leader High Constable,
which was one of the highest titles of France. Many of the
knights he rewarded with French lands.

After this, still more Scots joined the French, among
them the Douglas. But this Douglas was an unlucky man.
He was called "Tine-man", which means Lose-man, because
he always lost the battles in which he fought. When he
joined the Scots in France they seemed to become unlucky
too, and they lost battles instead of winning them.

The English King now took Prince James with him to
France hoping that the Scots would not help the French any
more when they knew that their own Prince was in the
English camp. Henry even asked James to command the
Scots to go home. But James would not. "Set me free," he
said, "then they will obey me. How could they acknowledge
as their King one who is in the power of another man?"

Henry was very angry at this answer and once when he
took some Scots prisoner he hanged them all, saying that
they deserved no better fate for they had fought against
their own King. This was not true, for James was only in
the English camp because he was forced to be there.

At last, in a battle against John of the Leaden Sword, as
Douglas called the Duke of Bedford who now ruled France
for the English King, the Douglas and nearly all of the Scots
were killed.

The King of France made the few Scots who remained into a Royal Guard and for many years the French King's Scots Guard was famous. But some people say that the French Scots Guard had been formed hundreds of years before in the days of King Achaius, the friend of Charlemagne.

No more Scottish soldiers went to fight in France. They had now a reason for staying at home. Their King had been set free and he had promised not to help the French.

Regent Murdoch had proved to be so weak a ruler that far from being able to govern the country he was not even able to govern his own sons. They were wild and wicked. They set their father at defiance and would obey neither the laws of God nor of man. At last they became so insolent that Murdoch cried out one day in passion, "Since you will not obey me, I will fetch one home whom we must all obey."

From that day he began to pray the English to release Prince James and in May 1424, after having been eighteen years in prison, he returned home.

Murdoch's rule had lasted only five years.

CHAPTER 53

James I – The Beautiful Lady of the Garden

WHEN King Henry of England took Prince James of Scotland prisoner, he did not treat him unkindly. No chains were put on his hands or feet nor was he thrown into a dark and horrible dungeon. He was shut up in a strong castle but he had a pleasant room in which to live. His window looked out on a pretty garden. There, early and late, Prince James would sit watching the trees and the flowers, and listening to the birds singing, and that brought great comfort to him in his loneliness.

King Henry, remembering that he had said that he could teach James French as well as any man, had him taught not only French but many other things. Prince James learned to read French, and English, and Latin, to sing, and to play upon the harp and organ. He was also taught to fence and to wrestle, to use bows and arrows and, indeed, to do everything that knights and nobles did in those days.

No doubt the hours seemed long to the little boy, shut up all day in one room, so he looked forward to the coming of his masters, and soon he grew to love his books better than anything else. Over and over again he read the pretty stories of Chaucer and of other great poets, and he filled his mind so full of beautiful thoughts that when he grew up he too wrote poems.

But in spite of all this James was very lonely. When he was a boy he longed for other boys to play with and as year after year went by and he grew to be a man, he longed more and more to be out in the great world, to go and come as he wished, to talk and laugh, to be merry and sad with other men and women, and to have his share in all the joy and sorrow, work and play of life.

Often he could not sleep and would spend the night trying to read and so to forget his misery. Then, as soon as the sun began to shine, he would go to his window and look out upon the fair world into which he might not go. And the sight of the blue sky and the green trees comforted him.

One May morning he rose very early and, opening his window, leaned out to breathe the fresh, clear air. He looked down into the garden with its green arbour set about with thick leafy trees and hawthorn hedges white with blossom and up to the sky where big fleecy clouds were sailing through the blue. All the world was bright.

The birds seemed so glad and joyous that after they had stopped singing, Prince James still leaned by the window, watching them as they hopped about, preening their feathers, twittering and playing with each other in the sunshine. They came quite close to his window for they were not afraid of the man with the sad eyes who watched them. And all the time Prince James was saying to himself, "What have I done that I should be cooped up here within these four walls with no one to love me, while the birds may fly about in the free air and sing to each other and love each other?"

Still full of these sad thoughts he looked down again into the garden. Suddenly all the blood in his body seemed to rush to his heart. For there in the garden walked the fairest lady he had ever seen. Her golden hair was crowned with a wreath of flowers, red, white and blue. Her dress glittered with gold and gems. Round her neck hung a great, red, ruby heart and oh! she was more beautiful than any fairy princess. Unable to move, the Prince stood and gazed at her.

As soon as he recovered himself, Prince James drew in his head quickly, lest he should be seen and frighten the beautiful lady away. But again he leaned out to watch her as she walked with her two ladies-in-waiting, and played about with her little dog.

Then, although the lady was far away down in the garden and could not hear him, Prince James knelt at the window and whispered to her. "Dear lady," he said, "you are so beautiful I cannot help but love you. Why did you come? I am only a wretched prisoner but be kind to me and love me too. If you will not, I must bear the pain all my life."

And so he knelt, and watched, and whispered, and envied the little dog she played with. "Dear birds," he cried, "where are your songs? You sang of love this morning. Where are your songs now? Why are you silent? Do you not see that the most beautiful lady in all the world is walking in the garden? Sing on again and make my lady cheer. Now is the time to sing, or else never."

It seemed as if the little birds understood, for they began to sing more sweetly than they had ever sung before, it seemed to the Prince. The beautiful lady stood under the trees, looking up and listening to their songs. And Prince James knelt by the window, watching and loving her more and more.

The beautiful lady had gone from the garden. To Prince James, life seemed darker and more dreary than before. All day he mourned and grieved, longing again to see the lovely lady. When night came he still knelt by the window, as motionless as any statue. At last, wearied both in heart and mind, he leaned his head against the cold stone and slept. And in his dreams he saw again the beautiful lady walking in the garden.

CHAPTER 54

James I – The Poet King:
How he Reigned and How he Died

To PRINCE James in his prison, the days were dark and long and dreary, but brighter days were near. Regent Albany died. His son, Murdoch, ruled weakly and badly. Scotland longed for a king again, and at last the prison doors were opened – Prince James was free.

In those days, when a prisoner was set free he had to be ransomed. That is, a large sum of money had to be paid for him. But as James had been unlawfully seized when the two countries were at peace, the English could not demand a ransom. Instead, they sent the Scots a bill for all that had been spent on educating and keeping their King. Just as if the Scots had wanted the English to keep their King from them all these years!

As soon as James was free, he married the beautiful lady of the garden – "his fair heart's lady", he called her. Her name was Jane Beaufort. She was a relation of the King and a very great lady. The English were glad that James wanted to marry this lady for they thought she would make him keep peace with England and not help the French any more. Lady Jane, too, loved Prince James. She had heard much about him at the English court. Perhaps that May morning she had glanced up at his window and seen him as he knelt to watch her while she walked in the garden.

They were married with great pomp and ceremony in London and then this King and Queen, a happy pair of lovers, travelled slowly northward to their kingdom. They were followed by a train of English knights and nobles who had learned to love James and as they neared the Borders, the greatest of the Scottish barons came to meet their King.

Then with rejoicing and feasting they moved on to Scone where the King and Queen were crowned.

James found the land in a dreadful state. Under Murdoch of Albany's weak rule, the nobles had grown more and more proud and unruly. Each acted like a king. No one thought of keeping the laws if he did not choose to do so. The land was little else than one wide den of robbers.

James set himself at once to bring order into this confusion. Two or three days after he was crowned he called a Parliament. He was busy himself and he kept his Parliament busy too. He went through all the laws, doing away with some, making others more plain and secure. He made the proud nobles show how they came to be possessed of the lands they held and many of them who had taken other men's goods and lands by force, were punished. "Let God but grant me life," cried James, "and there shall not be a spot in my dominions where the key shall not keep the castle, and the furze bush the cow, though I myself should lead the life of a dog to bring it about."

By this James meant that people should learn to keep the laws so well that cattle would not need to be watched and guarded, and that people might live quietly in their homes and not need an army of soldiers to keep them safe from attack.

Soon after James came to the throne, Regent Murdoch and his sons were seized, tried and condemned for the evil deeds that they had done while the King was in prison in England. They were first shut up in Stirling Castle and afterwards their heads were cut off.

For thirteen years James continued to rule wisely and sternly. He brought peace to the land and comfort to the people, but many of the proud nobles hated him because he had lessened their power.

The King had many enemies and chief among them was Sir Robert the Graham. One day in Parliament Sir Robert rose in his place and cursed the King, calling him a tyrant. For this and other misdeeds all his possessions were taken

from him, and he was banished from the land. Then he, and
others with him, formed a plot to kill the King.

It was wintertime and James, having made up his mind
to spend Christmas at the monastery of the Black Friars at
Perth, journeyed northward with all his court. As he was
about to step into the boat to cross the River Forth, he was
stopped by an old woman. "My lord King," she cried, "go not
over. If you cross this water you will never return again."

For a moment the King hesitated. The woman seemed so
earnest that he could not help being struck by her words.
"Go," he said to a knight who rode with him, "ask the
woman more nearly what she means."

The knight went, but he could make nothing of the old
woman. All she would say was that someone called Hubert
had told her to warn the King. "Heed her not, Sire," said the
knight, as he came back, "she is but a half-witted
grandmother."

So the King went on and thought no more of the old
woman and her warning, and soon the lively procession
arrived safely at Perth. Day after day was spent in
merrymaking. Christmas passed. The New Year came and
still the King stayed on.

One evening, after a day of feasting and pleasure, James
sat playing at chess with a knight of the court whom he had
nicknamed the King of Love. "Sir King of Love," he said
laughing, "I read not long ago that a king should be killed
in Scotland this year. That must be either you or me, for we
are the only two kings in the land. So I warn you to look to
yourself." The courtiers around laughed at the King's jest,
although there were some there who knew only too well
that his words would soon become true.

The court had been unusually happy that day. The
evening, filled with games, singing and storytelling had
passed quickly, so it was late before the last courtier had
gone, but still the King, dressed in a loose robe, stood by the
fire chatting with the Queen and her ladies before going to
bed.

But while the King and Queen had been merrily passing the time in song and laughter, Robert the Graham and his friends had been preparing their wicked plans. Logs of wood had been placed across the moat, the locks and bolts had been taken from the royal rooms and everything done that would make the entrance of traitors easy.

Now, as the King talked, a fierce Highland war cry was heard without. The clang of swords, the rush of feet, came to his ears. The gleam of torches in the courtyard without showed through the uncurtained windows.

At once the thought of treachery flashed upon the King's mind. He sprang to the door to fasten it. Alas! the lock was broken and the heavy bar used as a bolt was gone. Turning quickly to the window he tried to break or bend the iron bars with which they were guarded. But strong though he was he could not move them. That way there was no escape.

The noise and tumult were coming ever nearer and nearer. The terrified Queen and her ladies huddled in a corner, trembling. But one brave lady, Catherine Douglas, stood by the door, her arm thrust through the iron loops where the bolt should have been. She at least would do what she could to keep the traitors out. The King looked round hopelessly. What was to be done? His eye fell upon the tongs by the fireplace. Seizing them, he forced up a plank in the floor and, jumping down into the vault below, let the plank fall into its place again. He might have escaped that way for a little square hole led from the vault to the open air. But alas! only three days before, the King himself had given orders to have it built up, for when he played tennis in the garden his balls would often roll into the hole and be lost. So now he could only stand in the vault and wait, listening anxiously to the sounds above.

Scarcely had the King disappeared when three hundred Highlanders, armed with drawn swords, battle-axes and weapons of all kinds, rushed into the room. Brave Catherine tried in vain to keep them back. They broke her pretty white arm and rudely threw her from the door as they burst it open and dashed in. Ever afterwards, Catherine was called Catherine Barlass, because of her brave deed.

The room filled with armed men and the ladies, terribly frightened, ran away, trying to hide. The Queen alone was so struck with terror that she could not move. With pale face and staring eyes she stood gazing at the scene. One of the ruffians struck her and would have killed her, had not Robert Graham's son stopped him. "For shame," he cried, "what would you do to the Queen? She is but a woman. It is with men that we have to do. Let us on and find the King."

Then they swept through the rooms, leaving the Queen alone, sobbing bitterly. Everywhere they searched – in cupboards and wardrobes, under beds and couches, but nowhere was the King to be found. At last, mad with disappointment and anger, they turned and left the wrecked and ruined rooms.

Then the King, hearing no noise and thinking that all was safe again, lifted the planks which covered his hiding place and made ready to come up. At this minute the traitors returned. One of them had remembered the vault below the floor. "Ha," he cried in wicked glee, as he tore up the plank and saw the King, "the bridegroom is found for whom we came and for whom we have sought so long."

With his drawn sword in his hand one knight leaped down into the vault. The King caught him by the shoulders and threw him down. A second knight jumped down. But the King seized him too and threw him down.

King James was a mighty, strong man and he was fighting for his life. But he had only his naked hands with which to fight and his enemies were armed to the teeth. Then Sir Robert Graham, seeing how James struggled with the two men, also sprang into the vault, sword in hand.

Even James could not fight with three men at once. "Have mercy," he cried.

"Cruel tyrant, you never had mercy on the lords and nobles," replied Graham. "You shall have no mercy now."

"Then, for the salvation of my soul, let me confess my sins to a priest."

"You shall never have other confessor than this same sword," replied Graham fiercely and therewith he pierced the King through the body, so that he fell to the ground. Others followed the Graham, till the King lay dead with sixteen wounds in his brave heart.

Then the traitors sought for the Queen and would have killed her too. But she had fled to warn the people of the town who now came hurrying in. They came too late. The King was slain and the traitors fled.

CHAPTER 55

James II of the Fiery Face – The Story of the Black Dinner

JAMES I was killed in 1437 and his son, who was also called James, was then only six years old. He was, however, crowned at once for although some of the nobles had hated James I, he had been loved by most of the people and they willingly accepted his little son as their King.

Sir Robert Graham had thought and hoped that the people would bless him and love him for having rid them of a cruel tyrant. He soon found out his mistake. The people cursed him for his deed. Filled with terrible rage and hatred, they hunted him and those who had helped him till, in little more than a month, every man of them was taken prisoner. They were all put to death in most horrible and cruel ways. However bad their crime had been, we cannot help shuddering at the terrible punishments which fell upon the murderers. And Graham, instead of being remembered with love, was remembered with hate.

As James II was such a little boy, of course he could not himself rule. So several of the great nobles were chosen to rule instead.

These powerful men were jealous of each other and quarrelled, each trying to be greater than the other and each trying to get possession of the King.

The greatest of all the lords was Earl Douglas. Ever since the days of the good Lord James, the Douglas family had been growing more and more powerful. Now they were the greatest and proudest nobles in the land and they kept state like princes. Indeed, their houses were far more splendid and their servants far more numerous than the King's. Within their own lands, which were large and wide, they did as they liked. When the Earl Douglas rode abroad he was attended by a thousand knights and soldiers. He held a Parliament, made knights and waged war as if he were a king. What he desired he took. No man was strong enough to stand against him and all the wild young men of the land, seeking for adventure, flocked to join the Douglas soldiery.

This powerful earl was now made Governor of the kingdom. He died, however, in about a year and was succeeded in his earldom by his son, William. William was only seventeen but he was even more proud and grand than his father had been.

At first the Queen Mother, as Queen Jane was now called, lived with her little son, the King, in Edinburgh Castle. But soon she began to be afraid of Sir William Crichton who was Chancellor of the kingdom and Governor of the castle, and she feared that he meant to do some evil to the King. So she pretended that she wanted to go on a pilgrimage and, hiding James in one of her boxes, she ran away with him to Stirling Castle.

The Governor of Stirling, who was Sir William Crichton's rival, was greatly pleased to see the Queen and her little son for now, having possession of the King, he was the more powerful.

For about two years the Queen Mother and her son lived in Stirling and after the death of Archibald, Earl of Douglas, Sir Alexander Livingstone, the Governor of Stirling was made Governor of the kingdom. And he, having the King in his power, ruled as he liked, taking counsel of neither lord nor baron. This made Sir William Crichton very angry and he longed to get possession of the King once more. So one dark night, with about a hundred armed men he took his way to Stirling and there, near the castle walls, he lay in hiding, hoping to capture the King when he came out to ride in the morning.

As Sir William had expected, the King came out very early in the morning, accompanied only by a few horsemen. James rode happily along and before he knew what was happening, he found himself surrounded by armed men.

Very humbly and reverently they all bowed before the King who was greatly astonished at their sudden appearance.

Then Sir William came forward and spoke to James in a gentle, loving manner. "I pray your Majesty," he said, pointing to the gates of Stirling, "let me deliver you out of that prison. The Governor wickedly keeps you there to the hurt of your kingdom. Come with me to Edinburgh or to any part of Scotland that you please and I will keep you safe from all dangers and from the power of those who would do you hurt. For it becomes a prince to live freely, governing others, and not subject to any vassal's rule or correction. I speak for those who wish you well."

As Sir William spoke the King began to smile. He knew that in Stirling Castle he could not do as he liked. Both his mother and the Governor often said to him, "You must do this," or "You must do that," and he thought how nice it would be to do just as he liked. So he smiled. And seeing him smile, Sir William knew that he had got what he wanted. He knew that the King was willing to go with him. Laying hold of his bridle, he turned his horse's head towards Edinburgh. Then some of the King's servants and followers, who had come out to ride with him, came forward and tried to persuade him not to go with Sir William.

But the Governor's eldest son, who was also with them, bade them be silent. "It is vain," he said, "for us to strive with so many armed men. The more so as they mean no harm to the King. It is better to suffer this defeat than to attempt what is beyond our power." So the King was led away towards Edinburgh and his servants turned back to Stirling with the news.

The Governor was not at Stirling at this time but as soon as he heard of what had happened, he mounted upon his horse and came galloping back as fast as he could. He was angry with himself for not having kept the King more safely. He was angry with his friends, because he felt sure that some of them must have been in league with Sir William and helped him to capture the King. But this he was determined upon, that having been powerful he meant to continue being powerful. Yet he felt now that he was not strong enough to stand alone and he was undecided what to do. "Shall I join with the Douglas against Sir William," he asked himself, "or shall I make friends with Sir William and help him to put down the Douglas?"

In the end he made up his mind to make friends with Sir William. So they had a meeting at Edinburgh and pretended to forgive all the evil they had done to one another.

Soon after this a Parliament was called at Edinburgh. There, many complaints were sent from all sides of how the whole land was filled with murder and war, and how there was no peace nor rest for any man.

That the pride and lawlessness of the Douglas were to blame for much of this was certain. Crichton and Livingstone therefore made up their minds to rid the country of him.

He was so great and powerful that they dared not take him by force. So they wrote a kind letter to him. In this letter they told him in many fair words that his help was needed to rule the country and they begged him to come to Edinburgh to see the King.

The Earl was pleased with this letter and suspecting no treachery, rode to Edinburgh with his young brother, David, and a great company of followers. As they neared the city some of his knights began to suspect that all was not fair and honest. So they begged the Earl to turn back. But although the Earl was proud and haughty he was chivalrous and noble. "Do not speak to me of treachery," he said. "The Chancellor has treated me kindly. I will hear no evil of him."

So they rode on but the knights grew ever more and more uneasy and at last even David begged his brother to turn back.

Then the young Earl was angry. He spoke sharply to his brother, telling him that no great noble should pay heed to tale-bearing, and he commanded that no man in his company should again speak such words.

Then setting spurs to his horse the Earl galloped faster than before towards Edinburgh, followed sadly by his knights who dared speak no more words of warning.

The Earl and his brother were received with great joy. For a few days there was feasting and merrymaking. The King was delighted with his new companions. He was about ten years old now and he was very tired of having only grave, stern men about him. The Earl was young and handsome and he had such splendid stories of adventure to tell that the King grew to love him.

But while the Douglas feasted and played with the King, his enemies were making ready.

One day the Governor managed to send most of the Earl's soldiers out of Edinburgh. That night there was a great feast. All the most delightful dishes that could be thought of were prepared for the two young nobles. But when the dinner was over, when the last dish had been carried away, a great black bull's head was brought in upon a silver dish and placed before the Earl. The black bull's head was the sign of death.

Too late the Earl remembered the warning of his friends. Too late he saw that the Governor and the Chancellor meant him evil. He and his brother started up from the table and drew their swords. But armed men rushed in from every side. There was no escape. They were soon fast bound hand and foot.

Meanwhile the King wept and clung to them. He fell upon his knees before the Chancellor, and with tears and sobs begged him to save his new friends. But the Chancellor answered sternly, "Earl Douglas is your enemy. He is a traitor to his country. So long as he has life, the land can have neither rest nor peace. He must die."

So the two boys were hurried away to the courtyard of the castle and there their heads were cut off.

This was afterwards called the Black Dinner. It was indeed a black dinner for the Douglases.

CHAPTER 56

James II of the Fiery Face – The Fall of the Black Douglases

YOUNG William Douglas, who was killed at the Black Dinner, was succeeded by his uncle, James. He was so fat, and old, and idle, that he was called Gross James. But he did not live long and he was succeeded in the earldom by his son, William, who was prouder and fiercer than any of the Douglases had ever been.

The King was now growing up and he began to take the ruling of the kingdom into his own hands. War again broke out between England and Scotland. Douglas, although he was an unruly subject, was a fierce enemy of the English. He now marched with all his soldiers against them and fought so well that the King made him Lieutenant General of Scotland. But the Douglas became so proud and daring that King James was obliged to take this office from him again.

Terribly angry, Douglas went to his castle, vowing to avenge this insult. He defied the King in every way that he could. He leagued himself with other great lords against the King, wasting and destroying the lands of those who would not join with him.

This was nothing but rebellion and one gentleman called Maclellan refused to join. Douglas at once seized Maclellan and imprisoned him.

When the King heard of this he was very angry and at once sent Sir Patrick Grey, Maclellan's uncle, to Douglas with a letter asking him to release Maclellan.

As King, James ought to have commanded Douglas to let Maclellan go, but the Earl was so dreadfully powerful that the King dared not.

Sir Patrick Grey rode off with the letter as fast as he

could and arrived at Douglas Castle just as the Earl had finished dinner. Sir Patrick wished to deliver the King's letter at once but Douglas would not take it, though he greeted his guest with a great show of friendliness.

"Have you dined?" he asked.

"No," said Sir Patrick.

"Then you must dine first before we come to business. It is ill talking between a full man and a fasting."

So the Douglas called for beef and for wine, and set before his visitor the best that his castle could provide.

Sir Patrick sat down and ate well and heartily, for he was hungry after his long ride, and the Douglas sat beside him talking cheerfully.

But Douglas had guessed why Sir Patrick had come. Secretly he sent a message to his soldiers and while Sir Patrick dined, his nephew was led out to the green grass beside the castle. There he was made to lay his head upon a block and with one blow the headsman struck it off. Then a cloth was thrown over the dead body and it was left there alone.

At last, after much delay, Douglas broke the seal of the King's letter and read it. He sat some time as if thinking it over. Then, looking up, he said, "I thank you, Sir Patrick, for bearing to me this message from my liege lord. So far as it is possible he shall be obeyed."

Taking Sir Patrick by the hand, he led him out to the grassy courtyard. "You have come a little too late," he said, pointing to the dead body. "There lies your nephew, but he wants the head. Take his body and do with it what you will."

With a sad heart Sir Patrick replied, "My lord, since you have taken his head, dispose of his body as you please."

Then, filled with wrath and sorrow, he called for his horse and leaped upon it. Turning in the saddle, "My lord," he cried in a voice shaking with anger, "if I live, you shall be well rewarded for the deed you have this day done."

The proud Earl flushed scarlet from throat to brow. "Who

dares defy the Douglas in his castle?" he cried. "To horse, men, to horse, and after him."

Sir Patrick, seeing the Earl's fury, set spurs to his horse and galloped hard. After him came the Douglasmen thundering along on their mighty chargers. But Sir Patrick's horse was good and tried. He seemed to understand his master's danger and he galloped as he had never galloped before. It was a fast and furious race and not till the walls of Edinburgh came in sight did the Douglasmen give it up.

Sore at heart and weary of limb, Sir Patrick made his way to the King and told him his sad tale.

Angry and sorrowful too was the King when he heard the news. He knew not what to do with this wild, wicked lord. For it seemed Douglas had respect neither to King nor crown, and the very throne was in danger.

Yet Douglas and the King had once been friends. So at last James resolved to send for the Earl and to talk with him kindly and calmly, and try if he could not reason with him, and make him give up his wicked ways.

The King wrote a letter and sealed it with his great seal, asking Douglas to come to the court at Stirling and promising him that his life and liberty should be safe, in spite of all he had done. This letter was called a "safe-conduct", which means that it was the King's promise to the Earl that no one should attack or hurt him, and that he might safely come and go again to his own lands.

Trusting to this safe-conduct the great Earl came, bringing with him his five stalwart brothers and a large band of followers. The King received him kindly and gave him a fine supper, hoping by gentleness and friendliness to win him from his wild ways.

When supper was over, James drew Douglas aside in order to talk with him privately. At first they both seemed quiet and calm but as the King urged Douglas to give up his league with the other nobles, they both grew hot and angry.

"I will not break my bond for any man's asking," said

Douglas insolently. Then growing more and more angry, he poured forth a torrent of scornful words against the King.

James, who had a fiery temper, suddenly lost control of himself. Drawing his dagger, "False traitor," he cried, "if you will not break the bond, this shall." With that he struck the Earl in the body. Sir Patrick Grey, who stood near, remembering the threat he had made as he rode away from Castle Douglas, struck him down with his battle-axe. Others crowded round and soon the great Earl lay dead with twenty-six wounds in his breast.

This was a wicked action on the King's part and although it was done in a fit of passion, that was but a poor excuse for so unkingly an act, for James had given his word that Douglas should return safe to his own lands. It was an act too, which did no good, but rather evil, for the Earl had five strong brothers ready to avenge his death. Choosing James, the eldest, as their head they gathered their friends and followers together. Through the streets of the town, in scorn they dragged the King's safe-conduct tied to the tail of an old, broken-down carthorse. Then, as they could not storm the castle because it was so strong, they wasted the town with fire and sword. Their four hundred trumpeters blew upon their trumpets and heralds cried to all the four winds of heaven that never again would a Douglas acknowledge James as King or Prince, and that they should not cease to war against him till they were avenged upon him for his tyranny and treachery. Again the trumpets sounded, that all might know there was strife for ever between the Douglas and the King.

So was a mighty rebellion kindled. All Scotland rang with civil war. The throne seemed to tremble and almost at times there was doubt whether James Stewart or James Douglas should reign in Scotland. But at the height of its pride and splendour the Douglas fortune began to turn. Many nobles forsook the Earl's banner and joined themselves to the King. At last, one morning Douglas awoke to find his camp silent and deserted. Of the forty thousand men that he had led out scarce one hundred remained.

The struggle was over. The Earl broke up what remained of his army and fled to hide in the wildest parts of the Border lands where once he had ruled as lord. Then, with a few followers, he fled into England. Many years later he returned to Scotland and, old and broken, he died a monk in the Monastery of Lindores.

Thus ended the power of the Black Douglases.

The Earl of Angus, who was himself a Douglas, had greatly helped the King during this rebellion. Now he was rewarded by the title of the Douglas and by much of his land. So it was said that the Red Douglas put down the Black. But although the Red Douglases became famous, they never rose to such great power as the Black Douglases had done.

Now, at last, for some years the land had peace. James ruled firmly and wisely. People began to keep the laws. All seemed well. But alas, soon these happy days were over.

Although the English had long before been driven out of Scotland, the Border castle of Roxburgh had remained in their hands ever since the days of Edward III. James now made up his mind to drive them out of this last stronghold and he laid siege to the castle.

It shows how well James had ruled his land that all the chieftains flocked to his aid. Even Donald, Lord of the Isles, the wildest of them all, came with his men to help the King.

But the siege lasted long and the soldiers began to be weary of it. One morning they were cheered by the arrival of the Earl of Huntly with a fresh army. The King was so pleased at this that he ordered the gunners to load the cannon and bombard the walls once more.

In those days, gunpowder had not been long in use and people did not know how to make good cannon. They were made of pieces of iron, or wood, bound together. James was standing near one of these clumsy guns, watching the men fire, when it burst. Splinters flew in all directions. One hit the King and killed him where he stood.

So died King James II. He was only twenty-nine and had reigned twenty-three years. He was called James of the Fiery Face because he had a great red mark on one cheek. Perhaps he may have been also called so because he had a fiery temper, as we know he had, from the way in which he killed Douglas. That is the only bad thing we hear about him. Otherwise he was a good king.

In the Duke of Roxburgh's park at Fleurs, a hawthorn tree may still be seen which marks the spot where he died.

CHAPTER 57

James III – The Story of the Boyds

THE LORDS and barons were full of grief at the death of their King. The soldiers lost heart and they would have given up the siege. But the Queen, hearing of this, left off her weeping and her sorrow. Drying her eyes, she took her little son, James, by the hand and with him went to the lords, as they sat in council.

Sad, pale and beautiful she stood before them, with the little Prince beside her. "You must not give up the siege," she said. "For very shame you must not. Let not the death of one man take away all your courage from you. Forward, therefore, my lords. Shed the blood of your enemies for your King, rather than your own tears. Let it not be said that you needed to be encouraged by a woman, and that a widowed one. Rather, my lords, should you comfort her."

Cheered by these brave words, the nobles resolved to go on with the siege, and so fiercely did they assault the castle that the English, seeing no hope of help, yielded it. Then the Scots destroyed the castle, so that it should not again be a stronghold for the enemy.

The new King, James III, was only eight years old so the kingdom was ruled by Bishop Kennedy. In England, great churchmen were often also great statesmen but in Scotland Bishop Kennedy was the first great churchman to be a statesman. He ruled well and wisely but after six years he died. He was greatly mourned for, as an old history writer says, "He knew the nature of the Scottish men so that he was the most able of any lord in Scotland to give any wise counsel or an answer when the time occurred." Another says that his death was lamented by all men, as if they had lost a public father.

After the good Bishop died the great nobles, greedy of power, began each to flatter James and to try to get possession of him. Two of the boldest, Lord Boyd and his brother, Alexander, succeeded in carrying him off from those who had charge of him.

One day, as the young King, who was now fourteen, sat in his court at Linlithgow, Lord Boyd and his friends rushed in. They seized the King, placed him upon a horse and set out for Edinburgh. Gilbert Kennedy, the brother of the good Bishop, tried to stop them. He took the King's horse by the bridle and turned it again towards Linlithgow. But Alexander Boyd struck the old man with his hunting staff so that he dropped the bridle. Then the King and his captors rode on to Edinburgh and Kennedy turned sadly back to Linlithgow.

Lord Boyd had succeeded in gaining possession of the King but he was afraid that he might be punished for it. So when Parliament was sitting in Edinburgh he suddenly entered. Throwing himself at the King's feet he clasped his knees. "I pray you, my lord King," he cried, "declare before the lords and commons here assembled that you are not angry with me for having of late removed your Majesty from Linlithgow to Edinburgh. Declare to them that I have used no force nor in any way hurt your royal person."

James, having been told before what to say, replied, "My lords, far from being carried forth from Linlithgow by force, I do assure you that I accompanied my Lord Boyd and his knights of mine own free will and pleasure."

Whereupon Parliament agreed that Lord Boyd had done right and that in future he should take care of the King.

After this the Boyds grew quickly greater and greater. Land, money and power were given to them, till soon they were the most important people in the whole country.

But just as quickly as the Boyds had risen into power they fell again. It was proposed that James should marry Margaret, the daughter of the King of Denmark and one of Lord Boyd's sons went to that country to arrange about the marriage. While he was away the nobles talked to James. They told him many evil stories of the Boyds and showed him that he was being treated more as a prisoner than as a king. They succeeded in making him very angry with the Boyds and he turned entirely from his old friends, and gave orders that they should be seized and put in prison. Lord Boyd and his sons, however, were warned in time and they fled away, and died in a foreign land. But Alexander was taken prisoner and his head was cut off.

After this the King himself ruled. He married the Princess Margaret of Denmark and as her wedding present, her father gave the islands of Orkney and Shetland to the King of Scotland. These islands had been in the possession of the Norse King ever since the days when the fierce Vikings used to come to fight and plunder along the shores of Scotland. Now they were returned to the Scottish King, and ever since they have belonged to Scotland.

CHAPTER 58

James III – How a Mason Became an Earl

JAMES III was neither a soldier nor a statesman. He hated war and he hated pomp and ceremony and great crowds of courtiers and servants. He would have been better pleased had he been a simple gentleman who could live quietly, spending his time in reading and study. But in those days reading and study were not thought fit occupations even for simple gentlemen. War was the only fit occupation for gentlemen and knights, and so the King did not make friends with the great and warlike nobles, but with humble men whose tastes were like his own.

His chief friends were Cochrane, an architect, or as the proud nobles called him scornfully, a mason; Rogers, a musician; Leonard, a smith; Hommel, a tailor; and Torphichen, a fencing master. But his greatest friend amongst them was Cochrane, the mason.

It made the proud nobles very angry to see that the King preferred the company of such people to theirs. And they began to think that one of his younger brothers would have made a much better king.

These brothers were the Duke of Albany and the Earl of Mar. They were both tall, handsome men, splendid soldiers and knights, and quite unlike the King in every way.

Although they were so different, the King loved his brothers. But Cochrane the mason and his friends did not like Albany and Mar, so they began to whisper evil things to the King against them. They pretended that Albany and Mar were in league with witches and wizards, and that they would cause the King's death. The King was very superstitious as many people were in those days when witches and wizards were still believed in. He was timid too and soon grew so afraid of his brothers that he ordered them to be seized and put in prison. Albany, however, managed to escape to France and from there he went to England. Mar was taken and died soon after in prison, killed, it is said, by the King's orders.

Then, Cochrane, the King's favourite, became greater and greater. He received the dead Earl's money and lands, and henceforward called himself the Earl of Mar. The King allowed him to issue coins which, instead of being entirely of silver, were mixed with copper. The people were very angry at this, and they refused to sell their goods for "Cochrane's plaks", as they called them. They insisted that this money should be called in again. But Cochrane would not listen. "By heaven," he cried, "the day I am hanged it shall be called in, and not before."

The King would do nothing without his favourite's advice. If a man wished to ask anything of the King, he was obliged to flatter and to make friends with Cochrane. To be ruled by a mason was very bitter to the great barons, so gradually James lost the love of many of the greatest men of the kingdom and they began to plot together to rid themselves of Cochrane and the others who were the King's favourites.

At this time the King of England prepared to make war once more against Scotland. He meant to help the Duke of Albany, and to set him upon the throne instead of James. He thought this would please the Scots but, however angry they were with their own King, they had no mind to allow the King of England to interfere. So, when James called his soldiers together they came eagerly.

It was a very great army which gathered on the Borough-muir near Edinburgh and marched southwards. Besides foot soldiers and horsemen, the King brought some of the great cannon from Edinburgh Castle and over these, he made Cochrane captain.

Cochrane came to battle in very great state. He rode upon a splendid horse, a golden helmet was carried before him and in front of it marched four trumpeters, blowing upon golden horns. Behind him rode three hundred men clad in white. His tent was made of silk and even the cords were twined with silk and gold.

All this show made the nobles more bitterly angry than ever with Cochrane. Very early one morning as they were encamped at Lauder, they met together in the church there, to discuss how they might rid themselves of this upstart, as they called him.

They were all agreed that Cochrane must die. But how was it to be done? That was the question. He was powerful, he was brave, he was loved by the King, he was constantly surrounded by soldiers and servants. How was it to be done?

In this doubt and difficulty, one of the lords, seeing that although the nobles were discontented enough, they lacked courage and decision, told a story. "Once upon a time," he said, "all the mice met together to consult how they should defend themselves against their great enemy the cat. The cat was so big, and they were so small, that they could not kill him. And he prowled about so quietly on his soft paws that he was often close upon them before they had time to run away. At last, after much talking, they decided to hang a bell round his neck so that they should always be able to hear when their enemy was coming. But the plan failed, for no mouse could be found bold enough to hang the bell round the cat's neck."

As soon as this lord had done speaking Archibald, Earl of Angus, started forward. "There is no need of delay," he cried. "I will bell the cat." From this speech he was known ever after as "Archibald-bell-the-cat".

At this moment there came a loud knocking at the church door, which was barred and guarded.

"Who knocks thus loudly?" demanded the knight who kept the door.

"It is I, the Earl of Mar," came the answer.

"Ha!" cried Angus, "the victim has been beforehand with us. He saves us the trouble of seeking him. Unbar the door."

The heavy bolts were slowly pushed back, the door

swung open and Cochrane entered. He was, as usual, splendidly dressed. He wore a hunting costume of black velvet. Round his neck hung a heavy chain of gold, at his belt a golden horn set with jewels. He came forward with a haughty, careless smile.

Angus met him. "A halter would better become you," he cried, pulling the gold chain roughly from his neck.

"You have been a hunter of mischief long enough," said another knight, snatching at his horn.

Cochrane was not easily made afraid but he was astonished at this rough usage. "My lords," he said, "is this jest or earnest?"

"It is good earnest," they replied, "as you shall soon see. You and your fellows have taken too much advantage of our King this long while. Now that is at an end and you shall receive the reward of your misdeeds."

The fierce, stern nobles crowded round Cochrane and he was quickly bound hand and foot. Then a party of soldiers hurried to the King's tent. There they found all the other favourites. They seized every one of them except a boy called Ramsay. He clung to the King and James held him tight in his arms, and prayed so earnestly for his life that the nobles spared him. But all the others were led out to Lauder Bridge and hanged there in a row, with Cochrane in the middle.

Even at the last moment, Cochrane could not forget his grandeur and finery. He begged to be hanged with a silken cord from his tent and not with a hempen rope like a common thief.

"Thou art but a false thief and traitor," the lords replied, "and deserve no better." And instead of hanging him with a silken cord, they hanged him with one of horsehair which was thought to be more disgraceful even than hemp. As soon as he was hanged they made a proclamation, calling in all Cochrane's plaks. Thus his words came true.

So died the King's favourites, most of them for no greater fault than that they were low born.

CHAPTER 59

James III – The Battle of Sauchieburn

HAVING finished their cruel work the barons broke up the army and, taking the King, led him prisoner to Edinburgh Castle. All the nobles had been eager and willing to destroy the King's favourites but when it became known that some of their number were in league with Edward of England and with the Duke of Albany, and that they hoped to place the Duke upon the throne, the others were angry. So the nobles were divided into two parties, some for the King and some for the Duke.

But for a short time these quarrels were forgotten. Peace was made with England and Albany came to Edinburgh, demanding that the King should be set free. This was done but soon James found that he was really his brother's prisoner, for the Duke ruled and forced the King to do as he wished. Then Albany began again to plot with the King of England but this was discovered, and once more he was forced to flee to France.

The King was now again really free and he soon did many things which displeased his proud barons, and they became angry with him, and discontented with his rule. All those, too, who had helped to kill the King's favourites felt sure that some day James would punish them, so they rose in rebellion.

When James heard that the Lowland lords were gathering to battle he fled to the north leaving his son, James, whom he dearly loved, safe, as he thought, in Stirling Castle. "As you love honour and life," he said to the Governor, "let no man enter into the castle till I come again. Nor let the Prince pass out, nor meet with any man, but guard and keep him well." This the Governor vowed to do.

But the rebel lords came to him and promised him a great sum of money if he would give the Prince up to them.

"A halter would better become you" (page 211)

Sir Andrew with his two ships, The Yellow Carvel *and*
The Flower, *beat five of the English (page 217)*

And the Governor, forgetting his oath to the King, allowed the Prince to be led away to the camp of the rebel lords.

Then the King, having gathered an army of faithful men in the north, marched again to Stirling. But the Governor would not let him come into the castle.

"Then let me see my son," said the King.

"You cannot see him."

"Where is he?" asked the King, still calmly.

"He is with the rebel lords," replied the Governor.

Then the King was angry. "False traitor, you have deceived me, and if I live I shall be avenged upon you," he cried, and rode away.

Next morning, at Sauchieburn, not far from the famous field on which the Battle of Bannockburn was fought, the King's army and the rebels met. On both sides fluttered the royal banner, for in the one army was the King and in the other the Prince. James had never been a great soldier and now when he looked across at the royal standard and remembered that his dear son was in the army opposite, he had little heart for fighting.

But one of his nobles came to him, bringing a beautiful grey horse. "My liege," he said, "I pray you accept this horse. It is so swift that it will beat any in Scotland, so that whether you advance or retreat you are safe."

Then, taking heart, the King mounted upon the beautiful grey horse and led his men against the enemy. But when the battle began, when he heard the clash and clang of sword on armour and all the noise and turmoil of war, fear came upon him again and turning his horse he fled from the field. Over the plain of Bannockburn, where Bruce had fought and conquered, near to the bridge that Wallace had won, this poor King fled until he came to a mill beside the Bannock burn. There the miller's wife stood at a spring filling her pitcher with water. When she saw a splendidly armed knight come thundering along on his great warhorse, she was frightened. Letting her pitcher drop, she ran screaming away.

Startled, the King's horse reared and plunged and the King, who could not ride well, was thrown to the ground. There he lay, stunned with the fall and sorely bruised. Then the woman, seeing him lie so still, called to her husband and together they carried the King into the cottage and laid him upon a bed.

Presently he came to his senses again. Groaning and in much pain, he asked for a priest.

"Who are you?" said the woman.

"This day at morn I was your King," replied James sadly.

Hearing that, the woman, who seems to have been easily excited and frightened, ran out into the road wringing her hands, and calling out, "A priest, a priest for the King."

"I am a priest," said a man who came up at that moment. "Where is the King?"

The miller's wife, glad so soon to have found what she sought, took the man by the hand and led him quickly into the cottage where the King lay.

The priest knelt beside the King. "Are you sore wounded?" he asked bending over him.

"I know not but that I might recover," replied James, "but I desire to confess my sins and to receive pardon for them."

"This shall give you pardon," answered the man, and drawing a dagger, he stabbed the King to the heart again and again. Then rising, he lifted the dead King in his arms and went away, no one knew where. No one knew who he was, or whether he was a priest or not. He was never heard of more.

CHAPTER 60

James IV – The Story of a Great Sea Fight

KING James III was only thirty-five when he was murdered in 1488, having reigned for twenty-eight years.

The battle did not last long after the King had fled from the field. The rebels won the victory and, soon after, Prince James was crowned, under the title of James IV.

But at first no one knew what had happened to James III. At this time Scotland was beginning to be famous for her ships and her brave sea captains. Sir Andrew Wood, one of the bravest of these sea captains, was lying in the Forth with his ships. As the King could be nowhere found, the lords began to think that perhaps he had taken refuge in one of Sir Andrew's boats. So they sent messengers to Sir Andrew, asking him if the King were with him.

"He is not here," replied Sir Andrew. "Search my ship if you do not believe me."

So the messengers went back. But the Prince and the lords were not content. They again sent to Sir Andrew commanding him to come ashore.

Sir Andrew came as he was commanded. He was a very handsome man, and was grandly dressed. As he came into the room he looked so splendid that the Prince ran to him crying, "Sir, are you my father?"

"No," answered Sir Andrew, the tears running down his cheeks, "no, I am not your father. But I was his true servant, and the enemy of all those who rebelled against him."

At these words the Prince turned away sadly, for he had most unwillingly risen against his father.

"Do you know where the King is?" asked the lords sternly, for they did not like to be spoken of as rebels.

"I do not," replied Sir Andrew scornfully.

Still the lords did not believe him. "Is he not in your ship?" they asked again.

"He is not," replied Sir Andrew. "But would to God he were there safely, and I should defend and keep him from the traitors who murdered him. I hope to see the day when they shall be hanged for their evil deeds."

These bold answers made the lords very angry and when Sir Andrew had gone back to his ship they called all the sea captains of Leith together and ordered them to fight Sir Andrew and to take him prisoner.

But the captains refused and another brave sailor, called Sir Andrew Barton, spoke up bravely, "There are not ten ships in Scotland," he said, "fit to fight Sir Andrew's two, for he is well practised in war and his men are hard to beat on land or sea."

Later, Sir Andrew Wood came to great honour, for James IV was fond of ships and was glad that Scotland should have brave sailors like Andrew Wood and Andrew Barton.

James saw, too, that it was necessary for Scotland to have a navy. For an island lying in the sea must have ships to guard her shores and also to carry goods to other countries. People were at this time slowly beginning to learn that a country was richer and happier when at peace, and that it was much better to trade with other nations than to fight with them. They were also finding out that Europe was not the whole world and many brave sailors had sailed into far, unknown seas and discovered strange lands, and had come home with curious tales of the wonderful countries and peoples they had seen. So James built ships, and encouraged his people to fish in far seas and to trade with distant countries, and soon the Scottish flag was known and respected far and wide.

Among the ships which James built was one called *The Great Michael*. It was the greatest ship that had ever been known. All the carpenters in Scotland worked upon her for a year and a day till she was ready to put to sea. All the forests of Fife were cut down to get wood for the building of this monster which cumbered all Scotland to get her to sea, says one old writer. King James was so interested in this great ship that he used daily to go on board to watch how the work was going on and would often dine there with his lords. At last she was finished and sailed proudly out on the waters of the Forth. Then the King commanded that cannon should be fired at her sides to see if the vessel was strong enough to stand fire. And *The Great Michael* was so well and strongly built that the cannon did little harm to her.

The English, too, had great ships and they used to attack the Scots whenever they met upon the sea. They would even come right up the Scottish Sea, as the Firth of Forth was then often called. King James was very angry at this and he sent Sir Andrew Wood against the English; and Sir Andrew, with his two ships, *The Yellow Carvel* and *The Flower*, beat five of the English and carried their captains and men prisoner to the King.

When King Henry heard how his ships had been taken, he was very angry. He sent through all England, saying that whoever would go to fight Sir Andrew, and bring him prisoner, should have great honour and a thousand pounds in gold. So Stephen Bull, a daring sailor, said that he would go and would bring Sir Andrew, alive or dead, a prisoner to King Henry.

Stephen Bull, with three great ships, sailed away till he came to the Firth of Forth. There he found some fishing boats whose crews he took prisoner.

Then he sailed on again but still could see nothing of Sir Andrew. Very early one summer morning, however, an English sailor on the lookout saw two ships far away. Stephen Bull made some of the fishermen whom he had taken prisoner, climb the mast, so that they might see whether it was Sir Andrew or not.

But the fishermen, not wishing to betray their own countryman, said that they did not know.

"Tell me truly," said Stephen, "and whether we win or lose, you shall have your lives and liberty."

Then the men confessed that the ships were *The Yellow Carvel* and *The Flower*.

Hearing that, Stephen was very glad. He ordered a cask of wine to be brought up and all the men and captains cheered and drank to their victory, of which they felt sure. Then Stephen sent each man to his post and prepared to meet the enemy.

Sir Andrew Wood, on the other hand, came sailing along, little expecting to meet any English. But when he saw three ships coming towards him in battle array, "Ha," he said, "yonder come the English who would make us prisoners to the King of England. But, please God, they shall fail in their purpose."

He, too, ordered a cask of wine to be brought and every man drank to his fellow and, speaking brave words to them, Sir Andrew sent each man to his post.

By this time the sun had risen high and shone brightly upon the sails. The English ships were great and strong and had many guns, but the Scots were not afraid and they sailed on towards the English. Soon cannon boomed and the fight began. All that long summer day the battle raged, the heavy smoke darkening the blue sky. The people who lived on the shore watched and wondered, till at last night fell and the fighting ceased. But next morning, as soon as it was light, the trumpets sounded and once more the battle began. So fiercely did it rage, that neither captains nor sailors took heed of where the ships went. They drifted with the tide and the fight, which had begun in the Forth, finished near the mouth of the Tay. It ended in victory for the Scots.

Instead of being taken prisoner to Henry, Sir Andrew took Stephen Bull with all his men and led them before King James.

King James thanked and rewarded Sir Andrew greatly. Then he sent Stephen and his men back to England. "And tcll your King," he said, "that we have as manful men, both by sea and land, in Scotland, as he has in England. Tell him to send no more of his captains to disturb my people. If he does, they shall not be treated so well next time."

And King Henry was well pleased neither with the news, nor with the message.

CHAPTER 61

James IV – The Thistle and the Rose

WHEN James IV had reigned a little time he began to be very sorry for having rebelled against his father, James III. He spent much of his time in the Chapel Royal at Stirling, praying for forgiveness. As a punishment to himself he fastened a chain of iron round his waist. This he wore night and day so that he might ever be kept in remembrance of his wickedness and every year he added more links to the chain to make it heavier.

But although James did this he was by no means always sad and mournful. He loved sports and games and all the fine show of tournaments. He himself could fence and ride with the best. Often he held great tournaments at court to which not only his own nobles but famous knights from far countries came.

King James loved knightly games and amusements, but he loved his people too. Often he rode through his kingdom, quite alone and plainly dressed, so that none might know that he was the King. He would go into poor men's houses and sit and talk with them as one of themselves. Then he would ask them what they thought of the King and how he ruled. In this way he found out what troubles and wants the people had.

The King, too, sailed in his ships all round and among the islands of Scotland so that the wild people there, who had never seen a king before, were astonished at his grandeur. The Lord of the Isles and other Highland chieftains rebelled from time to time against him, and the Borderers were ever ready to break out into war. But James subdued them all, and he was so just and friendly that even those in the farthest corners of his kingdom came to know and love him. He was generous and spent liberally the hoards of money which his father had gathered, so that there was great love between the people and their King.

James at last made peace with England and married Margaret, the daughter of King Henry. All the people rejoiced greatly at this marriage and it was hoped that it would help to make a lasting peace between the two countries.

The Princess came from London surrounded by a splendid train of knights and nobles. King James, beautifully dressed, rode to meet his bride upon a fiery, prancing steed with trappings of gold. He and his nobles came dashing along at full gallop and when they met the Princess they reined back so quickly that the horses were thrown upon their haunches. This was to show how well they could ride.

Then to amuse Margaret a little play was acted. A knight appeared, with a lady who carried his hunting horn and led his horse. A second knight dashed forward, seized the lady and carried her off. A fight followed, in which the knights fought with great skill until the King threw down his glove and called "peace."

When they came to the city, the Princess mounted upon the King's horse and rode behind him through the streets, the people shouting and cheering all the way.

Afterwards came tournaments, balls and all kinds of merriments. In one tournament the King, calling himself the Savage Knight, appeared surrounded by fierce wild men dressed in skins of animals, and he fought so well that he conquered all who came against him.

At last the rejoicings were over and the people went to their homes, delighted with their lively, handsome, clever King and their lovely young Queen.

But the peace and goodwill between England and Scotland did not last long. Henry VII died and was succeeded by his son, Henry VIII. He was hot-tempered, as was James, so they soon found causes for quarrelling.

In those days there was a great deal of fighting on the seas between merchant vessels, even when the countries were at peace. Indeed many sea captains were little more than pirates. A quarrel arose between the English and the Scots, and the English captains went to their King to complain that they had been unlawfully stopped and robbed by Sir Andrew Barton the Scotsman.

So King Henry sent Lord Thomas and his brother, Sir Edward Howard, with two great ships well fitted with cannon and archers, against Sir Andrew.

As they sailed along looking for Sir Andrew, they met another ship. "Have you seen Sir Andrew Barton?" asked Lord Howard of the captain.

"Ay, that have I," he replied sadly, "but yesterday I was his prisoner and he has robbed me of all my goods."

"Do you know where he is now?" asked Lord Howard. "Only let me see him and I will fight him and carry him prisoner to our King."

"Heaven help you," cried the merchantman, "you little know what a man he is."

"Never fear," said Lord Howard, "I will bring him and his ships to England or he may carry me to Scotland."

So the merchantman turned his ship about and led Lord Howard to where Sir Andrew lay. Lord Howard pulled down the English standard, and instead, he tied a white willow wand to his masthead, as was the custom with merchant vessels. Then when they came in sight of the Scottish vessels, Lord Howard sailed past without saluting.

Now this was very rude. For just as we bow and take off our hats when we meet a friend in the streets, so, when ship meets ship upon the seas the captains make signs of greeting to each other.

When Sir Andrew saw the English ship sail past without saluting, he was angry. "What English churls are yonder," he said, "that show so little courtesy?"

He had two ships: a large one called *The Lion* and a little pinnace called *The Jenny Perwin*. So now he bade *The Jenny Perwin* "Fetch back yon pedlars now to me. I swear by the mass yon English churls shall all hang at my main mast."

The little pinnace sailed off, but Sir Andrew soon saw that it was no merchantmen with which he had to do but the King of England's ships of war. Fire flashed, cannon boomed and a fight, fierce and long, took place. Both sides fought desperately and well but the little pinnace was soon sunk. Sir Andrew cheered his men, Lord Howard his, but at last a keen-eyed English archer struck Sir Andrew and he fell forward on the deck. He was sorely wounded but he would not give in.

They never heard his whistle blow. Gallant Sir Andrew had fought his last fight and lay dead upon the deck.

Then Lord Howard, seeing that the Scottish leader was killed, boarded *The Lion* and took her. But when he saw Sir Andrew lying upon the deck he felt sorry, as brave men must at the death of a gallant foe. Yet he said, "If thou wert alive as thou art dead, I must have left England many a day." For he knew that if he had not killed Sir Andrew, he himself would have been carried prisoner to Scotland. Drawing his sword, he cut off Sir Andrew's head, and ordered the body to be thrown into the sea. Then greatly rejoicing, the English sailed home with their prize.

CHAPTER 62

James IV – Flodden Field

KING James had loved Sir Andrew and when he heard of his death he was sad, and angry too. He sent to King Henry, demanding that he should pay for all the damage and loss, and return *The Lion*.

"The death of a pirate can never be the cause of quarrel between princes," replied Henry haughtily, so the quarrel was made worse instead of better. There were many other causes for anger between the two kings. One was that Henry would not give up the jewels and money which his father had left to Queen Margaret when he died.

Then the French and the English began to quarrel.

The Scots had always been friends with the French. Now the Queen of France wrote a pretty letter to James calling him her knight, telling him that she was a lady in distress and begging him to fight in her cause, and to advance, if but three steps, into England for her sake.

James, as gallant a knight as ever lived, could not say "no" to such a letter, so in an evil hour he sent his fleet to France and determined himself to march over the Border into England. What became of the fleet is not known, and little more was heard of Scotland's splendid ships.

The King's wise men and counsellors tried hard to persuade him not to go to war with England. But James would not listen. He was very angry with Henry and the Queen of France had roused all his knightly feelings. He was determined to fight. So all over Scotland a proclamation was made that every man between sixteen and sixty should be ready, within twenty days, to pass with the King into England. And for love of their King a great army gathered to him. Yet still they tried to prevent him going to war.

One evening James knelt in the church at Linlithgow,

praying, when a man suddenly appeared before him. This man was dressed in a long blue robe with a linen belt about his waist and sandals upon his feet. His hair was long and fair, his face grave and commanding. Standing before the King, this man bent over him and spoke: "Sir King," he said, "my mother hath sent me to you, desiring you not to pass at this time where you propose to go. For if you do, you will not fare well in your journey, neither you nor any that are with you."

When the man had ceased speaking the King paused a moment in wonder. But even as he did so the figure vanished away, as if he had been a blink of the sun, or a puff of wind. Search how they might, no man could find him or any trace of him. It was thought by some that King James had really seen a vision of St John who had been sent to warn him. But many people think that it was merely someone who had dressed himself in this strange fashion in order to make the King believe that he had seen a vision, and so turn from his purpose.

But nothing anyone could do or say was of the least use and James, with his great army, passed into England. Queen Margaret, from her high turret chamber in Linlithgow Castle, sadly watched him go to fight against her brother.

King Henry was away fighting in France so the English army was led by the Earl of Surrey. Upon the field of Flodden in Northumberland the armies met, and a great battle was fought on the 9th September 1513.

Even at the last minute the lords tried to persuade the King to go away to a safe place and let them fight the English. But at this James was furiously angry. "My lords," he cried, "I shall fight this day against England although you have sworn the contrary. Though you should all flee from me and shame yourselves, you shall not shame me."

So the battle began and raged, and when night fell King James lay dead upon the field with all his best knights around him. Bishops and abbots, earls, lords and knights

lay there, having given, in vain, their lives to save their
King.

In Scotland, the women and the children and the old men
waited for news of their King and army. The Queen sat
lonely in Linlithgow, and wept and watched through the
long weary days. But at last one bright September morning
news came – news of disaster and death. Scotland was
turned into a land of tears. From castle to cottage, there
was scarce a home but where there was wailing for the loss
of some dear one.

CHAPTER 63

James V, the King of the Commons –
The Fall of the Red Douglases

ALL THE land was filled with mourning and fear – mourning for the King and all his gallant host, fear of the English. But in this terrible time the men who were still left showed themselves to be both wise and brave. They sent out a proclamation calling upon all who were fit to carry arms, to gather to defend their country. They forbade the women to weep and wail in the streets, for that did no good but only increased the misery. They told them rather to go to the churches and pray for help to the God of Battles.

The English, however, were not strong enough to follow up their terrible victory and their leader sent his soldiers to their homes. So the time of panic and despair passed away.

Then the wise men of Scotland gathered and crowned their little King, James V. He was only two years old and it was amid tears, rather than rejoicings, that the crown was placed upon his head.

At first the Queen Mother, Margaret, was made Regent. She was clever and beautiful but she was very young, being only twenty-four, and she soon married the young and handsome Earl of Angus, the head of the Douglas family and grandson of Bell-the-cat. This displeased many of the people. They thought that the widow of their King humbled herself in marrying a subject and they said that now she had no more right to be Regent. They remembered, too, that she was the sister of the King of England and they thought that she might wish to make friends with England. So they sent to France to ask John, Duke of Albany, to come to be Regent.

This John was the son of that Robert of Albany who had fled to France after rebelling against his brother, James III. He was therefore a cousin of the little King and, it seemed to most people, the best man to govern until the King should be old enough to rule himself. But Albany, having lived all his life in France, was far more of a Frenchman than a Scotsman. He was accustomed to the life of the French court and he was not very anxious to give up his idle life there in order to come to rule over Scotland. But many of his friends persuaded him that it was his duty. So he came, bringing with him a lively train of knights and nobles.

At first Albany seemed to rule well. Soon, however, it was seen that he was not strong enough for the hard task of governing such a fierce people as the Scots. He was neither clever enough nor brave enough, and the haughty manners of his French friends made both him and them hated.

The great Scottish nobles formed into different parties, each quarrelling with another and each struggling for possession of the King. Henry of England, who was always plotting to gain power in Scotland, secretly encouraged these quarrels. So gradually there arose two parties, one called the French and the other called the English. Albany was at the head of the French party, Angus and the Queen Mother at the head of the English.

Amid all this quarrelling the land was once more given up to lawlessness. In the islands, in the Highlands, on the border – where the greatest and fiercest families lived – there was bloodshed and robbery. Twice Albany gave up the task of governing this wild nation; twice he returned to it. But the Scottish people grew to hate him more and more. So a third time he went back to France, and this time he never returned.

Soon after the Duke of Albany had gone for the last time, Angus came into power. He took possession of the young King and ruled in his name. He filled all the posts with his own relatives and friends so that the Douglases did as they liked. No man dared oppose them. No man could get justice or redress unless he was a Douglas or a friend of the Douglases.

When James was sixteen he was declared old enough to rule. But although James was supposed to be King, he was really the Earl's prisoner. It was Angus who ruled the land

and he ruled the King too. The Earl made him ride through the country on pretence of doing justice and punishing thieves and traitors. But there was little justice done, and there were no greater thieves and traitors than in the King's own train.

King James hated Lord Angus and the Douglases, and the longer he was kept prisoner, the more he hated them. Several times the King's friends tried to free him but always in vain. The Douglases were too strong. "Your grace need not think to escape us," said one of them to the King. "If our enemies had hold of you on one side and we on the other, we should tear you to pieces ere we should let you go." This speech James neither forgot nor forgave.

At last the Douglases became so sure of their power that they grew careless of guarding their prisoner. One night they left him alone in Falkland Palace with only the captain of the guard and a few soldiers to watch him.

As soon as James knew this he made up his mind to escape. He was trembling with joy at the thought of being free, but outwardly he kept calm. Calling the head huntsman he gave orders for a hunting party next morning. "I shall make a great day of it," he said, "so tell all the gentlemen round about who have speedy dogs to be ready by four o'clock in the morning."

Having arranged everything with the huntsman, James called for his supper, "For," he said, "I want to go early to bed so that I can have a good sleep before the morning. Go you to bed too," he added to the captain, "for you will have good hunting tomorrow and must be up early."

Then the captain, thinking all was safe, set the watch and went to bed.

But the King was neither in bed nor asleep. Impatiently he waited and listened until all was quiet within the palace. Then when the last sound had ceased and all were asleep, he awakened a little page whom he might trust. "Go quietly to Jockie Hunt the stable boy," he said, "ask him for a suit of clothes and tell him to saddle three horses."

The page did as he was bid. Jockie, who was the King's friend, had long been willing to help him and was only waiting for an opportunity which had now come. Soon, dressed like a stable lad and mounted upon a swift horse, the King passed out of the palace gates with Jockie and his page. The guards let them pass. It was nothing unusual for servants to be sent on errands even at a late hour, and the guards knew too that preparations for a great hunt next day were afoot. So the three rode out without any questions being asked.

Once beyond the palace gates, the King set spurs to his horse and rode hard. Fast as the good horse galloped, it seemed but slow to the impatient King. The cool night air whistled past, the trees rustled and whispered, startled night birds flew across the path as the three galloped along, every stride bringing them nearer and nearer to freedom.

At last, just as day began to break, they thundered over Stirling Bridge. "Bar the gates," cried James to the warder. "Let no man pass as you value your life." Then weary but joyful he rode slowly on to the castle where friends awaited him.

Over the drawbridge and under the heavy portcullis he rode. With tired, happy eyes he watched the bridge rise and the heavy gate fall. Kneeling, the Governor presented him with the keys, while the soldiers shouted "God save your Majesty." He was King at last.

Worn out but happy, James went to bed with the keys of the castle safe under his pillow.

Meanwhile, late that night, George Douglas, the brother of the Earl, had returned to Falkland Palace.

"Where is the King?" he asked of the watchmen.

"His Majesty is asleep," was the reply. "He intends to go hunting tomorrow at dawn so has gone early to rest."

Douglas, hearing this, and believing all to be safe, went to bed also. But towards morning he was awakened by a loud knocking at the door. It was hastily opened. "Where is the King?" asked a man who stood there.

"He is in bed, asleep," replied Douglas, much astonished.

"No, no," replied the man, "this night he crossed over Stirling Bridge. I am sure it was he that I saw."

At that Douglas sprang from his bed and ran to the King's door. It was locked. Again and again he knocked but could get no answer. Then, putting his shoulder against it, he burst the lock and rushed into the room. It was empty. The window was wide open. The bed had not been slept in and upon it lay the fine clothes which the King had thrown off when he dressed himself in Jockie's shabby suit.

"Treason! Treason!" shouted Douglas, "the King is gone." Soon the whole palace was astir. High and low they hunted, but the King could not be found. "You shall have good hunting in the morning," the King had said to the captain. Now he knew the meaning of the King's words.

Post-haste a messenger was sent to the Earl with the news. Mad with anger, he hurried back to Falkland and, gathering their followers, the two brothers set out for Stirling.

But as they rode, a herald came galloping towards them. When he saw the Douglases he halted. Blowing his trumpet, he unfolded a paper and in a loud voice he read the King's proclamation. This proclamation forbade the Earl of Angus, or any of his kin or friends, to come within the space of six miles of the King, on pain of death.

Having listened to the King's command, the Douglases consulted together as to what had best be done. "Do not heed this fellow. Let us ride forward," said one. But the Earl and his brother decided that it would be wiser to obey the King. So, turning their horses, they rode sadly away. Their power was broken.

Soon afterwards James called a Parliament and one of his first acts was to send Angus and all his family into exile. "For I avow that Scotland cannot hold us both," he said. So the Red Douglases fell as the Black Douglases had fallen, and never more during the reign of James V did a Douglas have power in Scotland.

CHAPTER 64

James V, the King of the Commons – The Story of Johnnie Armstrong

NOW that James was free he began really to rule, and one of the first things he tried to do was to bring order to the Border lands. All about the Borders lived tribes of fierce, unruly men who were nearly always at war with the English or with each other. They never thought of tilling the ground or of rearing cattle for themselves, but when they were in need they rode out against their peaceful neighbours and stole from them anything they could lay hands upon.

The great lords were often the worst thieves. In one castle it was the custom, when the last bullock had been killed for food, for the lady of the house to place upon the table a dish of spurs. This was a hint to the lord of the castle that it was time for him to gather his men and ride out for more. Then the men would buckle on their armour, mount their horses and ride away.

In the gloaming of a summer night, or when the August moon was shining, some peaceful farmer would be roused by the trample of horses' hooves and the lowing of cattle. He would awake, perhaps, to find his cattle sheds empty, his barns ablaze and the thieves already far away. Or, if there was yet time to fight, he might be left dead or wounded beside his plundered homestead, while the robbers rode homeward, driving the good man's cattle before them.

Sometimes these raids were the result of quarrels between two families; they were vengeance for some real or fancied wrong. Sometimes they were mere lawlessness. One man wanted what another had, so he took it. Might was right. It seemed to these Border reivers that if a man could not protect his goods, they had a right to take them from him. That was quite natural and simple, and so unruly were the times that it was hard to make these reivers believe that they were in any way worthy of punishment.

But King James meant not only to make laws but to force the people to keep them. He loved justice and he set himself to protect the weak from the strong. So, under pretence of a great hunting expedition, he gathered a good company of knights and soldiers and rode to the Borders. And so quick was the King that he seized the greatest of the reivers and hanged them at their own castle gates before they were even aware of their danger.

But one of the greatest of them all, Johnnie Armstrong, he could not seize. This man was so much feared that the people far into England paid him money every year to be free from his attack. This was called "blackmail". So long as the farmers paid the money Johnnie left them in peace, but if it was not paid he plundered them without mercy.

Johnnie was very rich and lived in great state. He ruled like a king in his own countryside. He dressed very grandly, and when he rode abroad was attended by twenty-four men almost as fine as himself.

Johnnie had no fear of James and when he heard of his coming, he dressed himself in his best and rode to meet the King, to ask him to dine at his castle.

But James, instead of being friendly as Johnnie had thought he would be, was stern and angry. He was not pleased to see Johnnie so grandly dressed and followed by such a train. "What wants that knave that a king should have but the sword of honour and the crown?" he cried. "Take the traitor out of my sight and let him be hanged."

Then Johnnie begged hard for his life. "My lord King," he said, "I have ever been your true subject. Let me live and I promise to keep a band of forty true men always ready to fight for you."

"You must die," said James.

"I have never hurt a Scottish subject, man or woman," said Johnnie. "It is only the English that I rob. Let me live."

"You must die," said James, hard and stern as before.

"Had I known," said Johnnie at last, "that you meant to treat me so I should never have come near to you. I should have kept the Border side in spite of you, and of the King of England too. For well I know King Harry would give the weight of my best horse in gold to know that I must die this day."

But all that Johnnie could say was vain. He and his twenty-four gallant men were led away to die. No doubt many people were glad to be rid of these Border robbers. Yet although they were a great trouble to their neighbours they were also the defenders of their country against the English. So, many mourned for their loss, and were angry with the King. But James V, like James I, had sworn to bring order into his land, and "make the furze bush keep the cow."

CHAPTER 65

James V – The Goodman of Ballengiech

LIKE his father, James IV, James V was fond of travelling about in disguise among his people. Dressed very plainly and calling himself the Goodman of Ballengiech, he used to wander about quite alone, often having strange adventures.

One day while walking alone he was attacked by four or five men near Cramond Bridge. James at once drew his sword and defended himself, but although he was a splendid swordsman one against five was a very unequal fight. Fortunately, however, a farm labourer was threshing corn in a barn nearby. Hearing the noise, he ran out with his flail in his hand. A flail is a tool with which people used to thresh corn before ways of doing it by steam were invented. Seeing one man fighting against five, the labourer ran to his help and so well did he lay about him with his flail, that the five very soon ran away.

The labourer then took the King into the barn to rest. James was hot and dusty, and he asked the man for a basin of water and a towel so that he might wash his hands. This the man brought and while the King washed and rested he talked to the man, asking him questions about himself.

The man told James that his name was Jock Howieson and that he was a labourer on the farm of Braehead which belonged to the King.

"Well, Jock," said James, "if you could have a wish, what would you like best in all the world?"

"I would like to have the farm on which I work, for my very own," said Jock. "And who may you be?" he added.

"I am the Goodman of Ballengiech," said James. "I have a small post at the palace of Holyrood. If you would like to see some of the fine rooms, come next Sunday and I will show them to you. You have saved my life this day and I will willingly do what I can to give you pleasure."

Jock was delighted at the idea of seeing the palace and said goodbye to his new friend, assuring him that he would come on Sunday.

When the day came, Jock dressed himself in his best and set out for the palace. Arriving at the gate, he asked for the Goodman of Ballengiech, as he had been told to do. The King had given orders that anyone asking for the Goodman should at once be brought to him. Jock, who was feeling rather shy at the great house and all the finely dressed people he saw, was very glad when he met his friend.

James led Jock through all the grandest rooms of the palace. He was very much astonished at all he saw, and he amused the King by some of his remarks.

"Now," said James, after Jock had seen everything there was to see, "would you like to see the King?"

"That would I," replied Jock, "if he would not be angry."

"Oh, you need have no fear. I can assure you he will not be angry," replied James.

"But how shall I know which is the King?" asked Jock. "There will be so many grand nobles around him."

"Easily enough," said James. "All the others will take off their hats, only the King will wear his."

The King then led Jock into a great hall where many of the knights and nobles of the court were gathered together. He was rather frightened at so many grand people, but still he looked eagerly round for the King. "I cannot see the King," he whispered at last to James.

"I told you that you would know him by his wearing his hat," replied James, smiling.

Again Jock looked all round. At last his eyes came back to his friend. He was wearing his hat! So was Jock, for with his country manners he had forgotten to take it off. Jock stared at the Goodman for a minute, then slowly he said, "It must be either you or I that is the King then, for we are the only two that are wearing hats."

The King and the courtiers laughed at Jock's funny way of putting it, and Jock was very much astonished to find that the man he had been talking with in such an easy, friendly manner was the great King of whom he had heard so much.

James gave Jock the farm of Braehead as a reward for his bravery. In return, James asked that Jock, and his sons after him, should always be ready to present the King with a basin of water and a towel whenever he passed by Cramond Bridge, in memory of the day on which Jock had fought so bravely. This Jock readily promised and went home feeling very happy.

Ever since then, Braehead has belonged to the Howiesons, and nearly three hundred years after, when George IV came to Edinburgh, Jock Howieson's descendant appeared before the King carrying a silver basin and ewer and a beautiful towel, that he might perform the ceremony by right of which he held his lands.

CHAPTER 66

James V, the King of the Commons – His Last Days

DURING the whole of the reign of James V, his uncle, Henry, the King of England, tried to interfere with Scottish affairs. He kept spies in Scotland who told him everything that took place there. But neither James, nor the people, were willing to submit to Henry's interference.

You remember that in the old days all Christian people belonged to one Church. But after a time some people disagreed with the Pope and began to form a new Church. These people were called Reformers, or Protestants, and as far back as the time of Regent Albany, a Protestant martyr had died in Scotland.

Henry VIII did not like this new religion, but he had quarrelled with the Pope, so he told the people of England that they must no longer look to the Pope as head of the Church, but to their King. Having himself quarrelled with the Pope, and being always anxious to mix himself up in Scottish matters, King Henry tried to make his nephew, King James, also quarrel with him. He proposed to meet with King James at York so that they might talk the matter over and, although James had many reasons for not wishing to leave the Romish Church, he agreed to come for neither did he wish, at that time, to have war with England. And Henry was so hot-tempered that to refuse might have meant war.

In great state Henry travelled to York and for six days he waited there for James. But James never came.

The fact was, his wise men would not let him go. They did not trust King Henry and they were afraid of what he might do to their King.

After waiting for six days Henry turned home again,

furiously angry, and at once declared war against Scotland. He renewed the old and almost forgotten claim of overlordship and vowed to make himself King of Scotland.

Henry gathered an army and marched northward. James, too, gathered an army and marched to meet the English. He had reached the Border when news was brought that the English army had dispersed. In the heat of his passion, Henry had not laid his plans well. The weather was cold and wet for it was in the middle of November. There was nothing in all the land for either man or horse to eat so he was obliged to send them home again.

As soon as the Scots nobles heard that the English had turned back, they too resolved to go home. They had gathered to protect Scotland, not to invade England. Scotland was no longer in danger, so they would not fight.

But James now wanted to fight and he was very angry with the nobles when they said they would not. He implored, he threatened, all in vain. They would not go on. So at last, angry and disappointed, he too broke up his army and went back to Edinburgh.

But James could not give up his desire to fight his uncle and, making great efforts, he again gathered a small army and sent it into England. This army crossed the Border at a place on the west called the Solway Moss.

James had secretly decided to make the leader of the army a favourite of his, called Oliver Sinclair. So as soon as they had entered England, Oliver, standing upon a shield raised upon the shoulders of four strong men, read aloud the King's letter, or commission as it was called, bidding the soldiers accept him as their leader.

Murmurs, loud and fierce, broke from the soldiers as they listened. The captains, leaving their posts, gathered to talk it over. All discipline and order were at an end. The whole army was thrown into angry confusion.

Unfortunately, at this moment, a small body of English horse drew near. At once the English leader saw that the Scots were in disorder. What the reason was they cared not.

It was an opportunity not to be lost, and with levelled lances they dashed forward.

The Scots were utterly taken by surprise. With scarce an attempt to fight, they fled. Not knowing the country, many were caught in the Solway Moss, or marshy ground, and died there. Others were taken prisoner. It was not a battle but a rout.

The news filled James with despair. He was a crushed and broken king. Everything of late had gone wrong. His two sons had died, his nobles, he thought, had wronged and forsaken him. Now his army was shattered without striking a blow. For hours he sat alone, sullen and brooding. Once he had been merry and laughter-loving, now he would hardly utter a word.

The year was drawing to a close. "Where will you spend Christmas?" asked his courtiers and servants, "so that we may make preparations."

"Choose you the place," he answered sadly, "for I care not. But this I can tell you, that before Christmas Day ye shall be masterless, and Scotland without a king."

At last James became so ill that he would neither eat nor drink, but lay upon his bed, scarcely speaking.

As he lay thus, word was brought to him that a little girl baby had been born to him. But even that could give him no joy. "Is that so?" he said with a sigh. "It came with a lass and it will go with a lass." This he said, meaning that the crown had come to the Stewart family through a woman, Marjorie, the daughter of Robert the Bruce, who you remember married Walter the High Steward. Their son was Robert II, the first of the Stewart kings. James now thought that with his little daughter the crown would pass away from the Stewart family. But it did not.

A few days after this, on the 14th December 1542, King James V died. He died because his heart was broken and he did not care to live. He was only thirty years old. He had been stern and perhaps cruel to the nobles, and had made many enemies among them. But the people loved him.

To the poor, his palace gates were ever open. No one in poverty or distress ever came to him in vain, so that he was called the King of the Commons. During his reign, he had sailed all round his kingdom, going even farther than his father had done. He had made wise laws, he had encouraged trade and learning, and in every way tried to be a good king.

CHAPTER 67

Mary Queen of Scots – France

KING James V had been twice married, both times to a French lady. His first Queen, who was the daughter of the King of France, only lived about a month after she came to Scotland. He then married another French Princess, called Mary of Guise. Her little baby daughter, who was also called Mary, was only seven days old when James died, and she became Queen.

Once more the country was without a real head, and the quarrels and struggles for power among the great nobles became very bitter. There were two great parties. The Queen Mother, Mary of Guise, and a great churchman called Cardinal Beaton were at the head of one party and the Earl of Arran, who was chosen to be Regent, at the head of the other. The Roman Catholics followed Mary and Cardinal Beaton; the Protestants followed the Earl of Arran.

Henry of England pretended to be very sorry when he heard of the death of King James. But he was not really sorry for he now saw a new way of joining England and Scotland together. He proposed that the little baby Queen should be married to his son, Edward.

Of course a little baby could not be married but Henry wanted the Scottish people to promise that when she was old enough, she should marry his son.

The Scottish people did not love the English, but the Regent and many of the nobles had become Protestants and it seemed to them that it would be a wise thing for their little Queen to marry a Protestant Prince. So it was agreed that when Mary was old enough this marriage should take place. But the Queen Mother, Cardinal Beaton and all those who followed them did not like the arrangement at all.

Henry, however, was not content with this promise. He wanted to get possession of the little Queen and asked the

Scottish people to send her to England. The Scots would not hear of this and said she must not leave Scotland until she was at least ten years old. Then, as Henry still went on trying to get possession of Mary, the nobles took back their promise and said she should never be married to Prince Edward at all.

This made King Henry so angry that he gathered his ships and men of war and sent them to fight against Scotland. The Regent was a weak and foolish man, easily pulled this way and that, and never ready for anything. He ought to have known that Henry would be angry and he might have been prepared. But he did nothing.

One bright May morning, a crowd of white sails appeared in the Forth. The people watched anxiously, wondering what ships they might be. Soon they saw the royal standard of England fluttering in the breeze and knew that it had to do with their old enemy. Then cannon boomed and the red fires of war blazed till the fairest lands of Scotland were blackened wastes. It was a rough wooing. Too rough to suit the Scotsmen but not rough enough to conquer them. For two years the war went on, the French helping their old friends, until at last peace was made.

Cardinal Beaton now became very powerful and really ruled the land. But the Protestants were growing stronger and stronger. The Cardinal hated the Protestant religion and tried in every way to stop it from spreading among the people. By his orders, George Wishart, one of the boldest of the Protestants, was hanged and his body burned at St Andrews opposite the Cardinal's palace, Beaton himself sitting upon the walls and watching Wishart die.

This, and many other cruel acts, roused the hatred of the Protestant party and, three months later, sixteen men rushed one morning into the palace and murdered the Cardinal.

Many people, even of the Protestant party, were angry and grieved at this action. Yet they were glad that the proud, cruel Cardinal was dead.

And cruel though he was, Cardinal Beaton had helped to keep Scotland out of the clutches of Henry VIII.

Soon after this Henry VIII died and again the English people tried to force the Scottish people to let Queen Mary marry Prince, now King, Edward. Another great army was sent into Scotland and a terrible battle was fought in 1547 at a place called Pinkie, near Edinburgh. In this battle the Scots were defeated. It was the last time that they were ever defeated by the English in a great battle. But this defeat, instead of making the Scots agree to allow Mary to marry Edward, made them more determined than ever not to allow it.

All this time the little Queen, around whom there had been so much fighting, for whose sake so many brave men had died, knew nothing at all about it. She played in her nursery or in pleasant gardens with four other little girls who, like herself, were all called Mary. She was sent from place to place for safety and her little friends always went with her. Now it was decided to send her to France where she would be quite safe from the English.

So the Queen Mother kissed her little daughter, who was now six years old, and sent her away with her four little friends to the court of France.

Some time after this, Mary of Guise, the Queen Mother, was made Regent, instead of the weak Earl of Arran. She was a clever woman but she made many of the nobles angry by giving the chief posts to Frenchmen. On the whole, however, the land was more peaceful than it had been for some years.

Meanwhile the little Queen was growing up in France. Far away from the sounds of war and strife she led a cheerful, happy life.

Princes and princesses are sometimes very lonely. But little Queen Mary was not lonely. Besides her friends, the four Scottish Marys, she had as companions more than thirty French princes and princesses with whom she learned her lessons and played about. She was so pretty, so

*In some sunny palace garden the days passed happily for
the Queen and her Marys (page 245)*

Queen Mary and Knox had many talks together (page 249)

graceful and so clever, that everyone loved her. A great lady wrote of her, that "This small Queen of Scots has only to smile in order to turn all French heads."

Mary was taught to sing, and to play, and to dance, to ride and to hunt. She was also taught to sew and to embroider, and she could speak and write Latin and several other languages. So, sometimes at the lively French court, sometimes in some sunny palace garden the days passed peacefully and happily for the Queen and her four Marys. Then, when the Queen was fifteen, she was married to the Dauphin, the eldest son of the King of France.

Mary was now quite old enough to go home to Scotland to rule her own country, but she did not go. Among the many things that she had been taught, no one had thought of teaching her that a queen must work, and think, and live, for her people. So Mary stayed at the lively French court with her husband, the Dauphin, leaving her mother to govern Scotland.

Then the King of France died and the Dauphin became King, and Mary became queen of France as well as of Scotland. And Mary called herself Queen of England too, and used the royal arms of England. Her cousin, Elizabeth, was now upon the throne of England but Mary said she had a better right to the throne than Elizabeth. She never tried, however, to make the English people give her the crown, and calling herself Queen of England was merely an empty show. But it made Elizabeth very angry. So instead of loving each other, these two cousins, ruling over neighbouring countries, hated and despised each other.

But while Mary smiled and danced in France, dark and difficult days were coming upon Scotland. The Queen Regent was a Roman Catholic, and more and more of the Scottish nobles were becoming Protestants. Although the Regent tried to be friends with these Protestant nobles, it became every day more difficult. As the Protestants grew stronger, the Roman Catholics urged the Queen Regent to persecute and destroy them. The Protestant nobles, or

Lords of the Congregation as they came to be called, began to be afraid that the Queen Regent meant to take away the freedom of Scotland and make the land into a French province. At last these feelings grew so bitter that war broke out. This war was called the War of Reformation, or the War of the Congregation.

Chief among the leaders of the army of the Congregation was a man called Knox. He was neither a soldier nor a noble, but a preacher. He marched up and down Scotland preaching fiery sermons, stirring up the people till they tore down the altars and images in the churches and often, I am sorry to say, ruined the beautiful old churches themselves.

French soldiers helped the Queen Regent and the Catholics, and the Lords of the Congregation, finding that they were not strong enough, asked Queen Elizabeth to send soldiers to help them. This Elizabeth did. So for the first time was seen the strange sight of an English army marching into Scotland and being welcomed by the Scots. For some time the war went fiercely on, but the Queen Regent suddenly died, and soon afterwards the war came to an end.

The French soldiers were sent back to their own country in English ships and the Scots, who no longer wanted the help of the English, accompanied them to the Border, and there said goodbye to their dangerous friends.

Then a Parliament was called. This was a strange Parliament, for instead of making and discussing the laws of the land, they made and discussed the laws of faith and religion and made new rules for the governing of the Church. This Parliament declared that the Pope had no more power over the Church of Scotland, and it was made a crime for anyone to read or listen to a Roman Catholic service. Thus, by one stroke as it were, the Reformation in Scotland was made complete.

When Mary heard of what this Parliament had done she was very angry, for she was a Roman Catholic and loved the Roman Catholic Church. "I am your Queen," she said, "or so you call me. But you do not use me so. You have done what pleased yourselves." The Parliament was no Parliament, she said, because it had been called without the consent of the Queen. So she would not agree to anything it had passed. It might have ended in war between the Queen and her people, but just at this time Mary's husband, the King of France, died. As long as he lived, Mary was of great importance in France. Now that he was dead, and another king upon the throne, she found that the French people did not want her any more. She felt lonely and deserted, and so she resolved to go home to her own people; so she got on board a ship and sailed away to Scotland. But she found it very hard to leave France where she had been so happy. She knew little about Scotland and she was not sure if she would find friends there. She was only nineteen and she was going away for ever from the land and people she had loved.

All day long she leaned against the side of the ship watching the shores of France grow dim in the distance. When night came, she would not go down into her cabin, but ordered a bed to be brought on deck for her. It was a warm August night, there was no wind to fill the sails, so the ship lay becalmed. Very early in the morning, the Queen awoke to see faintly still the shores of France. But the wind sprang up and soon the last outline faded away. "Farewell, beloved France," she cried, as tears filled her eyes. "Farewell, I shall never see thee more."

CHAPTER 68

Mary – Darnley and Rizzio

IT WAS August when Queen Mary arrived in Scotland and landed in Leith, but the day was bleak and grey. A thick mist covered sea and shore, and as she arrived sooner than was expected, nothing was ready. But it soon became known that the Queen had come, and after some hours a few poor horses were got together and the procession started for Holyrood. It was not a very grand procession and everything seemed poor and plain to Mary after the splendour of the French court. Yet the people were glad to have their Queen among them once again and they did their best to show their gladness. Bonfires were lit and crowds gathered under the Queen's windows, singing doleful psalms and playing on instruments much out of tune. It was anything but beautiful music yet Mary was so good-natured that she would not have it stopped but said she liked the melody well, for she knew that the people did it to honour her.

Soon, however, Mary was to learn how fierce her subjects could be. She had made up her mind to allow the people to worship God in their own way, and she meant to worship in her way. But it had been made a crime for anyone to read Mass, as the Roman Catholic service is called, and when it became known that a priest was going to read Mass for the Queen in her own private chapel at Holyrood, there was a terrible uproar among the Protestants. "I will rather see ten thousand French soldiers landed in Scotland than suffer a single Mass," cried Knox. Another fierce Protestant buckled on his armour and rushed into the palace courtyard, shouting that every priest should die. But the Earl of Murray, the Queen's half-brother, Protestant though he was, put his back to the chapel door and with his sword prepared to defend it. Others joined him, and so the uproar ceased.

Afterwards, Queen Mary sent for Knox and talked to him. She wanted to be friends with Knox, but although Knox was a good man he was very stern and narrow. He could only see his own side and could not believe that anyone was right who thought differently from himself. Mary was clever and answered Knox and his arguments very well. But although they had many talks, they could never understand each other and could never be friends. Knox often preached against Mary, saying cruel things of her and her way of living, and yet, perhaps, with all his sternness, he had a kindly feeling for the young Queen and only spoke cruelly because he wished to make her better.

In spite of difficulties, the first few years after Mary returned to Scotland passed quietly. She was so beautiful and clever, that even stern Protestant nobles were glad to fight for their Catholic Queen.

Many men loved Mary and were anxious to marry her. But it was difficult to find a prince worthy of this young, beautiful Queen. At last she married her cousin, Henry Stewart, Lord Darnley. He was tall and handsome. "The handsomest long man I have ever seen," said Mary. He was cousin to Queen Elizabeth as well as to Queen Mary and, if neither of them should have children, he was the next heir to both thrones. So it seemed a good thing that Darnley and Mary should marry.

Darnley came from England, where he had been living, to visit Mary. They soon loved each other and were married.

Some people, especially the Protestants, were very angry about the marriage for Darnley, like Mary, was a Roman Catholic. Among those who were angry was the Queen's half-brother, the Earl of Murray. He and the chief Lords of the Congregation banded together and raised a rebellion. But Mary called her army together and, wearing a helmet upon her head, with pistols at her saddlebow and her husband beside her in gilded armour, she rode out to meet the rebels. She swept through the country, chasing them from place to place, till at last Murray and the other leaders fled into England. This rebellion was called the Run-about-Raid from the way in which the rebels were hunted about from place to place.

For a short time Mary and Darnley were happy. But soon the Queen began to find out that her "handsome long man" was only a silly, jealous boy. He was wicked as well, and instead of loving her husband, Mary grew to hate him, and became very unhappy. The people, too, would not allow Darnley any power as King. He was only the Queen's husband, they said. This made Darnley very angry with Mary for he thought she was to blame.

Among Mary's servants there was an Italian musician, named David Rizzio. He was clever and useful. He wrote the Queen's letters, advised and helped her in many ways and also amused her by writing poetry and music. The Queen also wrote poetry, and she became fond of Rizzio and made much of him. This made Rizzio very proud and haughty. He dressed in splendid robes and was insolent to the great lords who hated him because he was only a common man and a foreigner.

Darnley, too, hated Rizzio. He hated him so much that he made up his mind to kill him. He made friends with some of the nobles who were Rizzio's enemies and together they planned his murder. One windy March night the Queen and Rizzio, with a few of her ladies and friends, were sitting at supper in a tiny room off Mary's bedroom in Holyrood. It is such a tiny room that if you ever go to see it, you will wonder how so many people found room to sit there.

It was about seven o'clock. The curtains were drawn, the candles were lit and Mary sat talking merrily with her friends. But while they talked and smiled, the courtyard of the palace was filled with armed men who took possession of the great gates and closed them so that none of the Queen's friends might enter. Then, led by Darnley, they crept quietly up the secret stairway which led to the Queen's rooms and which no one but he might use.

Telling the men to wait, Darnley went into the room

alone. No one was surprised that he should come to see the
Queen and he sat down beside her, put his arm round her
waist and talked kindly to her.

Suddenly the door opened again. Mary looked up and
saw before her another of the conspirators called Lord
Ruthven. He had been very ill, but such was his hatred of
Rizzio that he had risen from his bed so that he might help
to kill him.

Ruthven's face was pale, his eyes were sunken and he
was so weak that he had to be helped up the stair. As he
stood in the doorway, gaunt and terrible in his armour, his
looks frightened the Queen so that she cried out in fear and
told him to be gone. But behind him crowded steel-clad men
with drawn swords and fierce looks.

"If it please your Majesty," said Ruthven in his hollow,
dreadful voice, "let yonder man Davy come forth from your
presence. He has been over long there."

"Ah," cried Mary, turning to Darnley with a bitter look,
"is this your work?"

"Nay, but I know nothing of it," replied Darnley.

Ruthven drew his dagger and Rizzio, pale with terror,
threw himself upon his knees trying to hide behind the
Queen. Holding on to her skirts he shrieked, "Save me,
save me!"

In a moment all was confusion. The little room was filled
to overflowing with armed men. The table was overturned.
As it fell, a lady caught up one of the candles upon it,
otherwise the room would have been left in complete
darkness. Roughly the men tore Rizzio from the Queen.
Ruthven himself took hold of her and, placing her in
Darnley's arms, bade him to take care of his wife, and her
to fear nothing.

Mary could do no more to save her favourite. Darnley
held her fast while the fierce soldiers dragged the poor,
trembling, shrieking wretch away.

They had meant to try him in some kind of a rough
fashion, but now that they had him in their power they

thought no more of a trial and as soon as he was out of the Queen's rooms they stabbed him to death. So eager were they that in the struggle they wounded each other, and at last left their victim lying in a pool of blood with fifty-six wounds in his poor body.

Weak and ill, Ruthven staggered back to the little room where Mary stood trembling and weeping with fear and anger. Too weak to stand, he sat down in the Queen's presence, hardly begging pardon for his rudeness, and called for wine.

"Ah, traitor!" cried the Queen, "how dare you come into my presence? How dare you sit when I stand?"

"Madam," he replied, "I do it not out of pride, but out of weakness of body." Then he told her that what was done, was done with the knowledge of her husband which, far from comforting the Queen, only hurt her the more. But not knowing that Rizzio was already dead, she still begged for his life.

Then one of the Queen's Marys came running in with a pale face and the news that Rizzio was killed. "And is it so?" cried Mary, dashing the tears from her eyes. "Then farewell weeping. Now will I study revenge."

CHAPTER 69

Mary – Bothwell

THAT night the Queen was kept a prisoner and Darnley acted as if he were the King. But he could not act like a king for long. He was as weak as he was bad, and no sooner was Rizzio dead than he began to be afraid of what he had done.

The Queen now feared her husband as much as she hated him. She knew that he had made the others murder Rizzio and she wondered at times if he would not murder her too. But in order to get away from the fierce men who held her prisoner she smiled on Darnley and hid her hatred, until at last he, who had led her enemies on, helped her to escape from them. One night in the darkness she fled away, accompanied only by Darnley and a few faithful friends. When morning dawned, her fierce jailers woke to find their prisoner gone.

Once more Mary was a queen, and free. She gathered her army and drove the traitors out of the country. Then she rode in triumph through the streets of Edinburgh – the same streets through which, but a week before, she had fled in darkness and in fear, and almost alone.

Soon after this, Mary had a little baby whom she called James. But Mary hated Darnley so much that she could not love her little boy. "He is too much your son," she said to her husband.

Although Mary hated her husband she could not live without being loved. She always tried to make people love her. And many people, both men and women, loved her very much and were ready to die for her. But the sad thing was that of all the men who loved Mary, none were strong enough, or noble enough to protect and help her. If Mary had found some strong, good, brave man to be her husband her life might have been very different and much happier. But the King of France had been a sickly boy. Darnley was a weak and foolish, not to say wicked, boy and all around her were men who plotted, and spied, and worked for their own ends, caring little for the happiness of Scotland or its Queen.

Now there came into Mary's life another man called James, Earl of Bothwell. He was a handsome, swaggering, brutal, brave man. He had lived a great deal in France and had fine manners and a light-hearted jolly laugh. He was bad but he was brave and Mary, who loved brave men and who was tired and sick to death of her foolish, cowardly husband, loved him. She heaped honours and favours upon this man who, an old writer says, was "as naughty a man as liveth and much given to detestable vices."

Mary's love for this swaggering Earl made Darnley very angry. He became sullen and sulky, would hardly speak to the Queen and at last went home to Glasgow to live with his father and mother. While there, he became ill of a dreadful disease called smallpox. When the Queen heard that he was ill she went to visit him, and it seemed as if their quarrels were forgotten and that they were friends again.

Darnley was quite pleased to be friends with his beautiful wife and when he was well enough he went with her to Edinburgh. But instead of taking him to the palace at Holyrood, Mary took Darnley to a little house called Kirk of Field, just outside the walls of the town. She said as he was ill, he would be more comfortable there. For the house stood high and was surrounded by a garden, whereas Holyrood lies very low.

Every day, Mary came and sat some hours with Darnley, talking with him and amusing him. Once or twice she spent the whole night in the little house, sleeping in the room below Darnley's. It seemed as if the old days had come back and they would be happy again. But alas! it was all a trap. While Mary talked and smiled with Darnley, Bothwell and his friends were laying their plans.

One night as the Queen sat with her husband, dark figures might have been seen passing and re-passing through the garden, carrying sacks upon their backs. The sacks were full of gunpowder – it was Bothwell's men who carried them and Bothwell who directed where they should be put. They were piled up in the Queen's room, right under Darnley's bed.

While this dark work went on, the Queen sat in the firelit room, in a high chair covered with purple velvet which gleamed red in the flickering light. Never had she seemed so beautiful and gentle to the sick man. She had said that she would stay all night, but she suddenly remembered that she could not for it was the wedding night of one of her maids and she had promised to dance at the feast. So she kissed Darnley and said good night, telling him that she would come again next morning.

Did she know what would happen before morning, or did she not? That is a question which has puzzled many wise heads for hundreds of years. Perhaps it will never be settled. But we would like to believe that the beautiful Queen knew nothing about those black bags of gunpowder, and that the plot and the guilt were Bothwell's only.

The dance went merrily on but Bothwell soon left it. He went to his room and changed his fine dress of velvet and silver for a coarse, dark suit. Then he hurried away to Kirk of Field.

The dance was over, the lights were out, everyone was quietly sleeping when the noise of a terrible explosion startled the whole town. People leaped from their beds in terror. What had happened? Soon it became known that Kirk of Field House had been blown to pieces. The King was dead.

The deed done, Bothwell had crept back to his room, thrown off his clothes and tumbled into bed again. There he lay, pretending to be asleep when he was aroused by the sound of hurrying feet, strange cries and loud knocking at his door. "The King's house is blown up and I trow the King is slain," cried the messenger, hardly able to speak for terror and excitement.

"Treason! treason!" shouted Bothwell, springing from his bed. Hurriedly he dressed and was soon out in the streets, at the head of a company of soldiers, riding towards the Kirk of Field.

But pretend how he would, Bothwell could not deceive the people. Everyone pointed to him as the murderer, and as Queen Mary still continued to be kind to him and let it be seen, even more plainly than before, that she loved him, the people grew angry with her too and called her murderess. All Europe rang with the horror of the deed. Queens and princes wrote to Mary, urging her to punish the murderers. So Mary at last yielded. Bothwell was brought to trial. But the trial was a mere farce. Riding upon the dead Darnley's favourite horse, Bothwell appeared with five thousand soldiers at his back. So the judges, afraid perhaps to do anything else, said that he was innocent.

But the people still believed him guilty. Pictures and writings, accusing Bothwell and his friends, were pasted upon the walls and doors of the public buildings of Edinburgh. Voices in the night cried out the names of the guilty ones. Yet Mary would neither listen nor see.

One day the Queen rode to Stirling to visit her little boy. On her way back, when she was very near Edinburgh, Bothwell suddenly came towards her at the head of eight hundred horsemen. The cold April sunshine gleamed on steel armour, sword and spear as Bothwell and his men dashed recklessly along. They surrounded Mary's small company. Right up to the Queen's horse rode the Earl and laid his hand upon her bridle rein. Without a struggle, without one cry for help, without one blow being struck, the Queen was taken prisoner by her bold and swaggering Earl, for he had sworn to marry her, "Yea, whether she would herself or not." Right about wheeled the horses and with clatter and jangle they started off again, not towards Edinburgh but towards Bothwell's strong castle of Dunbar.

It was like a fairy tale. The ogre had carried off the beautiful princess. But there was no knight in shining armour to rescue her and soon Mary married the ogre – just three months after he had murdered Darnley.

Bothwell was already married to another beautiful lady who had done him no harm, but he was so eager to be great, to have the power of a king, that he made the priests and clergymen say that he might put her away. Then he married the Queen.

For a few short weeks Mary seemed happy. Then dark days came again. Her new husband was brutal and coarse, and the people were angry that she had married the man who had killed her last husband.

But neither Bothwell nor Mary knew how angry the people were and when at last an army gathered against them, they were surprised and unprepared. They had left Dunbar, and the castle in which they were was not strong. It was surrounded by the enemy and Bothwell, rather than be taken prisoner by the nobles, fled away, leaving Mary alone.

But next night, when all was dark and still, a tall, slim page slipped out of the castle gates. A pony stood ready saddled. The page mounted and rode out into the darkness. Over wild moorland, by lonely ways, the page galloped on until he met with Bothwell and a few followers. Then it was seen that the tall, slim boy was no boy, but Scotland's beautiful Queen. At three o'clock in the morning she rode once more into Bothwell's strong castle of Dunbar.

Mary had come quite alone. At Bothwell Castle there was no lady, so the Queen had to borrow a dress from a servant. A short red skirt, a white sleeved bodice and a black velvet hat was all that could be found for her. Dressed in this, she rode out at the head of the little army which had now gathered to her.

Early in the morning, Mary took up her position on Carberry Hill, almost on the same place where the Battle of Pinkie had been fought twenty years before. Opposite, lay the army of the lords. All day long they lay there, neither side advancing or striking a blow for the lords did not wish to fight until the afternoon, when the sun would be behind them and the Queen's captains would not strike the first blow.

Hour after hour went past. The day was hot. Many in Mary's army were not soldiers but simple peasants. They grew thirsty and weary of waiting under the burning sun. Some of them went off to drink at the stream which flowed nearby. They never came back again. For one reason or another others left and, little by little, Mary's army grew smaller and smaller.

With tears, and threats, and smiles, and promises the Queen rode up and down before the soldiers. It was in vain. They would not fight. At last, sick and sad at heart, she gave it up. All was lost. There was nothing left for Bothwell but to fly.

So there, on this bloodless battlefield, they kissed each other and said goodbye. For the last time Bothwell bent over the Queen's hand; then he galloped off. Just one month after her marriage day, Mary was thus once more left alone. They never saw each other again. After a wild and wandering life of fierce adventure Bothwell died, mad, in a foreign prison.

Meantime, with tear-stained face and bitter words, Queen Mary turned to the rebel lords. She was their prisoner. "I render myself," she said, and one of them gravely and sternly took her horse by the bridle and led her down the hill to the rebel camp.

So, riding among her captors, the Queen returned to Edinburgh. Before her was carried a horrid banner, with a picture of the little Prince James kneeling beside the body of his murdered father. Underneath was the motto, "Judge and avenge my cause, O God". Through the streets she rode, the mob yelling and cursing, her fair face all soiled and wet with tears and dust, till at last she reached the kindly shelter of the provost's house.

CHAPTER 70

Mary – How the Queen Escaped and How she was Made Prisoner Again

THE Queen was now a prisoner and to keep her quite safe, the lords took her away from Edinburgh and put her in a lonely castle in the middle of a loch called Loch Leven. Then they wrote out two papers which they made her sign. One paper said that Mary gave up her crown to her little son, James; the other, that the Earl of Murray should be Regent until James was old enough to reign.

Mary did not want to sign these papers. But she was helpless; she seemed to have no friends left. Stern, grave men stood round her and it is even said that one, more fierce than the others, seized her arm so roughly with his iron-gloved hand that she cried out in pain. So Mary signed away her crown which had given her, she said, "Long, great and intolerable pains," and which left her, "vexed in spirit, body and senses."

A few days later, the baby King was crowned. He was scarcely more than a year old. The Earl of Mar held him in his arms as the crown was placed upon his little head. Two other lords, laying their hands upon the crown, promised in his name to fear God and to keep the laws. He was then made to touch the sceptre and the sword with his tiny fingers. John Knox thundered out a sermon and after it was all over, the little King was lifted from the throne and carried back to his nurse.

There was great rejoicing over the coronation of the new King. Bonfires blazed, cannon boomed and people shouted. In her lonely prison, Mary heard the sounds. "What is it?" she asked.

"The people rejoice for the crowning of the King," was the reply.

Then Mary laid her head upon the table and wept. Her reign was ended.

When Mary signed away her crown she was only twenty-five. Although she had become Queen of Scotland when she was seven days old, she had really ruled but six years, and into the last two of these six years had been crowded all the passion and sorrow of a lifetime. But she was still young and still beautiful and, if the rebel lords had triumphed for the time, there were still men ready to love her and to fight for her.

Soon, plots were formed to free the Queen. Secret messages and letters found their way within the prison walls. At last all was arranged. A washerwoman had brought some clean clothes to the castle. Mary changed dresses with this woman and, taking a bundle of clothes in her arms and drawing her hood well over her face, she passed the guards safely and stepped into the boat. The boat started to re-cross the loch again to the shore. Mary sat very still and quiet with her head bent. Perhaps she sat too still for one of the boatmen thought something was strange. "Let us see what manner of dame this is," he said and stooping forward he tried to peer under her hood. Queen Mary quickly put up her hands to cover her face. Alas, they were no workwoman's hands – they were long, slender and white. She was discovered and, in spite of all her tears and entreaties, the boatmen turned and rowed her back to the castle again.

But although they had failed once, Mary's friends did not despair. At last, with the help of a boy of fourteen, called Little Douglas, who lived in the castle, she escaped.

The keys of the gate of the castle were always placed on the table beside the Governor when he was at supper. But one night, while Little Douglas waited upon the Governor, he dropped a napkin and in picking it up he also picked up the keys. The Governor did not notice that they were gone and, as soon as he dared, Little Douglas left the supper room and hastened to the Queen.

A few minutes later, with beating hearts they were hurrying down the silent passages. No one noticed them; no one questioned them. The gates were safely passed and locked behind them. Mary's friends on shore were watching and they saw three figures glide quickly from the outer gate to the water's edge. It was Mary, with her little frightened maid and Douglas.

They sprang into a boat which lay ready and Douglas, bending to the oars, rowed as fast as he could away from the dark castle. Halfway across he paused and dropped the keys into the water. They were safe for a time from pursuit. So eager was Mary to reach the shore that she took an oar and helped to row. At last, breathless with excitement and delight, she sprang to land. In a moment her friends were round her. A horse was ready and, leaping into the saddle, she sped away.

Oh! the wild, sweet ride, through the cool night air. She was free again! A queen again! At every bound her horse carried her further and further away from prison. At every bound her heart grew lighter, her hopes rose higher. With only a few hours rest she rode half across Scotland to Hamilton, near Glasgow.

The news of the Queen's escape flew like wildfire through the land. From far and near, those who loved her gathered to her, till she was at the head of an army of six thousand men.

The Regent Murray was in Glasgow, not many miles away, and he too gathered his army and marched against his sister. At Langside, a village near Glasgow, a battle took place. It lasted only three-quarters of an hour and ended in the total defeat of Mary's troops.

On a little hill, about half a mile from the battlefield, the Queen stood to watch. She was full of hope and gladness. Eagerly she watched the fight sway this way and that. But when she saw her troops beaten and scattered, when she saw them at last put to utter flight, she lost all hope. Turning from the field, she too fled, never pausing until she was sixty miles away.

Mary knew not where to go. She feared to remain in Scotland lest she should again be put in prison. France, where she had been so happy, was far off. England lay nearer. Surely, she thought, Elizabeth, her cousin, would be kind to an unhappy sister queen. So to England she went.

Alas poor Mary! In her need and trouble, she had forgotten the years of hate and distrust that lay between herself and Elizabeth.

Elizabeth could not forgive Mary for having claimed the throne of England. She could not forgive her for being more young and beautiful than herself. She would not receive and would not help her cousin. Mary found that she had only escaped from a Scottish prison to be shut up in an English one.

Elizabeth had to give a reason for putting Mary in prison. She said it was because she had helped to murder her husband, Darnley. But whether Mary had killed her husband or not, Elizabeth had no right to imprison her for Mary was not an English subject, and the English Queen had no right to interfere between the Scottish Queen and her people.

There was a trial, held first at York and then at Westminster, to which Mary's accusers came but to which Mary was not allowed to go to defend herself. Among those who came to accuse her was her half-brother, the Regent Murray.

There was a great deal of talking but nothing was proved one way or another. And after a long time, Elizabeth said that although she did not doubt the truth and honour of the Regent, he had proved nothing against the Queen, and she had made up her mind not to interfere with Scottish matters. She said this but she kept Mary in prison while Murray was allowed to go back to Scotland with plenty of good English gold in his pockets.

For nineteen years beautiful Queen Mary was kept prisoner in England. From castle to castle she was moved about, always strongly and carefully guarded. She had still many friends, and again and again they plotted to free her but they never succeeded.

CHAPTER 71

James VI – King's Men and Queen's Men

THE Earl of Murray now ruled Scotland in the name of James VI who was still scarcely more than a baby. He had a hard task, for the whole country was divided between King's men and Queen's men, and was full of unrest and war. Murray had behaved meanly and cruelly to the Queen but now he proved to be a wise ruler. Indeed, he was called the Good Regent.

But if he was good, he was stern; many people hated him and a man called Hamilton of Bothwellhaugh swore to kill him.

Bothwellhaugh waited long but at last his opportunity came. The Regent, on his way from Dumbarton to Edinburgh, stayed one night at Linlithgow. Next morning he mounted his horse and rode through the town. This was what Bothwellhaugh had hoped for. In those days, many of the houses had outside staircases and wooden balconies jutting out into the street. Upon one of these Bothwellhaugh took his stand. The balcony was hung with cloth so that no one could see him. Upon the floor he placed a feather mattress so that no one below should hear his footsteps. At the garden gate behind the house stood a horse ready saddled and bridled. Having made all his preparations Bothwellhaugh, with his gun in his hand, stood and waited for the Regent.

The streets were so crowded with people come out to see the Regent pass, that he could go but slowly. That was all the better for Bothwellhaugh for his aim would be the surer. Heavily the minutes dragged along. At last the Earl came. Opposite the house in which Bothwellhaugh lay hidden the procession seemed to pause. A shot rang out. The Regent reeled in his saddle and fell. His work done, the unseen murderer fled through the garden, leaped upon his horse and sped away.

The Regent was not killed; though sorely wounded, he had strength to walk back to the palace and at first it was thought that he would recover. But soon it was seen that there was no hope and in a few hours he died.

There was much grief at the Regent's death. He was buried with great pomp in the church of St Giles in Edinburgh. John Knox preached a grand sermon taking for his text, "Blessed are the dead that die in the Lord."

Murray had been scarcely three years Regent and was killed on the 23rd January 1570. Six months of trouble and quarrelling followed. Then the Earl of Lennox, Darnley's father, was made Regent. But Lennox was a weak man – far too weak for these fierce times and soon the whole country was in a blaze of civil war. Fathers, sons and brothers fought against each other. The very children in their games took sides and fought, King's men against Queen's men.

The Governor of Edinburgh Castle, who was called Kirkcaldy of Grange, and who had been a King's man, suddenly turned round and became a Queen's man. With him was another, called Maitland of Lethington. He was very clever, and when you are older, you will read much about him and all he did during the reign of Mary. He had been one of Mary's greatest statesmen, but he was so changeable that a writer of the time called him a chameleon which is a little animal that takes the colour of whatever it lies upon. Now Maitland openly took the Queen's side and joined with Kirkcaldy of Grange.

The King's men tried to hold a Parliament in Edinburgh. But cannon thundered from the castle till they were obliged to leave and go to Stirling. There they held a Parliament and there, for the first time, the little King was brought and made to sit at the head of the table among all the wise men. He was only about five years old and could not understand what was going on. So seeing a hole in the tablecloth he began to play with it, sticking his fingers into it.

"What house is this?" he asked one of the lords who sat beside him.

"The House of Parliament, your Majesty," was the reply.

"Then this Parliament has a hole in it," said the little King, not knowing how true his words were and what a very large hole there was in his Parliament, and that it was indeed torn in two.

The war raged on. The Queen's men followed the King's men to Stirling and attacked them there. They were driven back but the Regent was hurt in the fight and died in a few hours. He had ruled for little more than a year.

A new Regent was chosen. This Regent was the Earl of Mar. He was a good man and he longed for peace. He struggled and worked so hard for it that he died, worn out, having been Regent only thirteen months.

The next Regent was the Earl of Morton. Under him the civil war grew fiercer than ever. Battles were fought daily, each side hanging their prisoners or cutting off their heads with dreadful cruelty. "No quarter," which means no mercy, was the cry on both sides and no quarter was either asked or given. These wars were called the Douglas Wars, from the Earl of Morton's name which was James Douglas.

The King's men were on the whole the stronger, but all this time the castle of Edinburgh had held out for the Queen. Regent Morton, however, resolved to take the castle, cost what it might. He had not cannon enough of his own so he sent to Queen Elizabeth of England and she, always willing to mix herself up with Scottish matters, sent him both guns and men.

Then the siege of Edinburgh began. Gallant Kirkcaldy, the bravest soldier of his times, held out for more than a month. But strong though the castle walls were, they could not stand against the fearful cannonade of the English guns. They crumbled to pieces, as if they had been sand hills washed away by the incoming tide. The wells within the castle became choked with the ruins. The soldiers at last had neither anything to eat nor to drink. Maddened with thirst and worn with hunger, they would fight no longer. There was nothing left but to yield.

So gallant Kirkcaldy and wise Lethington gave themselves up. Kirkcaldy was so brave that even the fiercest of the King's men begged that his life might be spared. But Morton, the stern Regent, had made up his mind that he must die. So this brave man, who was "humble, gentle and meek – like a lamb in the house but like a lion in the field, and beloved of all honest men," died, as so many another good man and true had died, in the cause of his beautiful and unhappy Queen.

Lethington was found dead one day. He had poisoned himself as the old Romans used to do, rather than be hanged by his enemies.

With the taking of Edinburgh Castle, with the deaths of Kirkcaldy and Lethington, the last hope of the Queen's men vanished. Morton had triumphed.

For five years Morton continued to rule. He was firm and brave, and gradually peace came to the land.

But the Regent was greedy. He loved gold and he wrung money out of the people in all kinds of ways till they began to hate him. The nobles hated him too for his pride, and when the King was about twelve years of age they persuaded him that he was old enough to rule. The Regent was taken by surprise. He saw that it was then no use to fight against the lords, so he gave up his office of Regent and went away to live quietly in his country house – the Lion's Den, the people called it.

But Morton had no thought of really giving up his office; he was only biding his time. One day he came posting back to court and once more got the boy King into his power. He was no longer called Regent, but he was ruler all the same. James, however, was growing up and he did not want to be ruled by Morton. Besides, he had two friends whom he liked so much that they could make him do as they pleased.

These were Esme Stewart, a Scottish gentleman who had lived nearly all his life in France, and a soldier called James Stewart. The King made one of these friends Earl of Lennox, the other Earl of Arran, and heaped many more honours upon them.

These two men hated Morton and soon James, listening to their counsels, had the Regent arrested and condemned to death because he had helped Bothwell to murder Darnley. There was no doubt that he had known something of the murder but so had Regent Murray and many of the other lords. It had all happened many years before and some of the conspirators, who were far more guilty than Morton, had never been punished. But all that did not save the Regent, and he was executed.

The lords, who hated Morton, were quite pleased at his death but they soon found out that instead of one ruler they had now two. For after the death of Morton, Lennox and Arran became greater and greater. And the more powerful they became, the more were they hated and dreaded by the nobles. At last, some of the lords resolved to rid themselves of Lennox and Arran and to get possession of the King.

James was fond of hunting and one of the nobles, called the Earl of Gowrie, asked him to come to his castle of Ruthven to hunt. James went and was received with great honour. But the invitation was a trap. Secretly the castle was surrounded by soldiers. Then the nobles went to the King and begged him to send away his favourites, swearing that they would no longer be ruled and oppressed by them.

Too late, James saw why he had been invited to that lonely castle far from his favourites. Instead of replying to the lords, he tried to leave the room. But one of the nobles placed his back against the door, roughly telling the King that he must stay where he was. At that, James began to cry with shame and anger.

But that did no good. "Better that bairns should greet than bearded men," said the noble sternly. So James had to submit. He was a prisoner.

When Arran heard of what had happened, he hurried to Ruthven, vowing vengeance on the lords. But as soon as he entered the castle, he was seized and thrown into prison. Lennox was banished and he returned to France, where he died.

James was now obliged to do as the lords told him. No doubt they were better friends and advisers than Arran and Lennox had been, but every day he grew more and more weary of being a prisoner. For although he was allowed to ride about and to hunt, and seemed to be free, he was really nothing but a prisoner.

At last he managed to escape from the lords and fled to the castle of St Andrews. As soon as he was within the gates, they were closed and guarded by his own soldiers. The King was master again.

While a prisoner, James had tried to make the best of things and he had pretended so well that the lords did not believe that he was very angry with them. They did not now think that he would punish them. But they were mistaken. James had been made to cry and had been called "a bairn", and he had neither forgotten nor forgiven. The Earl of Gowrie was beheaded and the rest of the lords who had helped him fled away to England. So ended the Raid of Ruthven, as it was called.

Arran, the King's favourite, now returned to court more proud and haughty than before. For two years he ruled as he liked, and his insolence and vanity became greater and greater.

At last the lords could no longer bear his insolence. Many of those who had fled to England returned and, gathering an army of ten thousand men, they marched to Stirling. Backed by rows of sharp swords and bristling spears, they forced James to listen to them and to take them into his council. Arran was driven from court and after living for some years a miserable, hunted wanderer among the hills and valleys of Scotland, he was killed by one of his many enemies.

CHAPTER 72

James VI – About the Death of Two Queens and the Joining of Two Crowns

ALL THESE years, while the King had been growing up Queen Mary, his mother, had been kept in England, a captive.

From castle to castle she had been moved. As the years went on she was treated more and more poorly, kept more and more closely a prisoner. For, although her own son had been taught to look upon her as an enemy, Mary had still many friends, and plot after plot was formed to free her and to place her upon the throne of England. But sooner or later every plot was found out.

The last and greatest of these plots was called the Babington Conspiracy. It was so called from the name of a gentleman called Babington who was at the head of it. The plot was discovered and Babington and all his friends were put to death in cruel fashion.

It was then decided that Mary too should be tried for her share in the plot.

She was at this time imprisoned in the castle of Fotheringay in Northamptonshire. There, forty of the greatest lords and gentlemen of England came for the trial.

In the great banqueting hall of the castle they gathered and with grave, stern faces sat awaiting the coming of their prisoner. At one end of the hall there was an empty throne with a canopy over it. This was not meant for Queen Mary but only to show where Queen Elizabeth would have sat, had she been there. At the side was placed a chair for Mary.

As Queen Mary entered the hall it was seen that she walked with difficulty, for the long years in damp prisons had made her lame. When she saw that she was not to be allowed to sit upon the throne, but only on a common chair, she looked proudly and sadly at the lords. "I am a queen," she said, pointing to the throne; "my seat ought to be there."

But there was no pity nor kindliness in all the stern faces as she looked round upon them. "Alas," she said, after a moment's silence, "here are many counsellors, yet there is not one for me." Then she quietly took her seat.

The trial began, if trial it could be called, for Mary was not allowed to have anyone to help her or to plead for her. She did not even know of what she was accused. It was one poor woman against forty stern men.

All that was said or done mattered little, for it was meant that Mary should die. So her forty stern judges condemned her to death. But Elizabeth, although she hated and feared Mary, although she would have been glad to hear that she was dead, did not want to bear the reproach of having put her to death. So she would not, at first, sign the death warrant, as the paper commanding a person to be put to death is called. Elizabeth gave her wise men and counsellors many hints as to what she would like them to do. She even tried to make Mary's jailer murder her. But although he was a stern, rough man he would not do so wicked a deed.

At last, seeing nothing else for it, Elizabeth signed the warrant.

Very quietly Mary received the news that she was to die. "When is it to be?" she asked.

"Tomorrow, at eight in the morning," was the reply.

She had only a few more hours to live. Her maids gathered round her, weeping bitterly. "Come, come," she said, "cease weeping and be busy. Did I not warn you, my children, that it would come to this? Now blessed be God it has come, and fear and sorrow are at an end."

She divided her money among her servants putting each sum into a little purse and writing the name of the person for whom it was intended on a piece of paper. She wrote letters and made her will, and at last lay down to rest.

Early next morning she was awake and dressed herself with great care. She wore a black satin dress and a long white veil and round her neck hung a golden crucifix. So, leaning upon the arm of one of the officers of the guard, she entered the great hall of the castle. It was crowded with people and bright with firelight. Upon a low platform, covered with black, stood a block. The last sad hour of all her troubled life had come and soon Mary, who was perhaps the most unfortunate queen who ever set foot upon a throne, lay dead. "So perish all the enemies of the Queen," cried the Dean of Peterborough, as the executioner held up the head. He was answered by the sound of tears. Mary was only forty-five, yet her hair was white and her face was the face of an old woman.

When all was over, dreary silence settled down on Fotheringay. For a moment there was stir and clatter in the courtyard as a horseman rode out of the gates and, turning his horse southward, galloped wildly. It was a messenger to tell Elizabeth that her great rival was dead.

But no welcome messenger was he. When the Queen heard the news she was very angry, or at least pretended to be angry. She put one of her advisers in prison and sent others away in disgrace. But she could not remove from herself the blame for she had signed the warrant.

Mary had not many friends left in Scotland. But Elizabeth, by putting her to death, made many into friends who had before been enemies. James had never seen his mother. He had been taught not to love her but rather to think of her as an enemy. But now he was angry. He would not receive Elizabeth's messenger and it seemed as if there might be war. There was none, however. James knew that if he went to war with England, many of his nobles would not follow him, and that he had neither men enough, nor money enough, with which to conquer England. He knew, too, that when Elizabeth died he was the next heir to the English throne. So in a little time he let his anger die away and became friends again with the English Queen.

Sixteen years later that English Queen lay dying. "Will you have your cousin of Scotland to reign after you?" asked her wise men. She did not speak, but made a sign which seemed to mean "yes."

But whether the great despotic Queen would or would not, the King of Scots was the rightful heir. He was the great-grandson of Henry VII, and there was neither man nor woman in all England who had so good a right to the throne.

As soon as Queen Elizabeth was dead a lady who sat beside her drew a ring from her finger. Going to the window she opened it. Below sat a horseman, booted and spurred. The lady threw the ring down to him and the horseman, knowing what it meant, turned his horse's head northward and galloped off to Scotland. Hardly pausing for rest, he rode day and night until he reached Holyrood Palace.

The King had gone to bed but hearing that a messenger had arrived posthaste from England, he rose again. So, dusty, travel-stained and weary, the messenger knelt to kiss the hand of his new King – the King of England, Scotland and Ireland.

A few days later, King James said goodbye to Scotland and set out for his new kingdom. It had taken the messenger who came to tell him that he was King just three days to ride through all the kingdom. James spent a month on the way. He crossed the Border at Berwick, the town over which, perhaps more than over any other, the Scots and English had fought and quarrelled, and which they had torn from each other again and again. Now the King was received with great rejoicings. Everywhere as he passed, balls, plays, hunting parties and all kinds of entertainments were got up for his amusement and, when he at length entered London, cannon boomed and bells rang and the people cheered until they were hoarse.

So at last, after hundreds of years of war and bloodshed, England and Scotland were joined. What almost every King of England since the days of Edward the Confessor had longed for, had come to pass. But not in the way they thought. Scotland was still unconquered. She had given England a king.

This union of the crowns, as it was called, happened in 1608.

CHAPTER 73

James VI – New Scotland

FOR many years, daring sailors had been making voyages into unknown seas, and many new lands had been discovered. When these sailors came home with their wonderful tales of unknown countries, those who listened to them longed to sail away to see these strange places for themselves. People who were discontented or unhappy, people who were poor, people who were restless and longed for adventures, people who were poorly treated because of their religion, all went over the seas hoping to find happiness or wealth, peace or excitement. So there arose in the New World, as it was called, a New England, a New France, a New Spain.

Scotland was a small country but for many years brave Scotsmen had been in the habit of leaving their own land to look for fame in other lands. In every country of Europe they were to be found fighting other people's quarrels. But now that the New World had been discovered, there seemed to be no reason why there should not be a New Scotland as well as a New England where Scotsmen, instead of fighting for other countries, might work for their own.

So in 1621, James gave a large piece of land in America to a Scotsman called Sir William Alexander. He also said that to encourage people to go to this new colony (as a new country which is peopled by an old country is called) he would make everyone who would go there, and who would take with him a certain number of others, a baronet. That is, he would give the title of "Sir" to him, and to his sons after him.

Sir William Alexander was a poet as well as a statesman and some people laughed at him. He was not content to be King among poets, they said, he must make himself King of some Newfoundland and, like another King Arthur, he must have his knights.

In spite of much laughter, Sir William went on with his plans. He called the land Nova Scotia, which is Latin and means New Scotland. After a good deal of delay he got a ship fitted out and sent off to New Scotland with colonists. But it was now so late in the year, and the storms were so bad, that when they arrived at Nova Scotia they could not land, but were driven back to Newfoundland, which lies not far off. There they landed and the ship in which they had come went home, leaving them in that far-off country.

During the winter they had many hardships. Their minister died and so did their blacksmith and most of the others scattered among the people of Newfoundland, trying to earn a living by fishing.

In the spring, the ship came back with more people and a colony was really started. They built a fort and a little town of wooden houses round it. But misfortune after misfortune came upon them and, after struggling for some years, Sir William gave up all his claim to the land to a Frenchman called de la Tour who had married an English lady. But de la Tour promised that the colony should still belong to the King of Scotland.

The French had also colonies in America and, after this, Nova Scotia changed hands many times. Sometimes it belonged to the French, sometimes to the British until at last, in 1713, it was given back to Britain and has had close links with Britain ever since.

Perhaps, for a long time, it has been forgotten that this was ever a Scottish colony. But the place where the first colonists built was for many years called the Scottish Fort and the place where it stood is still pointed out. The name, too, of Nova Scotia remains to remind us of it. If you look on the map of Canada you will see it.

In 1625 James VI died. He had reigned for fifty-seven years during nineteen of which his mother, Queen Mary, still lived.

He was not in the least like any of the gallant Jameses who had gone before him. He was something of a coward and he could not bear even to see a drawn sword. He was ugly and dirty and, it is said, never washed his hands. He was clever without being truly wise so that he has been called the "British Solomon" and "the wisest fool in Christendom".

Like James I and James V, James VI wrote books. In one of these books he set down his ideas of how kings ought to rule; in another, he wrote against smoking. Sir Walter Raleigh, one of Queen Elizabeth's courtiers, had made voyages into far countries and had brought back tobacco with him. It soon became the fashion to smoke. Many people thought it a strange fashion. James thought it a disgusting one and did all he could to stop it. "It was," he said, "a custom loathsome to the eye, hateful to the nose, harmful to the brain and dangerous to the lungs."

I am afraid that people did not pay much attention to him.

CHAPTER 74

Charles I – The King and the Covenant

As LONG as James VI was King of Scotland only he was guided and ruled a great deal by his nobles. But when he went to England he found the people there ready to flatter him and to make much of him, and he soon became very proud and haughty and tried to do exactly as he liked.

James had never cared for the Presbyterian Church, as the Church of Scotland was called, and when he went to England he joined himself to the Episcopalian or English Church. Presbyterianism was no religion for a gentleman, he said. And all the rest of his life he tried to force the Scottish people to do as he had done, but they refused.

James only came back to Scotland once after he became King of England. When he died, he was succeeded by his son, Charles. Charles had been on the throne eight years before he visited Scotland. When he did come, however, the people welcomed him with joy, and he was crowned at Edinburgh with great pomp and ceremony.

But Charles was grave, unsmiling and cold, such a king as the Scots had never had, so their gladness soon died away.

Immediately after his coronation a Parliament was held. Charles forced this Parliament to do as he wished, so that it was said that of the thirty-one acts passed, only three were not hurtful to the liberty of the people. And for the first time in all Scottish history, the King and his Parliament quarrelled.

Charles went back to England and, soon afterwards, with the help of the Archbishop of Canterbury, who was called Laud, he made a new Prayer Book which, he said, all the Scottish churches must use. This Prayer Book was even more like the Roman Catholic Mass Book than the English

*The Marquis looked so handsome, grand and grave that
everyone was full of sad astonishment (page 285)*

*While the minister preached and prayed, sentinels
kept watch (page 297)*

Prayer Book so that the people were full of fear and indignation. The King, they thought, was going to force them to be Roman Catholics again.

It was announced that the new Prayer Book would be used after the 23rd July. All over the country on that day people crowded to the churches. They were quivering with anger and excitement; their freedom and religion seemed both to be in danger. For this was an act of tyranny. It was done by the order of the King and the English bishops without consulting either the Scottish people or Parliament.

To the church of St Giles in Edinburgh came bishops, judges, magistrates and gentlemen, besides great numbers of the common people. The Dean entered wearing a white surplice instead of the plain black gown which the Scottish ministers usually wore. He opened the new Prayer Book which was large and full of pictures. That alone, to the stern Scottish Presbyterians who hated all pictures and images, was a sin.

The Dean began to read, but hardly had he uttered a few words when an old woman called Jenny Geddes, who sat near the pulpit, sprang up. "Thou false thief," she cried, "wilt thou say Mass at my ear?" And with that she flung the stool, upon which she had been sitting, at the Dean's head.

In a moment all was confusion. People rushed at the Dean and tore his white surplice from his shoulders. They beat him and ill-treated him till he fled for his life.

The Bishop of Edinburgh got up into the pulpit and tried to speak to the people. They would not listen. "A pope, a pope," they cried, "pull him down, stone him."

Soldiers were at last sent for and the church was cleared. The doors were locked and bolted, and the service was read to the few who were in favour of it, while the crowd without yelled and groaned, battered at the door and threw stones at the windows.

For a month after this, there was no service of any kind held in the churches. Neither the new nor the old Prayer Book was allowed to be used. The churches stood desolate and empty. But the people had no thought of giving in. They begged Charles to take away the hated Prayer Book. But he would not.

Then the people rose as one man to resist. They drew up a paper called the National Covenant in which they bound themselves to fight for their freedom of conscience. That is, for freedom to believe and to do what they felt to be right in matters of religion.

On the first day of March 1638, in Greyfriars churchyard in Edinburgh, the National Covenant was first signed. The paper was spread out upon a flat gravestone and noble after noble wrote his name. After them came ministers, gentlemen, tradesmen and people of all ranks, high and low. Never was there such excitement. Many wept as they wrote their names. Others cut themselves and signed in their own blood. Afterwards, noblemen and gentlemen carried copies of the Covenant with them all over the country, till thousands of names were added to the list.

The Covenanters, as these Protestants were now called, sent a letter to King Charles. They called it their Great Supplication. Supplication means humble prayer. It was sent back to them with the seal unbroken. The King had refused even to read it.

It was to be war then! The whole country was ready for it. In every town and village the rattle of firearms and the tramp of men was heard as the people gathered and drilled for the defence of their religion.

At last a great army was encamped upon a hill called Dunse Law. Their leader was Sir Alexander Leslie, a little, old, crooked soldier with the heart of a giant and the courage of a lion. The sides of the hill were covered with wooden huts and with tents. Before the tent of each captain fluttered a banner with the rampant lion of Scotland and the motto, "For Christ's Crown and Covenant".

But after all, there was no fighting. At the last moment Charles gave way. He promised the Covenanters the freedom they asked, and they sent their soldiers to their homes again.

CHAPTER 75

Charles I – How the Soldier Poet Helped the King

CHARLES promised the Covenanters freedom but he never meant to keep his word. Soon war broke out again. The Scots marched into England and there, instead of being feared as they used to be, they were greeted as friends. For many of the English hated the Prayer Book. These Puritans, as they were called, sided with the Scots. Charles was also quarrelling with his English Parliament. His army fought in a half-hearted way and soon it fled before the Covenanters. So the King was obliged to make peace, and the Covenanters went home triumphant.

The quarrels between Charles and his English Parliament now grew worse and worse. James VI had tried to be an autocratic king, that is, he had tried to do exactly as he liked. "The King can do no wrong," he said, and he had taught his son, Charles, to think and to say the same. At last the whole country rose in rebellion. This is called the Great Rebellion and in it English, Scots and Irish all took part.

It was a war for freedom and a war for religion that now began. On one side were the King and many of the lords and gentlemen who were Roman Catholics and Episcopalians, on the other side were the members of Parliament, the Presbyterians and Puritans and most of the common people. In Scotland, many of the nobles too, fought against their King but some fought for him. Chief among these was James Graham, Marquis of Montrose. Montrose was handsome and brave, a soldier and a poet. He was so noble and so fearless that he seemed more like a knight of ancient days than a man of his own time. He had been a Covenanter, and had fought for the Covenant. Now he fought for the King. Traitors change from side to side, yet no one has ever called Montrose a traitor because, although he was a Covenanter and a Presbyterian, he had never wished to overthrow the King, and although he now fought for the King he remained a Presbyterian to the day of his death.

When all the country rose in war, a great Scottish army marched into England to help the Parliamentarians. Montrose had been with the King's army in England but seeing that he could do no good there, he made up his mind to return to Scotland. He knew that in the Highlands there were many loyal men who would fight for the King if they had a leader. But how to get there was the difficulty. Between him and the Highlands stretched half the length of England and all the Lowlands of Scotland filled with the King's enemies. The King's enemies were Montrose's enemies and he knew that if he were caught he would certainly be killed. But no danger ever made Montrose afraid.

So he sang. Dressed like a groom, mounted upon a poor old horse and leading another by the bridle he rode behind two of his friends, as if he were their servant. In this way they passed safely through England.

When they came to the Border they were told that the traitor, Montrose, was somewhere near and that soldiers were searching for him everywhere. But in spite of that, they passed on. They had gone a little farther when a soldier came up to them. This man had fought under Montrose and, in spite of his disguise, he knew him quite well.

"My lord Montrose," he said.

But the Marquis calmly went on with what he was doing, pretending not to know that he was being spoken to.

"My lord," said the man again.

"What folly is this?" said one of the gentlemen, hoping still to deceive the man, "this is my servant."

But the man laughed scornfully. "What," he said, "do I not know my lord Montrose well enough? But," he added, humbly and respectfully, "go your way and God be with you whithersoever you go."

When the Marquis saw that it was useless to try to deceive the man he gave him some money and sent him away. Then, knowing from this adventure how dangerous it was to delay, he and his friends rode as fast as they could, sparing neither their horses nor themselves, till they reached the Highlands.

There, for some days, Montrose lay hidden, sleeping among the hills by night, hiding in a peasant's hut by day. At first, things seemed quite hopeless. But soon he heard that another of the King's friends had landed from Ireland, bringing with him about a thousand men. Montrose at once joined them and was received with joy as their leader. Then, with this little army, he began his battles for the King.

The men were badly clothed and scarcely armed at all. Their weapons were sticks and stones, axes and heavy Highland swords, called claymores. A few had rusty old guns but they had no cannon, and only three horses. But the men were fiercely and recklessly brave. Their leader had the courage of a king. Day by day the army grew. Montrose swept all Scotland, winning victory after victory, till all Scotland seemed to be at his feet, and he even hoped to march victoriously into England.

But the soldiers he had had to fight against were untrained and when the Scottish commander in England heard of what was happening in Scotland, he sent an army back from England to fight Montrose. Montrose marched southward to meet this army. But as he marched many of his Highlanders left him and so, when he reached a place called Philiphaugh, he had hardly more soldiers than when he had begun his victorious campaign. There, whilst Montrose himself was in the neighbouring town of Selkirk, his camp was surprised in the early morning by the Parliamentarians under Leslie.

For the first time Montrose, with his rough Highlanders, had to face tried soldiers. For the first time he was defeated.

So complete was his defeat that he fled back to the Highlands. There, for some months, he tried hopelessly to raise another army.

In England, meanwhile, many battles were being fought, sometimes one side winning, sometimes the other. But at last the Parliamentarians got the best of it. Then Charles, seeing that his cause was lost, gave himself up to the Scots. Even then the Scots would have fought for their King again if he would have allowed both England and Scotland freedom in matters of religion. But this Charles would not promise, so the Scots gave him back to the English and went home to Scotland.

When Montrose knew that the King was a prisoner and his cause hopeless, he fled away across the sea to a country called Holland. He went as he had come little more than a year before, disguised as a servant.

CHAPTER 76

Cromwell – How the Soldier Poet Died

WHEN King Charles had been a prisoner for about two years the English condemned him to death and cut off his head. Then they said they would have no more kings and they made a soldier called Cromwell, ruler, giving him the title of Lord Protector. When Montrose heard that his King was dead he was filled with grief and anger. Being a poet as well as a soldier he drew his sword, and with the point of it he wrote a poem full of sorrow and defiance.

> "I'll sing thine obsequies with trumpet sounds,
> And write thine epitaph in blood and wounds."

Not only Montrose but every loyal Scot was filled with grief and anger. Even the Covenanters who had fought against the King had never meant that he should be killed; they had hoped to force him to rule better. So now they proclaimed as King his son, Charles, and messengers were sent to Holland, where he had taken refuge, to ask him to come to Scotland to be crowned. These messengers made it plain to Charles, however, that they would only accept him as King if he promised to rule according to the law, and if he promised to sign the Covenant, and to leave them free in matters of religion.

These conditions did not please Charles. He wanted to be a despot like his father and to do exactly as he pleased. He thought that if he could conquer the land there would be no need to yield to these conditions. So he said neither "yes" nor "no" to the messengers of the Covenant, but hesitated and delayed.

He hesitated and delayed because gallant Montrose, with his poet's sword in his hand, was sailing back to Scotland. He was going to write his King's epitaph as he had said, in blood and wounds, and to set his son upon the throne.

Montrose landed in Orkney and then crossed to the mainland. But the people did not flock to his standard as they had done before. A few men of Orkney, a few foreign soldiers whom he had brought with him, one or two loyalist gentlemen – that was his whole army. It was not enough with which to re-conquer a kingdom and when this little company met the Covenanting army, the Orkney fishermen fled without striking a blow; the foreign soldiers fought for a while but they too gave in, leaving Montrose and his few friends to fight alone.

Many were killed, others taken prisoners but Montrose himself escaped. Changing clothes with a peasant he wandered about for several days, suffering much from hunger, cold and weariness. At last, utterly worn out, he was discovered by his enemies and betrayed, it has been said, to the Covenanters by a false friend for the price of a few bags of meal.

The Covenanters hated Montrose and now that they had him in their power they were very cruel to him. They mounted him upon a rough Highland pony with straw for a saddle and a rope for a bridle, and with his legs tied together led him from town to town dressed still in the ragged, dirty clothes in which he had been captured. Insults were heaped upon him. In every town and village the women and children came out to hoot and yell, and to curse at him as he passed. But through it all, the Marquis rode with calm dignity, showing neither shame nor anger.

At last they came to Edinburgh. The whole city was ablaze with excitement because this great enemy of the Covenant had been taken. Bells were rung, bonfires were lit and the streets were crowded from end to end as Montrose passed through them. Tied to a cart which was driven by the common hangman, he was led to prison. But so splendid and noble did he look that those who had come to jeer and laugh were silent; many were so touched with pity that they sobbed aloud.

There was not even the mockery of a trial. Montrose had been condemned before he reached Edinburgh but he was taken before the Parliament in order to hear his sentence. There he defended himself nobly. "I did engage in the Covenant and was faithful to it," he said. "When I saw that some people, under pretence of religion, intended to take the authority from the King and seize on it for themselves, I judged it my duty to oppose it to the uttermost. As to my coming at this time, it was by his Majesty's just commands. Be not too rash, let me be judged by the laws of God and the laws of this land."

But nothing that Montrose could plead was of any use. He was condemned to die.

Next morning the Marquis was awakened by the sound of drums and trumpets. It was the soldiers being marshalled to guard the streets, in case anyone should try to rescue him on his way to death. "What," he said, "is it possible that I, who was such a terror to these good men when alive and prosperous, continue still to frighten them when I am bound for death?"

He rose and dressed himself carefully, combing out his long hair. As he was doing this one of the men who hated him most came into his prison cell. "Why is James Graham so careful of his locks?" he sneered.

"My head is yet mine own," replied the Marquis calmly. "I will arrange it as I please. Tonight, when it will be yours, you may do with it what you like."

Once again, for the last time, he marched through the crowded streets. He was no longer dressed in his shabby old clothes but in a beautiful suit of velvet which his friends had been allowed to give him. Every window, every balcony, from the Tolbooth to the Grassmarket where he was to die, was thronged with people. Many had come to scoff, yet none scoffed. He stepped along the street with so great state, he looked so handsome, grand and grave that everyone was full of sad astonishment. Once only the silence was broken by the shrill laughter of a woman's voice. Even his enemies shed tears and owned him to be the bravest subject in the world. He looked more like a king than a felon condemned to shameful death.

The Marquis was not allowed to speak to the people, lest even at the last they should rise and rescue him. But to those around him he spoke, ending with the words, "I leave my soul to God, my service to my Prince, my goodwill to my friends, my love and charity to you all."

When the last moment came the hangman burst into tears, and a quivering sob broke from the crowd.

Montrose was only thirty-eight when he died. To the last he was a poet, and the night before he died he wrote his own epitaph:

"Scatter my ashes, strew them in the air.
Lord! since Thou knowest where all these atoms are,
I'm hopeful Thou'lt recover once my dust,
And confident Thou'lt raise me with the just."

CHAPTER 77

Cromwell – For the Crown

MONTROSE gave everything for his King, even his life, and his King rewarded him by forsaking him. He made no effort to save him from death and even denied that he had commanded him to make war in Scotland. There was little gratitude in Charles II and now, seeing that there was no other way to the throne, he signed the Covenant and accepted the crown from the hands of the men who had just killed his truest follower.

Scarcely a month after the death of Montrose, Charles landed in Scotland. Once more Edinburgh was ablaze with joy and riotous with the sound of cheers and bells as Charles signed the Covenant, listened to long and solemn sermons and promised many things.

He did not care what he promised, so long as he won the crown. But he soon found that he was treated more like a prisoner than a king.

Charles was very young. He was lively and merry, and he brought many friends with him who were as lively and as merry as himself. But these friends did not please the solemn, stern Covenanters, so they sent them all away. Instead of laughing, dancing and playing cards, Charles found himself obliged to go about with a grave face and to listen every day to long sermons. Once he had to hear no less than six sermons in one day. On Sundays, he was not even allowed to go for a walk.

Charles grew so tired of this dull life that one night he ran away. But the Covenanters followed him and brought him back. They saw, however, that if they wanted to keep their King, they must not treat him so sternly, and after that he had a little more freedom.

But the English Parliament had abolished kings and had made it a crime for anyone to call Charles King. So

Cromwell marched into Scotland to fight against the very men who, so lately, had been fighting for him.

But the Scots were ready. Encamped in a good place near Edinburgh, with plenty to eat and drink, they quietly awaited the English. For a dreary, rainy month Cromwell and his men lay opposite. There was little fighting; hunger, cold and wet did their work. Horrible disease raged throughout the English camp; men sickened and died by hundreds. At last, without having fought any great battle, Cromwell decided to go homeward.

Then the wary Scottish general made a false move. He left his safe position to meet the English and was surprised and defeated near Dunbar.

After this, Cromwell had no thought of going home. He marched on through Scotland, taking towns and castles. His unconquered Ironsides, as his soldiers were called, were everywhere victorious.

All this time, Charles had not been with the army. Now, while Cromwell was marching through Scotland, he was crowned at Scone. The crown was placed upon his head by the Marquis of Argyll, one of Montrose's bitterest enemies. Then, taking command of the army, the King marched into England leaving Cromwell in Scotland.

Charles hoped that the English Royalists would rise and join him, and that he would be able to make himself master of England while Cromwell was out of it. But no sooner did Cromwell discover what Charles was doing than he followed him.

At Worcester the armies met. Again the Royalists were defeated and Charles, seeing his cause utterly lost, fled in disguise. After many adventures and dangers, he escaped at last to France.

This victory Cromwell called his "crowning mercy" for by it the last hope of the Royalists was shattered.

When Cromwell went away from Scotland, he left one of his generals called Monk, with five thousand men, to carry on the war. One by one the towns and castles of Scotland yielded to him.

But one castle called Dunnottar held out bravely and would not yield. The English, however, were determined to take this castle for they knew that within it were the Regalia, that is the crown, sceptre and sword of state of Scotland and they wanted to seize them and carry them away to England.

So cannon boomed and roared, and shook the castle walls. Food grew scarcer and scarcer; death stared the brave defenders in the face. Still they would not yield.

The Governor of the castle was called George Ogilvie. He had married a beautiful and clever lady named Elizabeth Douglas. She was with him in the castle, and now that it was impossible to hold out any longer, she thought of a plan by which the Regalia might be saved from the English.

"Let me have the Regalia," she said, "and I will send them away to a safe place. I will not tell you where, so when the English ask you, you can truly say that you do not know."

George Ogilvie knew that he could trust his wife, so he gave the Regalia to her. She then carried them away to another brave lady called Mrs Granger, the wife of a minister. Together they wrapped the jewels up in bundles of linen. Then Mrs Granger asked the English general to allow her to leave the castle, and to take with her some bundles of linen which belonged to her.

The general gave her leave and Mrs Granger calmly walked out with her bundles, mounted upon her horse under the very eye of the general himself, and rode away. Indeed, as he was a polite gentleman, he helped her to mount and to arrange her bundles. No doubt the brave lady's heart beat fast, and she was terribly afraid of being found out, but she looked so calm and unconcerned that no one suspected what precious things were hidden away in these bundles.

As soon as Mrs Granger got beyond the English lines, she

rode fast until she reached her own home. Then she gave the Regalia to her husband and he, going secretly into the church at night, dug a hole under the pulpit and laid the jewels in and covered them over again.

When Mrs Granger had gone, Dame Elizabeth told her husband that the jewels were safe and he, knowing that it was useless to hold out any longer, surrendered to the English. And because they had fought so gallantly the English general promised him and all his soldiers their lives and freedom.

So, next morning, with drums beating and colours flying, the little band of soldiers marched out. There were only thirty-six of them. They were pale and thin, some of them were wounded and ill and scarcely able to walk. But they made a brave show and held themselves proudly for they had fought to the last for their King and they had saved his crown from the English. George Ogilvie's young son carried the royal standard. He was the last man to carry the King's colours in Scotland for many a day.

When the little garrison had marched out the English entered the castle. They searched everywhere for the crown jewels but nowhere were they to be found. Then, being very angry, they seized George Ogilvie and tried to force him to tell where they were. But he did not know. He could not tell and would not have told even if he could. In the cruel manner of the time, they tortured him to make him speak, but he would not. Then they tried to bribe him, but neither torture nor bribery were of any use and at last this brave husband and wife were put in prison.

Day or night they were never left alone. A sentinel was always beside them so that they could not say a word to each other without being heard.

At last, Dame Elizabeth became ill. Although she was so brave and bright, like a piece of true steel she could not bear the close damp prison. All that she had to suffer wore out her strength so that she died. Just before she died, and not till then, did she tell her husband where the jewels were and he promised never to tell the English. And he never did.

Long afterwards, when King Charles came back again to reign, the jewels were found safe in the church where the minister had hidden them. He and his wife were rewarded by a sum of money. George Ogilvie was made a baronet but Sir John Keith, a gentleman who had had nothing to do with hiding the jewels at all but whose name had been used to put the English off the scent, was made an earl.

It seems a pity that the right person did not receive the greatest reward but George Ogilvie and his wife, Dame Elizabeth Douglas, will always be remembered among the patriots to whom Scotland owes her unconquered crown.

CHAPTER 78

Charles II – How the King Came to his Own Again

AFTER the Lowlands of Scotland had yielded to Cromwell, the Highlands still held out and still fought. But at length the last Highland chief laid down his arms and Scotland formed part of the Commonwealth, as the government was now called.

Cromwell had abolished kings, now he abolished the Scottish Parliament. "There should be," he said, "only one Parliament for the whole kingdom which should meet at Westminster, and there Scottish and Irish members should come, as well as English."

Cromwell made many wise laws and under the stern rule of the Lord Protector the country gradually settled down into peace and prosperity. But this did not last long, for in 1658 Cromwell died. He had been a strong ruler. He had indeed made himself king in everything but name so that it seemed quite natural to the people to choose his son, Richard, to succeed him. But Richard Cromwell was a very different man from his father. He was neither strong enough nor clever enough to rule, and after a few months he gave it up and went away to his house in the country. There he lived quietly until he died many years later.

As soon as Richard Cromwell went away, quarrels began as to who should govern. In England, many of the people were tired of the stern rule of the Puritans for they made life very dull, calling innocent games and music wicked, and thinking it sinful even to dress in bright colours. They remembered that over the sea there was a king – the King whom the Scots had already crowned – and they began to long for him to come back. The Scots had never forgotten their King. They had been the first to rise against Charles

I but they had never wished to kill him, and they had been the last to yield to Cromwell. Under Cromwell they had found no more freedom than under Charles I, and now they too thought of the King over the water.

Monk, who had ruled Scotland for Cromwell, seeing how things were began to march to London with his army. He was a stern and silent man. He told no one what he meant to do, but for some time letters had been passing between him and Charles who was now living in France.

One day while Parliament was sitting, news was brought that a messenger with a letter from the King was without.

The King!

Not for ten years or more had there been a king.

The messenger was brought in and the letter was read. It promised that all those who had rebelled should be forgiven; it promised that if they would now receive their King, people should be allowed to believe what they thought to be right. When the letter had been read, the members rose up and shouted, "God save the King." The Commonwealth was at an end.

On the 29th May 1660 Charles II landed in England. When the news reached Scotland, it was received with frantic joy. People shouted and cheered and danced. Fountains ran with wine, and in Edinburgh alone thousands of glasses were broken after drinking the health of the King. For it was the fashion, after drinking the health of any great person, to break the glass so that it should never be used for any meaner purpose. And now so often was the King's health drunk that it was said that the noise of the breaking of glasses in the streets was like the clash of armies.

The coming of Charles II was called the Restoration. Now that the King was restored, the Scottish Parliament was also restored. Cromwell's idea that there should be only one Parliament for the whole kingdom, was a good one. But neither the Scots nor the English were ready for it and as soon as they could, they went back to the old way.

The Scottish Parliament always opened with a great

procession. The members met at Holyrood and rode in state to the Parliament house. This was called the Riding of Parliament. So on New Year's Day 1661 there was a solemn Riding.

The crown, which had been so bravely kept, was brought from its hiding place and with the sceptre and the sword of state was carried before the procession. The King was not there, but behind the crown rode a soldier called Middleton whom Charles had sent as Vice Regent, that is, in place of the King.

Then two by two came the nobles, riding slowly. They were all clad in splendid robes, and behind them walked gentlemen holding up their trains. Footmen and guards surrounded them and so, with beat of drum and blare of trumpet, they reached the ancient Parliament house.

Yet for all the solemnity and grandeur of its opening there never was a more wretched Parliament in Scotland. "It was a mad, roaring time," says a man who lived and wrote in those days. "And no wonder it was so, when the men of affairs were almost always drunk." So it came to be called the "Drunken Parliament".

This Parliament passed an act called the Rescissory Act, by which all the laws and acts passed since 1640, nine years before the end of the reign of Charles I, were recalled. So that by this act the Covenant, which had become the law of the land, was swept away; the Presbyterian Church and all its courts was disestablished; the freedom of religion, for which the people had fought so hard, was gone.

This was what Charles had set his heart upon. He hated the Presbyterians. He had neither forgotten nor forgiven the dreary life they had made him lead when he came to take the crown ten years before. The Marquis of Argyll, the greatest Presbyterian chieftain in Scotland, had set the crown upon his head. But Charles knew no gratitude and when the Marquis came to do honour to his King, the King would not receive him, but ordered him to be imprisoned in the Tower because he had rebelled against Charles I.

Argyll was afterwards sent to Scotland and there he was executed, as his great enemy Montrose had been. He met his death bravely. "I had the honour to set the crown upon the King's head," he said, "and now he hastens me to a better crown than his own."

The Marquis was executed partly in revenge for the death of Montrose. Yet Charles, when he came to Scotland, had denied that brave friend and follower and had pretended to be glad that he had been killed. Now, when it suited him, he ordered Argyll's head to be placed over the gate of Edinburgh, to blacken in the sun and wind, as that of Montrose had done.

CHAPTER 79

Charles II – The Church Among the Hills

IT SOON became quite plain that Charles, like his father and grandfather before him, was bent on making Scotland Episcopalian. The Presbyterians, seeing this, sent a minister called James Sharpe to London to beg the King not to force them to do what they thought was wrong. But Sharpe betrayed those who sent him. He went over to the King's side and, soon after he came back to Scotland, he was rewarded by being made Archbishop of St Andrews.

Then Charles ordered all the ministers in Scotland to become Episcopalian or to leave their churches. Three hundred and fifty left, rather than yield. So many churches were thus made empty that there were not enough clergymen to fill them. All kinds of ignorant men were then sent as "curates" to preach to the people, instead of their ministers. These men had "little learning, less piety, and no sort of discretion" and the people would not listen to them. Rather than do that, they followed their ministers into wild hills and glens and there, among the heather and the broom, they sang and prayed as well as in any church.

These meetings were called Conventicles. Conventicle is formed from two Latin words: *con* meaning together; and *venire*, to come – so that it means a coming together. To go to a Conventicle was against the law, and those who did go went in fear of their lives, for soldiers rode through all the country looking for such meetings. When they were discovered the people were killed, tortured, fined and ill-treated in every possible way.

Yet the Presbyterians would not give in. The more they were persecuted, the more they clung to their own form of worship.

At first people went to the Conventicles unarmed, so when they were discovered they were scattered and killed without being able to resist. But soon they began to arm themselves. Men went to these mountain churches with guns in their hands, helmets upon their heads and swords by their sides. And while the minister preached and prayed, sentinels kept watch, ready to give the alarm at the first sign of danger.

Among the lonely hills, under the open sky, the voices of men and women rang out and the words of the grand old psalms rose straight to heaven:

> "Unto the hills I lift my eyes, from whence my help
>   will grow,
> Eve' to the Lord which framed the heavens, and made the
>   deeps below.
> He will not let my feet to slip, my watchman neither sleeps.
> Behold the Lord of Israel, still His flock in safety keeps.
> The Lord is my defence, He doth about me shadow cast;
> By day nor night, the sun nor moon, my limbs shall burn
>   nor blast.
> He shall preserve me from all ill, and me from sin protect;
> My going in and coming forth He ever shall direct."

Then suddenly there is a cry from the watchers. Through the glen comes the glint of red coats, the gleam of steel.

The women fly for shelter, the men stand to their arms. The echoes of the hills are awakened by the sound of shots, the clash of swords, the cries of the wounded. Then silence falls again. All is over. The soldiers ride away with their prisoners. The lonely valley is once more still. Only on the trampled bloodstained heather, there lie those who have walked through the valley of the shadow of death, those who have gone to dwell in the house of the Lord for ever. Then when evening falls, sorrowing comrades creep back to lay them in their last resting place upon the lonely hillside.

Many a green spot among the hills was marked with gravestones, many a peaceful Sabbath morning was turned into a day of mourning and tears and, at last, maddened by cruelty and oppression, the Covenanters broke into rebellion. They gathered an army and about three thousand marched on Edinburgh. But finding that the people there were arming against them, they turned aside to the Pentland hills. There, at a place called Rullion Green, they met the royal troops.

The Covenanters were weary with long marching. They were hungry and wet. Most of them were but poor peasants, undrilled and badly armed. But cruelty had made them frantic and, filled with religious madness, they faced the enemy, singing the seventy-eighth Psalm:

"Why art thou, Lord, so long from us,
    In all this danger deep?
Why doth Thine anger kindle thus,
    At Thine own pasture sheep?
Lord, call Thy people to Thy thought,
    Which have been Thine so long;
The which Thou hast redeem'd and bought
    From bondage sore and strong.

Lift up Thy feet and come in haste,
    And all Thy foes deface,
Which now at pleasure rob and waste
    Within Thy holy place.
Amid Thy congregation all
    Thine enemies roar, O God!
They set as signs on every wall
    Their banners 'splayed abroad.

When wilt Thou, Lord, once end this shame,
    And cease Thine enemies strong?
Shall they always blaspheme Thy name,
    And rail on Thee so long?
Why dost Thou draw Thy hand aback,
    And hide it in Thy lap?
Oh, pluck it out, and be not slack
    To give Thy foes a rap."

The Royalists were led by General Dalyell – Bloody Dalyell, the people called him, because he was so fierce and cruel to the Covenanters. He was a strange, savage old man. After the death of Charles I he never cut his hair or shaved. His long white beard reached below his waist and his clothes were of so quaint a fashion that the children followed him in the streets to stare at him, as if he were a circus clown. He had fought in many foreign wars and now the psalm-singing was mingled with the sound of strange oaths as the armies closed.

The Covenanters fought with a desperate courage; twice they beat back the Royalist troops. But the King's soldiers were mostly gentlemen, well-drilled and well-armed. The Covenanters were wearied peasants, and at last they gave way and fled in the gathering darkness. Not many were killed in this little battle but the prisoners who were taken were put to death with cruel tortures.

In vain Charles tried to crush out the spirit of Presbyterianism. Middleton, who had ruled for Charles, had been cruel and bad enough but after him came the Duke of Lauderdale, a Scotsman, who made for himself a name to be hated by Scotsmen. He was a big, ugly, coarse, red-haired man. He hunted, and tortured, and killed the Presbyterians and all the time he was a Presbyterian himself!

A terrible Highland army, called the Highland Host, was now raised and sent against the Covenanters. For three months these wild mountain men did their worst. They robbed, plundered and burned, until at last even their masters grew afraid and sent them back to their mountains again. They went back loaded with spoil as if from the sacking of cities. Clothes, carpets, furniture of all kinds, pots and pans, silver plate, anything and everything upon which they could lay hands they carried off, leaving their wretched victims penniless, homeless wanderers.

The cruelty and horror of the time at last grew so bad that a company of nobles and gentlemen went to London to speak to the King and to tell him of the dreadful things which were happening. Charles listened to what they had to say, then he replied, "I see that Lauderdale has been guilty of many bad things against the people of Scotland but I cannot find that he has acted anything contrary to my interest."

So the persecution still went on. Archbishop Sharpe, the man whom the Covenanters had sent to plead with Charles, had become one of their bitterest enemies. He helped and encouraged Lauderdale and at last, some of the Covenanters, maddened with cruelty and injustice, killed him as he was driving along a road across a lonely moor.

Many of the Covenanters were sorry for this murder. But they were all blamed for it, and had to suffer much in consequence. When they had the chance and the power, the Covenanters did other cruel and wicked things. But they were mad, really mad, with suffering. They looked on all who were not of the Covenant as the enemies of God and sons of Belial, and to destroy them was a holy work. So the unhappy years passed on. Now and again Charles seemed to try to be kind to the Covenanters. Then there would come days even more cruel than those that had passed. Many poor wretches wandered in wild places, living in holes and caves, many fled from the country and took refuge in Holland. Still the days of battle and blood went on – the "killing time" it was called. At last, in 1685 Charles died. Charles was clever but he was a bad man and a bad king. How even his friends regarded him you can guess from the following lines which were written by one of them:

> "Here lies our sovereign Lord the King
>   Whose word no man relies on,
> Who never said a foolish thing,
>   And never did a wise one."

CHAPTER 80

James VII – A Forlorn Hope

CHARLES II was succeeded by his brother, James VII. At heart Charles had been a Roman Catholic although he did not dare to own it. James, more honest, openly confessed that he was a Roman Catholic.

Many Protestants who had been driven out of both England and Scotland had taken refuge in Holland. It seemed to them that now was the time to strike a blow and free Britain, for they knew that many of the people must hate and fear a Catholic king.

They agreed that the Duke of Monmouth, an English noble, should invade England and that at the same time the Earl of Argyll should invade Scotland. The story of Monmouth belongs to England's Story so I will only tell you here of Argyll.

On the 2nd May 1685, with three ships full of arms and stores, the Earl set out. His hopes were high but from the very beginning the expedition was doomed to failure. The men who came with him would not agree to obey him as their general. They all wanted to give orders. Some wanted to do one thing, some another. Much delay was caused by these quarrels and many mistakes were made. Argyll was not strong-willed enough to be a great leader. He could not carry men along with him and make them want to do what he knew to be best. So he yielded to his captains and, instead of staying in the Highlands of Argyllshire where he had landed and where he was sure of a great following of his own clan, he marched southward. But as he marched his little army dwindled away. Still, when at last he found himself face to face with the royal troops, he wanted to fight at once. The others did not. It was folly, they said, to fight such a great army with their few men. They advised Argyll rather to decamp in the night and try to reach Glasgow.

Once more the Earl yielded to his captains. To deceive the enemy his soldiers lit camp fires as usual and leaving them burning, marched away. But the night was dark and his guides mistook the path. Instead of leading the men aright, they led them into a bog. Terror and confusion took hold upon them. They scattered and fled in the darkness and although they had been a good army at night, in the morning there were scarcely five hundred left. Even they too melted away until the Earl was deserted and almost alone. Thus was his army shattered before a blow had been struck.

Accompanied by only one friend, the Earl went to the house of an old servant thinking that he would be safe there. But the man would not receive his former master and drove him from the door. So, hungry and weary, Argyll and his friend wandered away again. The Earl, disguised as a peasant, walked behind his friend as if he were his servant, hoping in that way to escape.

They had not gone far, however, before they were met by some of the King's soldiers. The Earl's friend tried to draw the attention of the men to himself so that Argyll might escape. But some of the men, suspecting that he was no common peasant, attacked him. They were near a little river and hoping to escape that way, Argyll sprang into the water. He got through the river and then turned on his pursuers with his pistol. But alas! in springing through the water the gunpowder had become wet and the pistol would not go off. The soldiers closed round him and a blow on the head brought him to the ground. "Unfortunate Argyll," exclaimed the Earl as he fell.

When the soldiers knew who their prisoner was they were sorry. They were paid to fight for the King, yet perhaps their hearts were with Argyll. But they dared not let him go again and so, bound hand and foot, the great Earl was led to Edinburgh and thrown into the Tolbooth.

Once before, Argyll had been in that prison. He had been seized and condemned to death for a little fault. But he had succeeded in escaping and had fled to Holland. Now it would have been easy to condemn him for treason and rebellion. But even in those fierce times, that would have meant a trial and delay. His enemies would suffer no delay so it was decided to condemn him on the old charge, and his head was ordered to be cut off.

An hour before Argyll was to die he lay down to sleep. He had always been in the habit of resting every afternoon and now on his last afternoon in life, he slept as peacefully as ever he had done. While he was sleeping one of his enemies came to see him, but when he looked at the Earl sleeping like a child, he hurried from the room and burst into tears.

"What is the matter?" asked his friends.

At first he could not speak. Then he said, "I have been to see Argyll and found him sleeping as pleasantly as ever man did, within an hour of Eternity; but as for me – " He could say no more.

At last Argyll awoke and, accompanied by his friends, he walked calmly to his death and there, as he himself said, "in the midst of clouds he found fair sunshine."

CHAPTER 81

James VII – The Battle of Killiecrankie

IF THE Covenanters had suffered under Charles II, they suffered yet more under James VII. "There will never be peace in Scotland until the whole country south of the Forth is turned into a hunting field," he had said. And this he seemed bent on doing. Lauderdale had long been dead but his place had been taken by James Graham of Claverhouse – Bloody Clavers, the people called him. He was a fine gentleman. He had a beautiful face and grand manners but he was as cruel as polished steel. His time of power, however, "the killing time", was drawing to an end. For thirty years the terrible war of religions had racked Scotland but now it was almost over.

James VII was a despot. Despot is a Greek word for master but it has come to mean a cruel, hard master. The English would not suffer a despot and they hated Roman Catholics, and when they saw that James was bent on making the whole country Roman Catholic once more, they rebelled.

Mary, the eldest daughter of King James, had married William, Prince of Orange who lived in Holland. He was a Protestant Prince and had given a refuge to many Protestants who had fled from persecution. So now the people of England sent to Prince William and asked him to come to take the throne of England. He came and James, finding himself deserted even by his own family, fled away to France. Never was revolution so sudden and bloodless. Almost without a struggle, William and Mary became King and Queen of Britain. This was called the Glorious Revolution.

James had reigned only three years when he fled in 1688.

In Scotland, however, the revolution was hardly so bloodless as in England. In spite of all his cruelties, there were some who still clung to James and fought for him as their King. These people came to be called Jacobites, from *Jacobus*, which is Latin for James.

Chief among the leaders of the Jacobites was Claverhouse who was now called Viscount Dundee. From being a butcher of defenceless men and women he turned into the gallant leader of a lost cause. Men gathered to his standard until he had an army of six thousand, chiefly Highlanders. At a place called Killiecrankie a battle between the Jacobites and the royal troops was fought.

The two armies met and lay opposite to each other all day. Dundee and his Highlanders lay on a slope above King William's troops. Mackay, the leader of King William's army, dared not attack, and Dundee would not until the sun had gone down and no longer dazzled his soldiers' eyes. At last, about seven in the evening, he rode along the lines giving orders. The Highlanders threw away their plaids and their leathern socks so that they might charge more easily. Then, as Dundee gave the order to advance, they cheered wildly.

From the King's army came an answering cheer, but it was faint and spiritless. "Courage," cried Locheil, one of the Highland chieftains, "the day is ours. That is not the cheer of men who are going to win." Then he too threw off his shoes and charged barefoot with his clan.

On they came to the skirl of the pipes. Slowly at first they advanced, then faster and faster, till they broke through the royal lines, scattering them to right and left.

Dundee rode at the head of his few horsemen. But they did not follow him quickly enough. He stopped and rising in his stirrups took off his white plumed hat to wave them onward. At that moment a ball struck him. He swayed in his saddle and was caught in the arms of a soldier as he fell to the ground.

"How does the day go?" he asked.

"Well for the King," replied the man, meaning King James, "but I am sorry for your lordship."

"It is the less matter for me," said Dundee, "seeing the day goes well for my master." Then he died.

But the Highlanders swept on. Claymores flashed and fell. Highland dirks did fearful work, and the southron troops fled in utter confusion and dismay. In vain did Mackay try to rally his men; they could not stand against the mad onslaught of the Highlanders.

The Jacobite victory was complete, but their leader lay dead upon the field and it was worse than a defeat for them. When the news was told to William and he was urged to send an army to the Highlands he replied, "There is no need, the war ended with Dundee's life." And so it did. Some more fighting there was but the cause of James was lost. Leaderless, the Highlanders grew dispirited and returned homewards. But many of the gentlemen carried their swords and their misfortunes to France to share the exile of their King.

CHAPTER 82

William III and Mary II – The Story of the Glen of Weeping

ALTHOUGH the fighting ceased many of the Highland chieftains were slow to accept William and Mary as their King and Queen. At last William made a proclamation, offering pardon to all the chiefs who, before the 1st January 1692, would take the oath of obedience to him, and saying that all those should be punished who did not take the oath.

One by one the proud chieftains gave way and took the oath. Only one old man, Macdonald of Glencoe, as he was called from the name of the lonely glen in which he and his clan lived, would not give in. But suddenly, finding that he alone of all the clans was holding out, he too made up his mind to take the oath and hurried to Fort William, the nearest big town.

He arrived there on the 31st December. But to his dismay he found that he had come to the wrong town and that there was no one there to whom he could swear obedience to the King. Too late, Macdonald began to realise what he had done. He burst into tears and prayed the Governor to receive his oath. But the Governor was powerless; he was sorry for the old man, however, and sent him away to Inveraray, the right town, with a kindly letter to the sheriff, saying that he hoped this lost sheep would be received.

Once more Macdonald started off, but at this time the Highland roads were always very bad. Now in midwinter they were almost impassable. Through the cold and snow, Macdonald trudged bravely on. The shortest way to Inveraray led him within a mile of his own house. He would not even turn aside one mile, but passed it by. But hurry how he would, it was the 6th January before he reached Inveraray – just six days too late.

When the sheriff knew for what Macdonald had come, he looked grave. "It is too late," he said. But Macdonald was so earnest and begged so hard, that at last the sheriff let him take the oath, and the old chieftain started home again feeling safe and happy.

But the Master of Stair and the Marquis of Breadalbane, who were helping to rule Scotland, hated the Highlanders and particularly the Macdonalds of Glencoe. They had hoped that some of the clans would hold out so that they might have a chance of punishing them. They were really angry when they discovered that all had taken the oath. They resolved that as Macdonald had taken it too late he should not escape.

So the King was never told that Macdonald had taken the oath. He was made to believe that he and all his clan were a set of robbers, and that there would never be peace in the Highlands until they were utterly destroyed. And the King signed a letter giving orders for their destruction.

It is said that William did not read, or did not understand, the paper and that he did not know what he was doing when he signed it. But he ought to have known.

Having the King's permission, the Master of Stair set to work. But he did not go about it openly. He meant to root out the Clan Macdonald thoroughly and the letters he wrote are filled with a horrid joy. "To plunder their lands and drive off their cattle," he wrote, "would only render them desperate. They must all be killed, and the manner of execution must be sure and secret."

Sure and secret he meant it to be. So on the 1st February, one hundred and twenty soldiers appeared marching down the glen. As soon as their red coats came in sight, Macdonald's sons went out to meet them and ask them if they came in peace or war. "In peace," they said. The new barracks at Fort William were so full that there was no room for them, so they had been sent to quarter in Glencoe.

The Macdonalds believed the men and welcomed them as visitors. For a fortnight they lived together. All the

St George's Cross

St Andrew's Cross

Union Jack

St Patrick's Cross

Union Flag of
England & Scotland.

The flags of the United Kingdom (page 320)

hospitality that the little glen could provide was pressed upon the guests. Every day the officers passed some of their time at the chieftain's house. Every evening they gathered round his cheerful fireside, playing cards and games. Glencoe means "glen of weeping", but during these short winter days it was a glen of smiles. No thought of treachery disturbed Macdonald; he was sure of the King's protection.

At four o'clock one dark morning the glen lay silent and, except for the shriek and howl of the wind, not a sound was heard. But over the snow, dark forms were stealing. Suddenly a shot rang out. A few minutes more and the silent glen was echoing from end to end with the sound of gunshots and the cries of fear and pain.

The soldiers were at their deadly work. Nor did it take them long, for they had only defenceless men, women and children to deal with. In the darkness, almost in their sleep, they murdered the men who had treated them as friends and brothers. None were spared – old men and children alike met the same fate. Half clad, many fled through the darkness and the snow. Some reached safety, others died miserably in the lonely glens and mountain paths. As the soldiers butchered and robbed, they set fire to the cottages and soon the dark sky was lit up with the glare, and the crackle and roar of the flames mingled with the cries of the dying.

Then when their work was done the murderers marched away, driving before them the sheep and cattle of their dead hosts, leaving Macdonald and thirty or more of his clan to lie stiff and cold in the silent, lonely glen – the Glen of Weeping – the Valley of Tears, as it was rightly called.

The news of this deed was everywhere received with horror. It did great harm to William. The Highlanders, who had been inclined to live peaceably under his rule, were once more stirred to hatred against him. The Massacre of Glencoe, as it was called, perhaps brought more friends to the banished King than anything else which happened during the reign of King William.

CHAPTER 83

William III – Fortune's Gilded Sails

IF YOU have more pennies than you know what to do with, you put them into a savings bank and, if you leave them there long enough, other pennies are added to them. These other pennies are called interest. But the man at the bank, when he takes your pennies, does not lock them up in a cash box and leave them there. If he did, you would never get interest any more than if you put your pennies into a box at home. The interest does not grow by magic. When you put your pennies into a bank you really lend them to the people who manage the bank. They use them to buy and sell and so make more money, and they are then able to give you interest, that is, they pay you for having lent them your money.

Of course you cannot buy much with a few pennies, but when hundreds and thousands of people all put their money into the same bank it comes to a large sum, and with this large sum the bank managers are able to do great things. In this way money is "circulated", that is, instead of lying in a box locked up doing no good to anyone, it passes from one person to another, making everyone richer and more comfortable.

There are many things about banks and banking that are very difficult for little people, and indeed for grown-up people too, to understand, and I am not going to try to explain them. They are so difficult that up to the time that I have been writing about, there were no proper banks in Britain, where people could put their money and be sure that it was quite safe. But at this time a clever Scotsman called William Paterson went to London. He was so clever, that he made the English people listen to his ideas about banks, and very soon the Bank of England was started. When it was founded in 1694 by William Paterson, people were very much afraid that their money might be stolen, so the King was asked to send some soldiers to guard the house which was used as offices. This the King did and, until 1973, in London every evening you could see soldiers march into the courtyard of the Bank of England to keep guard all night over the people's money. However, they no longer do this.

But besides being a banker, William Paterson was a merchant. He saw that the English made a great deal of money by trading with other countries and by founding colonies in far lands. He saw no reason why Scotland should not do the same and, from being a poor country, become a rich country like England.

When he was young, Paterson had travelled a great deal. He had sailed far away over the sea, and had seen many a strange land. Now he formed the plan of founding a Scottish colony on the narrow neck of land which joins North and South America.

If you look on the map you will see that the land, at a place called Darien, is very narrow indeed. It seemed to Paterson that this was a splendid place at which to form a colony. On the one side was the Atlantic, on the other the Pacific Ocean, and the narrow neck of land between them might be made the centre of all the trade of the world. To get to India, ships had to pass round the stormy, dangerous Cape of Good Hope. But with a Scottish colony at Darien, that would no longer be necessary. Ships would then sail across the Atlantic; they would unload at Darien; in one day the cargoes could be carried across the narrow neck of land to ships on the other side. In this way time would be saved, danger avoided, all the trade of the world would pass through Darien which would become the gate of the sea and the key of the universe.

It was a glorious idea and looking far into the future, Paterson seemed to see Scotland made great and splendid by her merchants.

Scotland was still sore and angry with the memory of

Glencoe, and those who were at the head of affairs welcomed any plan that would take people's thoughts away from that dark deed. The Master of Stair, although he could not understand why people hated him instead of looking upon him as a hero, saw that he had made a mistake, and he did his best to help Paterson.

The King, too, would gladly have had the people forget Glencoe, so he gave them leave to form a company, which was to be called the Company of Scotland, trading with Africa. This Company was to be allowed to found colonies and to build cities, harbours and forts. If their ships were taken or hurt by the ships of other lands the government promised them help and support, besides other favours.

All Scotland was full of excitement. Everyone who had saved a little money brought it to the Company, hoping that their few savings would come back to them like a golden harvest. English people too wanted to join and sent money. Everything went well. Then suddenly some of the people in England became jealous. They got a foolish idea into their heads that if the Scots became wealthy and did a great deal of trade in far countries, it would hurt the English and make them poorer. They wanted to keep all the trade and wealth to themselves and so they made up their minds to stop the Scottish Company being formed.

This was very greedy and very unjust, but so strong did the feeling become that at last the English Parliament asked the King to stop the Company of Scotland because it would spoil English trade. And the King, instead of standing by the Scots who were as much his people as the English, said that he had been ill served in Scotland and hoped that some remedy might be found for the evils which seemed likely to arise from this new Company. When the English Parliament and the King talked like this, the English people became frightened and would give no more money to the Scottish Company.

The people of Holland, King William's other country, also wanted to join the Company but when they saw that it was likely to lead them into a quarrel with the English, they too drew back.

In spite of all this opposition the Scots resolved to go on with the Company, and the people were so enthusiastic and eager about it that although Scotland was a poor country, all the money which was needed to start with was soon gathered.

Everyone was full of hope and excitement and everyone thought that his fortune was made. It was known that gold was to be found at Darien and they had visions of their ships coming home laden with the precious metal.

When enough money had been gathered the company bought five ships from the Dutch and in them twelve hundred men and women set sail from Leith for the new colony.

It was a bright, sunny day in July when they started. All Edinburgh seemed to come to see them off. The quay was crowded with people who had come to bid their friends farewell and to wish them good luck. There were tears and laughter, prayers and blessings as last goodbyes were said, last handshakes given. Then the five vessels sailed out into the waters of the Forth, and never did ships carry a burden of more happy hopeful hearts.

After many weeks upon the sea the colonists at last safely reached Darien in the beginning of November. Darien was inhabited by Indians. They were a savage people but they received the new settlers kindly and, in return for some of the goods which the colonists had brought with them, they gave them land upon which to build.

The colonists at once began to build a town which they called New Edinburgh, and a fort which was called New St Andrews. The country they called Caledonia which is an old name for Scotland.

For a time things seemed to go well. Everyone worked with a will. All day long the sound of axe and hammer was heard and the little town of wooden houses grew rapidly. But while the colonists were busy building, the weeks and months slipped past. The food which they had brought with them was nearly all used up. Anxiously they turned their eyes towards the sea, watching for a ship bringing the food which had been promised from Scotland. No sail appeared. Day by day the portions served out to each man grew smaller and smaller. The work went on slowly, for men who are always hungry cannot do much. Still they hoped and still they watched, but no white sail glimmered on the calm blue sea.

You know that near the Equator the world is very much hotter than in what is called the temperate zone, where the British Isles lie. Darien lies near the Equator. When the colonists arrived it had been wintertime and they found the climate very pleasant. Now summer had come. The terrible tropical sun blazed down upon these tired, hungry men. There was no coolness anywhere. Inside the little houses it was dark and close, outside, a burning torment. At night, foul mists rose from the marshes round bringing deadly sickness with them. Struck down by hunger and disease, hundreds died. Every day, with sad hearts, the colonists laid some tired comrade in his last resting place.

But although Scotland was far off, there were English colonies in America quite near. So now the Scottish settlers sent to them, asking for food and help. But the English colonists had been told that the Scottish settlers had come to Darien without leave from the King, and that therefore they must not be helped. This was not true but the English colonists believed it and refused their starving fellow subjects the slightest aid. They let them die.

The savage Indians were kinder and brought fish and wild animals which they had caught to the hungry white men. But all that they could bring was not enough. Day by day more and more died and at last, filled with despair, the few who were left went on board one of their ships and sailed away from the dreadful place.

Meanwhile, in Scotland there had been a very bad harvest. It was so bad that there too many people were starving and there was no food to spare to send to Darien. But the Scots, feeling sure that their settlers would be able to get food from the English colonies, were not greatly disturbed. At length the bad time passed and a fresh fleet, carrying new stores and thirteen hundred men, set out for the golden land of Darien.

They had a bad passage and one of the ships was wrecked on the way. But at last they sighted land and all the difficulties and dangers were forgotten in the thought of the glad meeting with their comrades.

But as they neared the shore their hearts sank. No flag fluttered from the silent fort; no gun answered their salute. No smoke rose from the deserted town; all was silent and still. The new colonists landed. Instead of shouts of welcome, they heard only the scream of sea birds. Instead of a busy, prosperous town they found a ruined fort, shattered houses, grass grown streets.

It was a sad beginning, but the new colonists would not despair. They began to rebuild the ruined town and to cultivate the fields which had even in so short a time grown wild again.

Two months later another ship arrived bringing three hundred soldiers. These came none too soon, for the Spaniards who had founded a colony nearby, seeing that King William would give his people no help, threatened to attack the Scots.

Already disease and death had begun to waste the little colony a second time and daily their numbers grew smaller. The Spaniards then determined to crush them altogether, and gathered an army of sixteen hundred men and eleven battleships.

With only two hundred men the Scottish captain, whose name was Campbell, marched against them. He surprised the Spaniards, defeated their whole army and put them to flight, killing many of them. Then, with his gallant little army, he marched back again to Fort St Andrew, only to find it bombarded by the Spanish ships.

For six weeks the little fort held out. They had no food left, the Spaniards had cut off their supply of water, they had no more shot, even the pewter plates and dishes having been melted down to make balls. All the officers and many of the men were killed, when at last Captain Campbell surrendered.

The Spaniards were so filled with admiration for their gallant foes that they allowed them to march out with all the honours of war.

One morning the gates were opened and with banners flying the sad little company marched down to the harbour. There were so few of them that they could only man one ship. They chose one called *The Rising Sun*. With what glad hearts, with what high hopes they had set sail in that same ship. Now, with broken hearts and crushed hopes they crept on board again. *The Rising Sun*, which had seemed such a good name, now seemed a mockery.

The men were so weak and ill that they could not raise the anchor. They were so helpless that had the Spaniards wished, they could have killed them every one. But instead, they helped them to raise the anchor and to steer the ship out of harbour, and at last they sailed away. Of all those who had gone out so full of hope, not more than thirty broken, worn men ever reached home again.

So ended William Paterson's brilliant dream.

CHAPTER 84

Anne – How the Union Jack was Made

EDINBURGH was rejoicing at the victory over the Spaniards, when close upon the heels of that news came the news of the utter ruin of the Darien Colony.

The whole land was filled with tears and anger. Almost every family had lost some dear one, almost every household was made poorer. All the money which had been so eagerly given towards the forming of the Company had been thrown away. It had cost Scotland more than three hundred thousand pounds.

Perhaps the Darien scheme would never have succeeded. It was a dream too splendid, an undertaking too great for a poor country. The climate of Darien was one in which it was almost impossible for men used to a cold country to live. Although the Spaniards made no outcry until they saw the Scots forsaken by their King, perhaps they really had already claimed the country. But at the time the Scots would allow no such defence. The feeling from end to end of Scotland was that the failure of the colony was due to English jealousy, and to that alone. All the old bitter hatred between the two countries was stirred to life.

Then it was that King William and many wise men saw that the only way to end this bitter feeling was to draw the two countries closer together – to make them one. For although one king ruled the two countries there was no true union between the peoples. But neither Englishmen nor Scotsmen were ready for union and in 1701 King William died. Queen Mary had died six years before him and Princess Anne, Queen Mary's sister, now became Queen.

As Queen Anne's children had all died before she came to the throne, there was no near heir to the crown except her brother, the young son of James VII. But he was a Roman Catholic and therefore could not reign. And in case there should be quarrelling as to who should succeed, the English decided that it would be better to settle the question while Anne lived. So they passed an act called the Act of Succession, giving the throne to the descendants of Elizabeth, the daughter of James VI, who had married the King of Bohemia, or the Prince Palatine, as he was perhaps more often called.

The Scottish Parliament, on the other hand, passed an act called the Act of Security which left it very doubtful indeed as to who they would have to reign over them when Queen Anne was dead. This frightened the English for they saw that if one king ruled over England and another over Scotland, the old days of war and bloodshed would soon be back again.

Even as it was the two countries treated each other badly. They seized each other's trading vessels and annoyed each other in every way. Many of the English saw that it must either be union or war. It was cheaper to let Scotland have a share in English trade than to fight, so they became eager for union. But most of the Scots still hated the thought of it. It meant giving up their Parliament and joining the English Parliament. To many that seemed like giving up freedom – the freedom for which they or their fathers had fought for hundreds of years.

"What! shall we in half an hour yield what our forefathers maintained with their lives and their fortunes for many ages? Are none of the descendants here of those patriots who defended the liberty of their country, who helped the great King Robert? Where are the Douglases and the Campbells? Where are the peers and the barons, once the bulwark of the nation?" asked one old lord, and the tears came to the eyes of many who heard him as they thought of all the gallant struggles for freedom that their country had lived through.

But the friends of the union saw clearly that whatever Scotland might lose, she would gain much more, and that in the long run union would not mean bondage but a truer freedom. So they would not give up their point.

The Scottish Parliament met yet once more. For the last time there was a solemn Riding. From every corner of the kingdom the nobles and the people crowded to Edinburgh. Up the High Street the lords and members of Parliament rode, in all the splendour of their glittering robes, each with his train of gentlemen and servants. Trumpeters and heralds followed, then the crown and sceptre carried before the Lord High Commissioner, who took the place of the Queen. The streets were lined with soldiers and behind them crowded the people with angry, anxious faces, cheering those who were against the union, cursing those who were for it, as they passed. Then the doors of the grim old Parliament Houses closed upon the lively procession and the streets were once more left to the surging, passionate crowd.

Within the Parliament Hall there was noise and anger enough while the question of union was debated. Tongues said bitter things, hands were laid on sword hilts, eyes flashed hatred. But at last, hard common sense, helped on by the glitter of English gold, broke down all resistance.

It was agreed that England should give Scotland a large sum of money. This money was to help to repay what had been lost over the Darien scheme – lost by "misunderstandings and unkindnesses between the two kingdoms" and also to make up to Scotland for having now to take a share of England's national debt. But, it is said, much of this money was used to bribe the lords and to buy their votes for the union. This was not very grand or noble of the lords, yet money has often been put to a worse use, for in the long run the union was a good thing.

It was agreed that each country should keep its own religion and its own law courts, but that they should have the same money, the same flag, the same Parliament and the same king. It was also agreed that the crown and sceptre of Scotland should never be taken out of the country and, in case that the English should be tempted to take them, the Scots locked them up in a strong box. This box was put into a room in Edinburgh Castle. The window was barred, the heavy door was locked and padlocked and there, for many years, the famous Regalia, the crown which had been placed upon so many wise and so many foolish heads, the sceptre which had been held by so many strong and so many feeble hands, remained shut away from sight until its very existence was almost forgotten.

The patron saint of Scotland is St Andrew, and the flag of Scotland was a white St Andrew's cross upon a blue ground. The patron saint of England is St George and the English flag was a red St George's cross on a white ground. To make one flag the two crosses were placed one on the top of the other and they made something very like the Union Jack, but not quite. The flag that is known and respected all over the wide world was not complete until about a hundred years later when Ireland's red St Patrick's cross was added to the other two.

James VI used to sign his name in French – Jacques. It sounds rather like Jack so his flags came to be called the Jacks, and when the two were made one it was called the Union Jack, and has been called so ever since.

On the 22nd April 1707 the Scottish Parliament rose for the last time. "That is the end of an old song," said one of the nobles, and we may believe that he said the jesting words with a heavy heart.

On the 23rd October of the same year, the first British Parliament met. And so at last the two nations who had been enemies always, who had in three hundred and fourteen battles killed more than a million of each other, were made one. You may be sure that they did not settle down into friendship all at once. Indeed, a few years later the Parliament of Britain proposed that the union should be broken, and the proposal was only rejected by four votes in the House of Lords.

CHAPTER 85

George I – For the King Over the Water

QUEEN Anne died in 1714. She was the last of the Stewarts. The last of the long line of kings who had sat upon the throne of Scotland for nearly four hundred years. She was succeeded, as had been arranged by George, Elector, or King of Hanover who was the great-grandson of James VI.

King George was fifty-five when he came to the throne. He was a thorough German and could speak no English. Although he had known for some years that he would one day be King of Britain he had taken no trouble to learn the English language nor did he trouble to do so after he came to the throne.

King George was allowed to take possession of the throne quietly but there were many people, both in England and in Scotland, who did not give up the hope of once more having a Stewart to reign over them. Queen Anne's brother, James, who was called the Pretender, was living in France, "over the water". When the King's health was drunk, the Jacobites, as the people who clung to the Stewart cause were called, would pass their glasses over the water jug, silently drinking, not to the king upon the throne, but to the king over the water. They wore white cockades or rosettes which was the badge of the Pretender, and here and there the people of a town or village would pluck up courage and proclaim King James VIII. But no one paid much attention to these doings, and it was not until George I had been upon the throne about a year that a rebellion broke out.

This rebellion is called "The '15", because it took place in 1715.

One of the chief Jacobite leaders was the Earl of Mar. He, pretending that he was going to have a great hunting party, invited many of the Highland chieftains to his house. But it was only a pretence. Having gathered the chiefs together

Mar made a speech to them, begging them to fight for their true King. And there, in a lonely Highland glen, the standard of the Pretender was set up, and amid cheers and shouts James VIII was proclaimed.

As the banner fluttered out on the breeze the golden ball fell from the top of the pole. This frightened the Highlanders very much for they thought it was a sign of bad luck. But in spite of this men flocked to the standard and soon Mar found himself at the head of an army of nine or ten thousand men.

King George too gathered an army which, under the Duke of Argyll, marched against the Jacobites. At a place called Sheriffmuir the two forces met. Mar had far more soldiers than Argyll and if he had attacked at once he might have swept Argyll from the field. But Mar was not a good general. Instead of attacking Argyll he called a council of war.

"Shall we fight or not?" he asked.

"Fight, fight," cried the Highlanders.

So Mar agreed to fight, and when the soldiers heard the news they threw their bonnets in the air and shouted for joy.

The Highlanders were fiercely brave but they needed a leader, such a leader as Mar was not. "Oh for an hour of Dundee!" cried one of the chieftains when he saw how things were mismanaged and opportunities lost. Gallant Montrose or cruel, proud Dundee would have led them to victory. But the Battle of Sheriffmuir was neither a victory nor a defeat, for while one half of Mar's army routed Argyll's men, the other half ran away and both sides claimed the victory.

"If we have not gained a victory," said one chieftain, "we ought to fight Argyll once a week till we make it one."

But Mar did not fight. He waited and day by day his army became weaker for the Highlanders, growing disgusted at doing nothing, went home again. Day by day Argyll's army grew stronger.

In the Lowlands of Scotland and in the north of England the Jacobites also rose. But they too had no wise leader and almost without a struggle they laid down their arms again. Many of the chief rebels were taken prisoner and sent to the Tower of London, and one of them, Lord Derwentwater, was afterwards beheaded for his share in the rising.

And all this time the Jacobites were fighting and rebelling for a man that they had never seen, for James remained in France. But at last he came to Scotland and the hearts of the Highlanders rose again.

"Now," they said, "we will live more like soldiers. Now we will be led to battle instead of mouldering away doing nothing."

But they were soon disappointed. James was no soldier. He was handsome, cold and grave. He never smiled and hardly ever spoke, so that even his followers called him "Old Mr Melancholy". This was not the kind of king that the Highlanders had expected. "Can he speak at all?" they asked angrily, and although he was brave enough they began to think that he was a coward.

"Why did the King come?" they asked.

"Was it to see his subjects butchered like dogs, without striking a blow for their lives and honour?"

"If he is willing to die like a prince, he will find ten thousand men in Scotland ready to die with him."

James had not come with any very great hopes and now he was disappointed to find his army so small. He grew more and more gloomy, and when he heard that Argyll was marching upon him he burst into tears. "Weeping," said a friend when he heard of this, "is not the way to conquer kingdoms."

Weeping was not the way to conquer kingdoms and neither was James of the stuff of which conquerors are made. He gave it up. He ran away to France, taking with him the Earl of Mar and leaving the men who had risked everything in his cause leaderless and despairing. "King James VIII" had been in his country just six weeks.

When the Jacobites heard that their King had deserted them, they were filled with grief and anger. In disgust and despair they threw away their arms and, scattering as quickly as they had gathered, they fled, some back to their homes, to their wild glens and mountains, others to the Orkney Isles, and from there to France. The rebellion was over.

CHAPTER 86

George II – A Story of Smugglers

KING George I died in 1727 without having ever visited Scotland. He was succeeded by his son, George II. George II was hardly less German than his father but he could speak a little English and, although people did not like him any more than they had liked George I, he was quietly accepted as King.

England and Scotland seemed to be settling down peaceably into one kingdom, but there was one great cause of discontent in Scotland and that was the taxes and custom duties which since the union the Scottish people, as well as the English, had to pay.

You know that a great many things are done by Government for the good of the country. But to do these things money is needed. So in order to get this money people are taxed. Supposing the Government needed some money, Parliament might say, "We will put a tax of twopence on tea." Then tea would cost twopence more than it did before, and the extra twopence would go to Government to pay for things the country needs. Or they might say, "We will put a tax of one shilling on cats." Then everyone who had a cat would be obliged to pay the Government one shilling. People sometimes think that taxes are very hard and even unjust but, after all, if the country is well governed and Government does good things with the money, the people really get their money back again and sometimes a great deal more.

Long ago, however, people did not see this. They thought taxes were a great burden and they did all they could to avoid paying them.

Nearly all the things which came from foreign countries such as wine, spirits, silk, tea and tobacco were taxed. When a ship arrived laden with these things, a revenue officer, as the man who collected the taxes was called, went on board and received the money before the goods were allowed to be taken ashore.

In order to avoid this many ships, instead of coming into a harbour or port, went to lonely places on the shore where there were caves known only to the captain and crew. There, on a dark and moonless night, they would silently unload. The goods they had brought would be safely stowed away in the caves, ready to be carried inland as soon as it was safe. Then they would haul up their anchor again and make off before it was daylight. The people who did this were called smugglers because they smuggled the goods into the country without paying duty.

The smugglers were very clever and sometimes they would bring great cargoes of tea and tobacco hidden under such things as fruit or fish which were allowed to be brought into the country free. The revenue officers would go on board the ship and search to see if there was anything contraband, but the smugglers were so bold and clever that they were seldom found out.

Contraband comes from two Latin words, *contra*, "against", and *bandum*, "a proclamation", and means that the goods were brought into the country against, or in spite of, the King's proclamation.

Nearly everyone, rich and poor, laird, farmer and minister helped the smugglers. They helped and protected them, hid the goods they brought and warned them when the revenue officers were near. And everyone bought and used these smuggled goods. Of course this was breaking the law but no one seemed to think that it was wicked.

About this time there was a famous smuggler called Andrew Wilson. He had been a baker, but had given that up and had taken to smuggling which was much more exciting and interesting than making bread. He was so clever at smuggling that the revenue officers became very anxious to catch him. After trying a great many times they did catch him and not only took away the goods he had, but made him pay a large sum of money as a punishment. Andrew Wilson thought that this was very unjust. He considered that he had been robbed by the Government and made up his mind to rob the Government in revenge.

Taking a boy called George Robertson with him, he broke into the revenue officer's house and stole about two hundred pounds. But the soldiers were called out to hunt for Robertson and Wilson and soon they were caught and put into prison.

Nowadays no one is hanged for stealing but in those days it was quite common, and so Robertson and Wilson were condemned to death.

But while they lay in prison they managed to get hold of a file and with it they cut through the iron bars of their little prison window.

The window was very small and Wilson was a great big man. So Robertson proposed that he should go first, and from the outside try to pull out some of the stones so as to make the window larger. Wilson, however, would not hear of that. He insisted on going first. But he was too big. He stuck fast in the window and could neither get back nor forward. In vain he struggled, in vain Robertson pushed and pulled. While they were straining and striving, the jailers came. They were caught and after this they were watched and guarded so carefully that there was no hope of escape.

Wilson was very sorry that he had not allowed Robertson to go first and felt that by being so obstinate he was the cause of the poor boy's death. In those days it was the custom to take prisoners who were condemned to death to church upon the Sunday before they were to die. They sat in a pew specially meant for them and were carefully guarded by warders.

On the Sunday before Wilson and Robertson were to be hanged many people came to church, for no one thought that they had been very wicked. Everyone was sorry for them and curious to see the great smuggler.

The service was over and the people were slowly filing out of the church when Wilson suddenly sprang, like a wild cat, upon the warders. With each hand he gripped one by the throat then, crying out, "Run, Geordie, run," he seized another with his teeth.

For a moment Robertson stood stock still, hardly realising what had happened. Then hearing cries of "Run, run," all round him he dashed the fourth warder to the ground, and in a moment disappeared through the crowd.

Wilson could not keep hold of three men for long. He was soon overpowered and once more taken back to prison. But Robertson got right away and search how they might, the warders could not find him.

The magistrates were very angry about this escape but the people were glad. They were delighted too with Wilson's strength and courage, and hoped that now he would not be hanged. But the magistrates were more determined than ever that he should die and so, a few days later, through streets lined with soldiers he was led to death.

The whole town was full of people ready for a riot, but it was not until Wilson was dead that they broke out. Then they began to throw sticks and stones at the executioner and to attack the city guard.

Captain Porteous, the captain of the city guard, was a brutal, surly man. He now became madly angry and ordered his men to fire on the crowd. He himself seized a musket from a man nearby and gave the example by firing first.

As the soldiers obeyed, several people fell dead or wounded. With an angry yell the crowd rushed upon the soldiers who were obliged to retreat to their barracks, firing on the crowd to protect themselves as they went.

So angry were the people that Captain Porteous was taken to prison and charged with having given the order to fire upon the crowd. He denied that he had done so but few believed him, and he was condemned to die.

The people of Edinburgh were eager for revenge and

were glad when they heard the sentence. But when it became known that the sentence was a mere farce and that Captain Porteous would very likely be pardoned, they were furious. Sullen, angry faces were seen everywhere and threats of vengeance grew louder and louder as the days passed.

But Captain Porteous paid no heed. He laughed, and swore, and drank as usual, careless of what people thought. One night he gave a supper to his friends in prison. They were drinking and laughing together when a jailer rushed in, breathless and pale, to tell them that a huge mob had surrounded the prison and that men were battering upon the doors and calling aloud for Porteous.

Blow after blow fell upon the great door but it would not yield. Without, the mob yelled and cursed. Within, seized at last with fear, Porteous cowered and trembled.

At length the blows ceased. Had the mob given it up? No. The door could not be forced, so it must be burned. Quickly bundles of wood, tar barrels, anything that would burn easily were brought and piled against it. The bonfire was lit and at last the great door gave way. Over the burning mass, trampling the ashes, scattering the flames, the mob rushed straight to where they knew Porteous was imprisoned.

Too late he had tried to escape. He was found hiding in the chimney, clinging to an iron grating half way up. He was torn from his hiding place and hurried through the streets by the angry crowd till they reached the place where Wilson had been hanged so short a time before. There they hanged him.

It was a weird sight. The town was in darkness, for there were no lights. But torches blazed on sword and battle-axe, lighting the wild figures of the people and the dark, pale face of their victim.

When all was over, the crowd scattered as quickly as it had gathered. The city sank to rest again and, except for the empty prison with its ruined door and the dead body of Porteous in the silent marketplace, no sign of a riot remained. It had been the most orderly mob that was ever known. Money even was left for the rope, which had been taken from a shop, with which to hang Porteous.

No one was ever punished for killing Captain Porteous. Who led the mob could never be found out. Parliament was very angry when news of it reached London. They talked of throwing down the walls of Edinburgh and taking away the gates in punishment, but the Scottish members grew so angry at the thought of this indignity that it had to be given up.

So ended the Porteous riot, as it was called.

CHAPTER 87

George II – The Story of How Prince Charlie Came Home

IN 1716 James Stewart fled back to France, a hopeless man. Nearly thirty years later in 1745 his son, Charles, returned, full of youth and hope, ready to fight once more for the crown. He was just twenty-five; he was lively and handsome, and for many a year he had made up his mind to win the kingdom for his father. Once, when he was walking by the shore, his hat blew off into the sea. Some of his friends began to get a boat out to go after it but Charles stopped them. "It is not worthwhile," he said, with a laugh, "I shall soon have to go to England to fetch my headpiece."

But when Charles landed in the north of Scotland, one July day in 1745, he had no money and very few followers. At first the Highland chiefs, remembering the misfortunes of thirty years before, were unwilling to help Charles.

"Go home," said one old chief, "for here you can do no good."

"I have come home," replied Charles. "I will rather skulk among the mountains of Scotland if I have only six men with me, than return to France."

"Lochiel," he said to another unwilling chief, "may stay at home and learn his Prince's fate from the newspapers."

"But no," cried Lochiel, "if you are resolved to fight, I will fight too. I will share the fate of my Prince, and so shall every man over whom I have power."

So with brave words and smiles and winning ways, the young Prince made his way to the hearts of the fierce Highland chiefs. Little by little the Jacobite army grew, and once more the Stewart standard was set up. To the sound of the pipes it fluttered out on the Highland breeze. It was of red silk and bore the words *Tandem Triumphans* which means: triumphant at last.

As the standard was raised the Highlanders cheered and
threw their bonnets in the air till it seemed as if the sky
was darkened with them. The white-haired Jacobite
Marquis – the "high minded Murray" – who held the
standard was so old that he had to be supported by a friend
on either side. But, although he was so feeble, he loved the
Stewarts. He had begged to have the honour of rearing the
standard and was ready to lose his life and all that he had
for his Prince.

When King George heard that Prince Charlie had landed
in Scotland he ordered one of his generals, Sir John Cope,
to march against him. He also offered a great reward to any
who would take the "Pretender" prisoner. Charles replied to
this by offering a reward to anyone who would seize the
"Elector of Hanover".

After the setting up of the standard Prince Charles and
his army marched southward. At five o'clock one morning
Lochiel and his men marched into Edinburgh and amid the
sullen silence of some and the cheers of others, "James
VIII" was once more proclaimed.

A few hours later the Prince himself rode to Holyrood.
The air rang with cheers, and crowds of people crushed
round him, eager to touch his hand, or even to kiss his
boots. That night, the old state rooms of the palace, silent
so long, rang again with sounds of music and laughter. For
Charles gave a ball and all the lovely ladies and gallant
men of Edinburgh gathered to do honour to their Prince.

Two days later, in the grey of early morning, Charles
placed himself at the head of his troops, for Sir John and his
army were not far off.

"Gentlemen," he cried, drawing his sword, "I have
thrown away the scabbard."

By that he meant that having now drawn his sword to
fight for the crown, he would never sheathe it again until he
conquered or died, and cheer upon cheer rent the air as the
men heard his brave words.

That night Prince Charles slept upon the field among his

followers. Very early next morning they were up, and before the royal troops were ready they attacked them. In about five minutes, the King's army was utterly defeated and was flying from the field, their leader with them.

The Highlanders lost very few men but the slaughter of the royal troops was dreadful. "See your enemies at your feet, sir," said one of his officers to Charles.

"Alas," replied the Prince sadly, as he turned away, "they are my father's subjects."

After the Battle of Prestonpans, as this battle was called from the name of the place near which it was fought, Charles returned to Edinburgh. There he spent a few days gathering men and money, giving balls and parties and winning hearts with his smiles. Bonnie Prince Charlie he was called. The women loved him for his bonnie face and winning ways, and the men because he was daring and manly. "He could eat a dry crust, sleep on straw, take his dinner in four minutes and win a battle in five," they said.

Ladies danced with him and prayed for him, and sold their jewels to get money for him, and every man who had a sword laid it at his feet.

At last Charles made up his mind to march into England and fight for his crown there. But the Highland chieftains did not wish to go. They wanted to stay in Scotland and fight for Scotland only, and they tried hard to persuade the Prince not to go either.

"I see, gentlemen," said Charles at last, "that you are determined to stay in Scotland and defend your country, but I am not the less resolved to try my fate in England though I go alone." So the chieftains gave way and the march into England began.

But although Charles met with little opposition, the English Jacobites did not rise to join his standard as he had expected. No one resisted him; he took several towns as he marched along but there was no excitement, no enthusiasm as there had been in Scotland. After a long, weary march the Jacobite army reached Derby, and there the chieftains insisted on turning back. In vain Charles urged and implored them to go on. "Rather than go back," he cried, "I would wish to be twenty feet below ground." But they would not listen to him.

So the long weary march back began.

Meanwhile, had the Prince only known it, London was awaiting his coming in fear. The King was ready to flee. And if the King had fled there is no doubt that many who now quietly looked on, waiting to see what would happen, would have taken sides with the Prince and Britain might once more have had a Stewart King. But for good or ill the Prince turned back.

On the march south he had been cheerful and merry, gladly sharing every hardship with his men. Now he was gloomy, sullen and broken-hearted. And the men themselves, when they heard that they were to march back, were full of grief and rage. After many hardships, after two months' march through bitter winter weather, the wearied army reached Glasgow. But the Stewart cause was lost and the Prince a broken man.

At Glasgow the hopes of the Prince revived a little and he marched northward, intending to take Stirling Castle. King George had sent another general to replace Sir John Cope who had run away from Prestonpans, and at Falkirk another battle was fought in which the King's soldiers were again defeated. But the Highland chieftains, instead of following up this victory and besieging Stirling, advised the Prince to march northward. And again, sorely against his will, the Prince was obliged to listen to them.

When the King heard that Charles had beaten another general he was very angry and resolved to send his own son, the Duke of Cumberland, to fight the rebels.

On Culloden Moor the two armies met. On Culloden Moor the last hope of the Stewart cause was lost. The royal army was rested and fresh, well-drilled and well-armed. The Jacobite army was weary, hungry, ragged and desperate.

In a few minutes Prestonpans had been won. In a few minutes Culloden was lost. But after Prestonpans Charles had been pitiful to the wounded – "they are my father's subjects," he said. After Culloden, Cumberland treated the fleeing and the wounded with such merciless cruelty that ever after he was called the "Butcher". Yet the men he slaughtered were his father's subjects too.

Charles would have been glad to die on Culloden with his faithful followers but two of his officers took his horse by the bridle and led him from the field. His life was saved but his cause was lost, and he was a hunted man with the price of thirty thousand pounds upon his head.

This rebellion is called "The '45", because it took place in 1745.

CHAPTER 88

George II – The Wanderings of Bonnie Prince Charlie

FOR five long months Prince Charlie wandered in the Highlands and islands of western Scotland. He suffered hunger, and cold, and wet, but through it all he was cheerful and brave. No house was safe for the whole country was full of soldiers searching for him. He hid in rocks and caves by the seashore, or slept among the heather. Often he had no food at all for a whole day at a time, other days he had only raw oatmeal.

Many times Prince Charlie was nearly caught but he escaped danger after danger. For although the money offered for his capture would have made many a poor Highlander rich beyond his wildest dreams, not one tried to earn it. Instead, they risked their lives and their freedom to help and save him.

Among the many people who helped Prince Charlie a beautiful lady called Flora Macdonald is perhaps the most famous. With great danger to herself, she went to him when he was hiding on the seashore and the King's soldiers were all around seeking for him. Dressed as her maid he travelled safely for a few days and managed to escape from the island on which he was at the time, and to go to another.

When Flora Macdonald could no longer help the Prince he found other people ready to do so, and for some time he lived with seven robbers called the seven men of Glenmoriston. These seven men had fought at Culloden and now, afraid to return to their homes, they led a wild life among the mountains. They hated the Butcher Duke and his soldiers, and they attacked them and stole from them whenever they could. Once, four of them attacked and put to flight seven of the Duke's men, and another time they attacked a whole troop of soldiers and carried off from them a herd of cattle which they were driving to the camp.

The Prince was nearly starving when he came among these wild men for he had had nothing to eat for two days. He was afraid to tell who he was and pretended that he was the son of a Highland chieftain. In spite of his ragged clothes, however, the seven men knew the Prince at once, but far from wishing to hurt him they were delighted, and bound themselves by a most solemn oath to help him in every way. "May our backs be to God and our faces to the Evil One, may all the curses that the scriptures do pronounce be upon us and our sons after us, if we do not stand firm to the Prince in the greatest of dangers, or if we tell to any man, woman or child that the Prince is in our keeping till once his person is out of danger."

And so well did they keep this oath that the Prince had been safe in France for a year before they told anyone that he had been with them.

Charles lived for several weeks with these wild men. They soon became good friends, the robbers loved and served the Prince and did everything that they could to make his life more comfortable.

His clothes were very old and ragged so they waylaid a servant who was travelling with his master's clothes and stole them for the Prince. They went in disguise to the nearest town to hear the news and buy newspapers, and once one of them brought a pennyworth of gingerbread back with him, thinking it would be a great treat for the Prince!

Charles, on his side, insisted that he should be treated as one of them. He made them keep on their bonnets instead of going bareheaded before him. And instead of calling him "Your Highness" they called him Dougal.

The robbers admired the Prince because he could climb, shoot and hunt as well as any of them, and sometimes would help to cook the dinner.

Charles could speak no Gaelic and the seven men could speak no English, so one of the Prince's friends had to translate all that was said. It was agreed that the Prince should not say anything that could not be translated to the men, and that the men should not say anything which could not be translated to the Prince. Charles in this way found out that they all used bad words and swore dreadfully. He scolded them for this and at last, when they saw that he was really sorry about it, they gave up swearing altogether.

About this time a young man called Roderick Mackenzie who had fought for Charles and who was very like him, was also wandering and hiding among the hills and valleys. While the soldiers were hunting for the Prince, they found Mackenzie. When they tried to take him prisoner, he defended himself bravely and fought hard for his life, but at last a soldier struck him to the ground. Then seeing that he must die and hoping to serve his Prince to the last, he cried out, "Villains, you have slain your Prince." The soldiers thinking that they had really killed the Pretender cut off Mackenzie's head and sent it to London, so for a time the search for Charles was not so keen. But the mistake was soon found out.

Charles at last felt he must leave his kind robber friends and try once more to escape to France. They loved him so well that they tried hard to make him stay. But he would not and at length, after some more adventures, he managed to escape on board a French ship. Twenty-three gentlemen and more than a hundred common men went with him. As they sailed away from their beloved land, tears dimmed their eyes, but hope was strong in the hearts and they swore one day to return and conquer.

But they never came again.

Many of those who had fought for Charles died on the scaffold. Many who had helped him to hide and escape were imprisoned. Among these was Flora Macdonald, but two years later she was set free. Even while she was a prisoner, people flocked to see her, glad to speak to and shake hands with so brave a woman, and there was hardly a woman in all Scotland who did not envy her for having been able to help the Bonnie Prince.

And so Bonnie Prince Charlie goes out of our story. The end of his life was sad. He lived an exile and a wanderer in foreign lands, and died far from his own country.

In the great church of St Peter in Rome there is a monument, placed there, it is said, by King George IV, upon which there are the names in Latin of James III, Charles III, and Henry IX, kings of England. They were kings who never ruled, and who are known in history as the Old Pretender, the Young Pretender and Henry, Cardinal of York, who was the younger brother of the Young Pretender.

CHAPTER 89

George III – About a Greater Conqueror Than Kings

WHEN Prince Charlie led his army to Derby and back again the men walked all the way, and it took two months to go and come. Now, if anyone wished, he could go to Derby and back again in one day – by rail. But in the days of Prince Charlie, and for long after, there were no railways, and to walk was the only way in which an army could move from place to place.

But as Prince Charlie marched northward a little boy of ten, with his head full of stories of Bruce and Wallace, watched eagerly for a sight of the gallant Prince, and all his life he remembered the time of "the forty-five".

This little boy was called James Watt. He was not very strong so he had not been sent to school as other little boys are. He spent most of his time at home with his mother who taught him to read. And as soon as he could read he devoured every book that he could lay hands on. As James could not play about like other boys his mother gave him paper and pencil, and he would spend hours amusing himself by drawing. Often too, he would pull his toys to pieces and make them up again into other things. And often he would spend hours seemingly doing nothing.

"I never saw such an idle boy as you are," said his aunt, one day, as he sat by the fire watching the kettle boil. "Take a book or employ yourself usefully. For the last hour you have not spoken a word and have done nothing but take off the lid of the kettle and put it on again, or hold a spoon over the steam watching how it rises from the spout and catching the drops as they fall."

But James was not idle. He felt that there was power in the steam, but how to make use of it he did not know and his childish brain was trying to find out.

When Watt grew up he tried to earn a living by making mathematical instruments – that is rules, compasses and other things which are required for making very careful measurements. But many people did not buy these things and Watt did not make much money. So he began to think of making money in other ways, and all his spare time was spent in trying to find out what steam could be made to do. At last he came very near inventing a steam engine which would work and be of some use. Watt became so excited and interested about it that he neglected his real business and at last gave it up altogether. He was poor, ill and in debt, but kind friends helped him and lent him money so that he might go on making his models and experiments. By this time he was married, and he began to be very unhappy because he was so poor and could not give his wife everything to make her comfortable. But she was a brave woman. "Do not make yourself uneasy," she said, "though things should not succeed as you wish. If this engine will not do, something else will. Never despair."

And Watt did not despair, and after twenty years of work and failure and disappointment, he at last succeeded.

Watt has been called the improver of the steam engine, but he might almost be called the inventor of it. The steam engines which were known before Watt's were clumsy things and of little use. It was Watt who showed people that steam could be made to hammer iron, cut steel, pump water, drive the weaver's loom and the spinner's wheel, and later, it was people working with Watt's ideas who laid down rails and sent trains to thunder from one end of the kingdom to the other, and ships to sail up and down our rivers and across the far seas, heedless of wind and tide.

There never was a greater conqueror than steam. It changed the face of the whole world, and time and distance took a new meaning. It was the power of steam which brought the lonely Highlands into touch with all the busy life of towns. It gave work to millions of men; it brought comfort and wealth to thousands more; it did more than anything else to break down the boundaries between Englishman and Scotsman, and not only between Englishman and Scotsman, but between Britons and the people of all the world beyond our island shores.

James Watt himself did not dream of all the wonderful things steam would do, but before he died the first steamboat had been launched upon the Clyde. This boat was called *The Comet*. It was invented by another Scotsman called Henry Bell and was launched in 1812. But even before that, a little pleasure steamboat had been tried on Dalswinton Loch in Dumfriesshire, when all the country folk came crowding to see the wonderful new sight of boat driven by "reek". For many years the hammer echoed along the shores of Clyde and from there, great battleships, or monster floating cities, were launched to carry the thunders of war or the gifts of peace the world over.

CHAPTER 90

George IV – God Save the King

GEORGE II died in 1759 and was succeeded by his grandson, George III. He reigned for sixty years and was succeeded in 1820 by his son, George IV. I have not told you very much about these kings because most of the interesting things which happened belong to the story of Britain and you will read of them in British histories.

You remember, in the time of Anne, when the kingdoms of England and Scotland were joined together, the Regalia of Scotland were carefully locked up and hidden away. So carefully were they hidden away that many people thought that they were lost for ever. At last the King was asked to allow the strong room to be opened so that the Regalia might be searched for.

The King gave his consent and one morning several gentlemen went to Edinburgh Castle to look for the crown.

The door of the strong room was opened and inside the chest was found. There were two locks on the chest and as the keys had been lost, the King's smith was sent for to break the locks. As the blows of his hammer fell, the chest seemed to give back a hollow, empty sound.

Among the gentlemen who stood round watching and waiting anxiously was Mr Walter Scott. He was a writer of books. He wrote stories of Scotland and Scottish life which are read not only by Scotsmen but by people all over the world. He also wrote a History of Scotland for his grandson which he called *Tales of a Grandfather* and some day, when you are a very little older, you might read his History and his other stories too. George IV thought so much of Mr Scott's books that he made him a baronet and so we remember him not as Mr Scott but as Sir Walter Scott.

Sir Walter loved Scotland and everything that belonged to Scotland, and while the locks of the chest in which the

Regalia lay, were being broken he waited with an anxious heart.

At last the heavy lid was lifted and there, to the delight of everyone, lay the Regalia, just as they had been hidden away more than a hundred years before. As soon as it was known that the jewels were safe the royal standard was hoisted on the castle and the cheers of the soldiers were echoed by hundreds of people who had gathered in the streets, waiting for the news.

Since then the Regalia have been placed in a room in Edinburgh Castle where everyone may see them. And when you go to Edinburgh, as you may some day, you may climb the castle rock and look at the crown and sceptre and sword of the Ancient Kingdom.

About two years after George IV came to the throne he paid a visit to Scotland. Except for "the King over the water" it was the first time that a king had visited Scotland since the days of Charles I, and although George IV was neither a good man nor a great king, the people welcomed him with joy.

It was resolved to remove the Regalia from the castle of Edinburgh to Holyrood Palace so that they might be carried before the King when he rode in state to the castle. This was done with much ceremony. A great procession of lords and gentlemen went to the castle, the gates of which were found fast shut. A herald blew his trumpet. "Who is there?" asked a voice from within the castle.

"The King's Knight Marischal," replied the herald. "He comes to receive the Regalia which are placed within your castle. He demands admission in the name of the King."

"Throw open the gates and make way for the King's Knight Marischal," cried the voice from within.

The gates were then thrown open and the Knight Marischal, followed by other great people, marched in.

When he came out again the Knight Marischal carried the Regalia on a velvet cushion, the band played "God save the King" and so, with banners flying and bagpipes playing, the Regalia were carried in state to Holyrood, through streets crowded with cheering people. There they were kept, guarded night and day by twelve gentlemen, until the King's visit was over, and they were then taken back again to the castle.

The King sailed to Scotland in his yacht *The Royal George*. When he anchored at Leith, Sir Walter Scott went out in a boat to welcome him.

"What!" said the King when he heard that he was there. "Walter Scott, the man in Scotland I most want to see. Let him come up."

So Sir Walter went on board and knelt to kiss the King's hand, and George called for wine and drank to his health.

Next day the King drove through the streets of Edinburgh. He wore a thistle, a sprig of heather in his hat and was dressed in Stewart tartan, and the people cheered him for a true Scottish King. For a few days there was great excitement, bonfires and fireworks, balls, parties and processions. Then the King went back to England.

And here I think I must end, for Scotland has no more a story of her own – her story is Britain's story.

It was Highlandmen who withstood the enemy at Balaclava; it was the sound of the bagpipes that brought hope to the hopeless in dreadful Lucknow; it was Scotsmen who led the way up the Heights of Abraham; it was a Scotsman, David Livingstone, who first brought light into Darkest Africa; and it was another Scotsman, General Gordon, who there laid down his life for the Empire. So you must read the rest of the story of Scotland in the story of the Empire. For Scotsmen did not do these things alone. They were able to do them because they stood shoulder to shoulder with their English brothers, and fought and laboured, not for themselves, but for the Empire, and so Scotland shares in the glory of the Empire, and adds to it.

List of Kings from Duncan I

	Reigned		English Kings who reigned at same time	Began reign
Duncan I	6 years	1034 to 1040		
			Harold I	1035
Macbeth	17 years	1040 to 1057	Hardicanute	1040
			Edward the Confessor	1042
Malcolm III	36 years	1057 to 1093		
			Harold II	1066
			William I	1066
			William II	1087
Donald Bane	6 months in 1093			
Duncan II and Edmund	6 months in 1094			
Donald Bane again	3 years	1094 to 1097		
Edgar	10 years	1097 to 1107		
			Henry I	1100
Alexander I	17 years	1107 to 1124		
David I	29 years	1124 to 1153		
			Stephen	1135
Malcolm IV (The Maiden)	12 years	1153 to 1165	Henry II	1154
William I (The Lion)	50 years	1165 to 1214	Richard I	1189
			John	1199
Alexander II	35 years	1214 to 1249		
			Henry III	1216
Alexander III	37 years	1249 to 1286		
			Edward I	1272
Margaret	4 years	1286 to 1290		
No king for 2 years		1290 to 1292		
John Baliol	4 years	1292 to 1296		
No king for 10 years		1296 to 1306		
BRUCES				
Robert I	23 years	1306 to 1329		
			Edward II	1307
			Edward III	1327
David II	42 years	1329 to 1371		

	Reigned		English Kings who reigned at same time	Began reign
STEWARTS				
Robert II	20 years	1371 to 1390		
			Richard II	1377
Robert III	16 years	1390 to 1406		
			Henry IV	1399
Regent Albany ruled 15 years		1406 to 1419		
			Henry V	1413
Regent Murdoch ruled 5 years		1419 to 1424		
			Henry VI	1422
James I	13 years	1424 to 1437		
James II	23 years	1437 to 1460		
James III	28 years	1460 to 1488		
			Edward IV	1461
			Edward V	1483
			Richard III	1483
			Henry VII	1485
James IV	25 years	1488 to 1513		
			Henry VIII	1509
James V	29 years	1513 to 1542		
Mary	25 years	1542 to 1567		
			Edward VI	1547
			Mary I	1553
			Elizabeth I	1558

James VI reigned for 58 years from 1567 to 1625. Until 1603 he reigned over Scotland only. In 1603 he became King of Great Britain and Ireland.

Charles I reigned 24 years from 1625 to 1649.

THE COMMONWEALTH

The Commonwealth lasted 11 years from 1649 to 1660.

STEWARTS

Charles II	25 years	1660 to 1685
James VII	3 years	1685 to 1688
Mary II and William III	5 years	1689 to 1694
William III alone	8 years	1694 to 1702
Anne	12 years	1702 to 1714

HANOVERIANS

George I	13 years	1714 to 1727
George II	33 years	1727 to 1760
George III	60 years	1760 to 1820
George IV	10 years	1820 to 1830

Index